Brother Lamech, Johann Peter Miller, Joseph Maximilian Hark

Chronicon Ephratense

a History of the Community of Seventh Day Baptists at Ephrata, Lancaster County,

Penn'a.

Brother Lamech, Johann Peter Miller, Joseph Maximilian Hark

Chronicon Ephratense
a History of the Community of Seventh Day Baptists at Ephrata, Lancaster County, Penn'a.

ISBN/EAN: 9783741122620

Manufactured in Europe, USA, Canada, Australia, Japa

Cover: Foto ©Lupo / pixelio.de

Manufactured and distributed by brebook publishing software
(www.brebook.com)

Brother Lamech, Johann Peter Miller, Joseph Maximilian Hark

Chronicon Ephratense

OF

SEVENTH DAY BAPTISTS

AT

Ephrata, Lancaster County, Penn'a,

BY

"LAMECH AND AGRIPPA."

TRANSLATED FROM THE ORIGINAL GERMAN

BY

J. MAX HARK, D. D.

LANCASTER, PA.
PUBLISHED BY S. H. ZAHM & CO.
1889.

TRANSLATOR'S PREFACE.

In offering to the public the following translation of the *Chronicon Ephratense*, a few words of explanation seem called for.

Of the original, probably not more than twenty copies are known to be in existence; and these, with possibly a few exceptions, are in the hands of collectors and antiquarians. To them its chief value lies not only in the great rarity of the work, but also in the fact that it is one of the most interesting specimens of book-making in Pennsylvania to be found anywhere, the paper, printing, and binding all being of strictly native production, the handiwork of the Solitary Brethren of the Community at Ephrata whose history it so quaintly and naively narrates.

It is believed, however, that the work has also a larger interest, and an intrinsic value of its own, as an exceedingly frank and ingenuous contribution to our knowledge of the peculiar and wholly unique social and religious condition, and entire spiritual life, of a very considerable part of the early settlers of Central and Southern Pennsylvania. The otherwise incomprehensibly heterogeneous social and religious life of that populous, prosperous, and important part of the State of which Berks, Lancaster, Lebanon, York, and Dauphin counties are the representatives; the strange variety of dialect, dress, social habits, religious beliefs, and sectarian organizations, to be met with in those counties to-day; are all readily accounted for as soon as we become acquainted with the history of the people and their surroundings, to which the *Chronicon* introduces us. Nor does the picture given us of the intense moral earnestness, the power of self-denying endurance, the hard-working industry and ascetic simplicity of life, the blindly stubborn pertinacity of these original "Pennsylvania Germans," leave us in much doubt as to where their successors of the present received their habits of strict economy and frugality, untiring toil, shrewd thriftiness, and patient, all-conquering perseverance, by which they have succeeded in making "the wilderness" and "desert" of a hundred years ago to enjoy to-day the proud distinction of being "the garden spot of the State." To the historian and social economist, therefore, as well as to the antiquarian, this hitherto all but inaccessible "Chronicle of Ephrata" has more than a passing interest and no inconsiderable worth, even while it appeals still more personally and directly to the thousands of general readers throughout the State and country, whose family names show them to be related by more or less direct ties of kinship to those stern old Brethren and Sisters of a by-gone age.

Who "Lamech and Agrippa," the authors of the Chronicle, really were, is utterly unknown. From their narrative itself we learn that "Lamech" was a member of the "domestic household," that is, a married Brother. The same is undoubtedly true also of "Agrippa," for the name does not occur in the list of "Solitary Brethren," or unmarried men, given in the volume. As to the real identity of the two, it is a secret that has been well kept. Tradition gives no hint or clue for our enlightenment. The future is not likely ever to reveal it.

The few foot-notes which the translator has taken the liberty of adding, are invariably distinguished from those of the authors by being enclosed in brackets. The full names of persons referred to in the text by their initials only, have for their authority the pen and ink annotations on the margins of one of the earliest copies of the *Chronicon*, now in the possession of Messrs. S. H. Zahm & Co. They appear to have been made by one who was contemporary and personally acquainted with most of the people and events referred to in the volume, and are unquestionably entirely reliable.

When we speak of "one of the earliest copies," collectors will understand that we refer to the fact that there were evidently three issues of the *Chronicon :* the earliest one had a blank space left on the title-page for the seal of the Community ; the next had the seal, printed on a separate piece of paper, pasted over this blank space ; and the third had it printed in its proper place directly on the title-page. A fac simile of the original of this curious old seal is given on the second title-page of the present volume.

The original narrative is written in a German so peculiar as almost to deserve to be called a distinct dialect. It has, of course, been impossible to reproduce in English all the involved sentences, ungrammatical constructions, local idioms, mystical expressions, and ecclesiastical words and phrases, peculiar to the Ephrata Community, and conveying a meaning to them often quite foreign to that which ordinary correct usage gives them. The translator has, however, attempted—he fears with but very partial success—

to render them into a correspondingly quaint, antiquated and unnatural style and language, to make his version as curiously un-English as the original is un-German, so far as this might be without becoming wholly unintelligible. He has been at special pains to reproduce the literal meaning of the original with scrupulous fidelity; if he has also to any appreciable degree preserved its peculiar "flavor," he will be content, even though for this he had to sacrifice every trace of literary elegance and grace.

J. M. H.

LANCASTER, PA., AUGUST, 1889.

CONTENTS.

TRANSLATOR'S PREFACE, ...Page iii
CONTENTS,..Page vi
AUTHORS' PREFACE,..Page xii

Chapter I.
Concerning the Awakening among the Pietists, Baptists, and Inspired; the Superintendent's Birth, his Bringing-up, Conversion, etc.,..Page 1

Chapter II.
The Superintendent is Banished from the Palatinate, and Comes to the Inspirationists,..Page 7

Chapter III.
The Superintendent Travels in Pennsylvania, and Lives There in Solitude,..Page 13

Chapter IV.
The Superintendent is Baptized in the Apostolic Manner; and Soon after Follows the Separation from the Baptists in Germantown,..Page 21

Chapter V.
The New Congregation Establishes Itself upon the Doctrine of the Holy Apostles, and Elects the Superintendent as Its Teacher,..Page 31

Chapter VI.
Concerning a New Awakening in Falckner's Swamp, and the Transactions with the Baptists Connected Therewith,...Page 38

Chapter VII.
The Sabbath is Introduced in the Congregation; Wherefore the Latter is Brought under the Judgment of the World; Besides Many Other Disturbances,..Page 44

Chapter VIII.
The Two Baptist Congregations Separate Entirely; and the Brethren at Conestoga give their Baptism back again to the Others,..Page 48

Chapter IX.
The New Congregation, Impelled by Holy Zeal, Grows, and the Sweet Savor of Its Walk and Conversation is Spread Abroad, ...Page 53

Chapter X.
The Tempter Tries to Instigate a Persecution by Raising a Cry of Immorality, ...Page 57

Chapter XI.
Concerning the Superintendent's Official Course in the Congregation, Until the Founding of Ephrata, ...Page 61

Chapter XII.
How Ephrata was Founded, and Ordained for the Settlement of the Solitary, ...Page 64

Chapter XIII.
Concerning a New Awakening at Tulpehocken, ...Page 70

Chapter XIV.
Ephrata is Occupied by the Solitary of Both Sexes; Divine Worship is Instituted, and the Communal Life Introduced, ...Page 76

Chapter XV.
New Persecutions are Commenced; In Part by the Members of the Congregation, ...Page 82

Chapter XVI.
The House of the Solitary is so Constituted as to Oppose the World in Everything. A Visitation of the Baptists Arrives at the Settlement, ...Page 88

Chapter XVII.
An Awakening Takes Place in the Congregation of Baptists at Germantown, the Most of Whose Members Join in the Awakening at Ephrata, ...Page 95

Chapter XVIII.
The Brothers' Convent, Named Zion, is Built, ...Page 106

Chapter XIX.
The Title of Father is Given to the Superintendent; and Concerning the Quarrels that Arose on Account of It, ...Page 113

Chapter XX.

A House of Prayer is Built in Zion; Besides Other Occurrences which Took Place in the Congregation and Settlement about the Year 1740, ...Page 119

Chapter XXI.

Concerning the Spiritual Course of the Church in the Settlement; and the Various Prophetic Gifts, ...Page 129

Chapter XXII.

Concerning the Temporal Course of Events among the Brethren in Zion, and How They Lapsed into the World. Item, the Superintendent's Co-Worker Dies, ...Page 137

Chapter XXIII.

Contains the Disputes which Occurred Between the So-called Moravian Brethren and the Congregation in Ephrata,...Page 145

Chapter XXIV.

A New Convent for the Sisters is Built, Called Sharon; the Singing Schools Come into Vogue at the Settlement, ...Page 157

Chapter XXV.

Concerning the Domestic Contentions in the Settlement, Up to the Time when the Eckerlins Moved into the Desert,......Page 170

Chapter XXVI.

The Brotherhood Recovers again from the Various Tribulations Caused by this Separation. New Church-Work Takes Place in Philadelphia, Besides an Awakening Among the English People, ...Page 187

Chapter XXVII.

The Mills of the Solitary are Destroyed by Fire; A Book of Martyrs is Printed for the Mennonites; the Domestic Household Undertakes a Reform with the Help of the Solitary; and a Nursery is Established to Lead Boys to a Spiritual Life,
Page 209

Chapter XXVIII.

Concerning an Awakening in Gimsheim, in the Palatinate, Which Brought Many People to the Settlement. Very Special Circumstances Connected with a Drought in Pennsylvania,...Page 218

Chapter XXIX.

Continuation of the History of the Eckerlins to Its End,...Page 224

CONTENTS. ix

Chapter XXX.

How the Country was Visited by War, and How the Solitary in the Settlement Fared by it. About the Quiet in the Land. Also, the Prior's Office is Given to Another Brother,...Page 235

Chapter XXXI.

The Community at Ephrata is Extended by an Awakening, for which Two Brothers of the Baptist Congregation, George Adam Martin and John Horn, Prepared the Way,...........Page 242

Chapter XXXII.

Concerning Various Strange Affairs which Occurred in the Country about the Same Time, and in which the Superintendent was Interested,...Page 263

Chapter XXXIII.

Concerning the Last Circumstances Connected with the Life of the Superintendent, and How at Last He Laid Aside His Earthly Tabernacle,..Page 278

Chronicon Ephratense,

CONTAINING THE

BIOGRAPHY OF THE VENERABLE
FATHER IN CHRIST,

Friedsam Gottrecht,

THE LATE FOUNDER AND SUPERINTENDENT OF THE SPIRITUAL
ORDER OF THE SOLITARY IN THE BARONY OF
LANCASTER IN PENNSYLVANIA.

COMPILED BY

BR. LAMECH AND AGRIPPA.

He is like a refiner's fire and like fuller's sope: he shall purify the sons of Levi, and purge them as gold and silver.—MAL. III : 2, 3.

For the time is come that judgment must begin at the house of God : and if it first begin at us, what shall the end be of them that obey not the gospel of God? And if the righteous scarcely be saved, where shall the ungodly and the sinner appear?—I PET. IV : 17, 18.

EPHRATA: PRINTED ANNO MDCCLXXXVI.

AUTHORS' PREFACE.

Unto the Saints and Beloved of God, the Firstlings of His Grace and Followers of the Lamb whithersoever He goeth, who were born of the seed of the Mother above, be Grace and Peace from Him who was, and is, and is to come.

Since early times men have endeavored to establish and maintain unity of spirit in the Christian Church, and with God, by means of councils, creeds, and confessions of faith, but in vain; for the separation between God and fallen man was far too great to be overcome by such external measures. To restore harmony, God had to come down from heaven, take upon Himself Adam's fallen humanity, and be killed for it upon the cross; and after He had pledged Himself to this important work, in the baptism received from John, He took His guilt from Adam and upon Himself, and since then the discord which existed between God and man has fallen upon Him, since He became the surety, and had to make good again that wherein man had offended. Therefore, what associations soever may be found among the various divisions of the Christian Church, there are none of them valid except that one in which, through the sacrifice of His own life, wrath was propitiated and turned into love, and of which He Himself in His baptismal water-bath was the founder; wherefore also he could say: That they may be one, even as He and the Father are one (JNO. XVII, 17), and herein appears His priestly character, whereby Adam's schism and hurt are healed again.

Now, after the Son entered upon His suretyship He had to surrender His God-right, and lay aside His divinity, otherwise He could not have been Mediator between the two parties; this Paul declares (PHIL. II, 8). He humbled Himself. What trials He had to undergo from the Father, from the time of His Mediatorship, it hath not pleased the Spirit to reveal, although searchers in the Spirit find occasion enough therefore in the Scriptures of the New Covenant. Then first the Spirit led Him into the wilderness to be tempted of Satan (LUKE IV, 1), which is equivalent to: Now wrestle with the prince of cruelty. In HEBR. IX, 14, also, it says expressly that the Spirit was actively coöperative in

His sacrifice upon the cross. He Himself, the Son, likens His Father to a vine-dresser and Himself to the vine; and how the latter is treated by a vine-dresser is well known. And though through all He maintained His oneness with the Father, and ever avowed that He and the Father were one, nevertheless the trials between His Father and Him finally reached their utmost, for otherwise Adam's disobedience to God could not have been avenged; yet, since there was no offence in Him, He could resign Himself absolutely into the Father's hands. And because this wondrous process has been transmitted by Him to His followers He could say to them: Blessed is he who shall not be offended in me.

If one reads the story of His crucifixion carefully one sees that at that time God was in league with His enemies; for they were faithful servants to Him, though in His plan of wrath, and carried out what His hand had determined for Him. Therefore, also, He loved His twelve chosen witnesses all the more fervently in His lone condition, for they had endured with Him in His sufferings; and He could say to them: With desire have I desired to eat this passover with you. That, however, the Son here was conscious of the whole God-determined plan concerning himself, cannot well be doubted, for He Himself said to Pilate: Thou couldest have no power at all against Me, except it were given thee from above. (JNO. XIX, 10). But at last the trial became so severe that He said: My God, my God, why hast Thou forsaken me? By thus being forsaken He was made a curse completely; for from whom God withdraws His communion he is accursed. Here, too, He was finally consecrated unto His high-priesthood, to which His previous wonderful works had contributed but little. Had He been conceived of the seed of man, the severe trial of the wine-press would have aroused in Him, if not wrath, yet at least righteousness, so that He would have called for vengeance, as was the case with those martyrs who on that account were not allowed to come as an offering upon the altar, but had to wait under the altar for their redemption. But He had within Him the tender well-spring of the eternal Mother, wherewith He propitiated the Father and turned His wrath into love; therefore also He lost not His confidence in Him; but commended His spirit into His hands. And now when everything seemed to be lost, He, as an High Priest crowned with honor and praise, embraced all His foes in His high-priestly prayer, and said: Father, forgive them, for they know not what they do, words which sooner or later will surely be fulfilled in them. This was the last and greatest miracle which the faithful Servant, according to Isa. LIII, performed upon earth. Had He failed in this work, wrath might indeed have been propitiated by His sacrifice, but He would have fallen short of adorning paradise, and the Mother would not have accepted Him. Therefore also with this high-priestly prayer the drama was so wonderfully changed that He could give the thief the assurance that he should to-day be with Him in paradise.

Now, beloved reader, had the first Adam successfully endured the trial of God in this process, the tempter would not have dared to destroy the union between God and him. But the preaching of the serpent implanted such a suspiciousness against God in him and his entire race that the leading of the cross, which Jesus Christ hath introduced by His manifestation in the flesh, is now treated with ridicule and scorn by all the children of Adam. If henceforth this union of the saints upon earth with God is not again to be attacked by the tempter, as was done in Adam's case, it is necessary that the plan for the temple structure of the Holy Ghost in the New Covenant be taken from that union which subsists between the Father and the Son. And as the Son, as the head of the church, endured the trial of suffering ordained for Him by the Father, for which reason the napkin lay separate from the linen clothes at His burial—so the sufferings of His body, the congregation, which yet remain are not all fulfilled. And since at the present time the sufferings of the body of Christ have reached a high degree, we may well question whether the time be not at hand in which the church will have to sing her Eli, Eli, Lama, from the cross, after the pattern of her Master, when God will openly forsake her, even as He there forsook His Son, and will ally Himself with Babel; which will be the consummation of the trial of the church of Christ on earth, in which she shall be preserved in her priesthood.

Then, when her temptations shall have reached even to the omnipotence of God, for her, too, as for Christ, the scene will be changed, so that she will enter upon the promise vouchsafed unto the thief. For mark well, reader, the union of Christ with His congregation is unto the angel of envy a thorn in the eye; unto all eternity he shall not be able to destroy it, as once he did with Adam. It is the chain wherewith the dragon will be bound, as they will also then have the honor to bind kings in chains and robbers with fetters of iron (Ps. CXLIX, 8), whereupon the rich of the earth shall be overthrown, and along with the redemption from captivity of the eldest son, as the seed of Israel, Shiloh or Messiah shall enter upon His dominion, the rod of the oppressor being broken, and universal peace shall reign among all the remnant of the people. And since in these times the sufferings of the people of God have increased so greatly, who shall blame us for supposing that the times of refreshing from the presence of God are even at the door, in which the spiritual Israel shall be led into the promised land by Joshua, or Jesus?

But to come to the point; it should be known that the unity of the spirit among the saints upon earth is as incomprehensible as God Himself. This the Superintendent has remarked in his hymns, declaring that the bond of unity in the Congregation gathered under his service had something incomprehensible in it, otherwise it would long ago have been scattered by the tempter, who raged so fiercely against it. His whole leading and teaching implies that human wisdom and reason have been made foolishness, which foolishness, however, is wiser than the wisdom of this world; wherefore, also, so much controversy and strife have arisen within the organization. It is, nevertheless, to be said on behalf of the actors in this long spiritual drama that they have been uniformly sensible, and in part also God-fearing persons; although all this could not suffice, because no mere human virtue without the cross can gain entrance into the kingdom of God. Wherefore even their falls, which served to humble them, should rather be excused; for no one has ever melted gold without finding some dross. And if the good no longer appears with the same excellence as, say, sixty years ago, when the favor of God so specially manifested itself, we yet are not to infer that it is wholly lost; but rather that it has only taken refuge under reproach from false lovers, lest the pearls be cast before swine and be trodden under foot by them.

Before we close this preface we cannot refrain from yet expressing our great sorrow that so little is being done to defend the Christian religion against the Turks, Jews, heathen, atheists, antichrist and naturalists; all which hath its cause in this, that one has become alienated from the Spirit, and has entrusted the eternal treasure to mere earthly reason. Thus everything is sought to be made comprehensible, and everyone with unwashed hands, and without repentance or conversion, sets himself up as judge thereof, as though he had no need of any further enlightenment of the Spirit, but knew all things already, though understanding nothing. Against such impertinent fellows we have raised, by the foolishness contained in this work, a bulwark which neither they nor any other Deist or Atheist shall overcome to all eternity. And as they will not condescend to this foolishness, neither shall they attain to the treasures which lie hidden underneath it. Be this of our preface and of the entire work

THE END.

In the Settlement at Ephrata,   BROTHER AGRIPPA.
April 14th, 1786.

CHRONICON EPHRATENSE.

CHAPTER I.

CONCERNING THE AWAKENING AMONG THE PIETISTS, BAPTISTS, AND INSPIRED; THE SUPERINTENDENT'S BIRTH, HIS BRINGING-UP, CONVERSION, ETC.

It is still fresh in the memory of all that, with the beginning of the present century, important changes in the realm of the church took place in many lands, especially in Germany. A great many people, of all ranks, separated themselves from the common forms of worship, and were in general called Pietists. But as only the three known church-parties were included in the religious peace, the Pietists everywhere began to be proceeded against with much severity. On this account many of them went back again into the pale of the church, and were therefore denominated Church-Pietists. The rest for the most part went back to the districts of Marienborn, Schwarzenau, Schlechtenboden, etc., whose rulers had themselves been awakened, and so took up the refugees and granted them liberty of conscience.

Among the Pietists gathered together in that region, two congregations were soon formed whose principles were radically different and contrary; namely, the Community of True Inspiration and the Baptists of Schwarzenau. As the Superintendent's relations were intricately involved with these congregations they will often have to be referred to. The Schwarzenau Baptists arose in the year 1708; and the persons who at that time broke the ice, amid much opposition, were Alexander Mack, their teacher, a wealthy miller of Schriesheim an der Bergstrasse, (who devoted all his earthly possessions to the common good, and thereby became so poor that at last he had not bread enough to last from one day to the next), his housekeeper, a widow Noethiger, Andreas Bone, John George Hoening, Luke Vetter, Kippinger, and a gunsmith, whose name is not known. These eight associated themselves together, chose one of their number by lot as baptist, and then, according to the doctrine brought from heaven by Christ, baptized one another that same year, in the running stream of water that flows by Schwarzenau. Who their first baptist was has never become known.

From these eight persons are descended all the various kinds of Baptists among the High-Germans in North America, who now are scattered from New Jersey to Georgia; but whether they were the first who restored immersion, as a candle to its candlestick, in Germany, that is a question demanding closer investigation. It is asserted that the godly Hochmann agreed with them on the subject of baptism, but as they carried the thing out while he was under arrest, he could not afterwards insist upon it any more; probably, too, their sectarianism was a hindrance to him. Certain it is that God was with them at that time. Neither was there any difference between them and the congregation afterwards founded at Ephrata, except with reference to the Sabbath, and it is affirmed that Alexander Mack once publicly declared: "We now lack nothing anymore, except the Sabbath, but we have enough to carry already." They had their goods in common, and practiced continence, though, it is said, they did not persevere in this zeal longer than seven years, after which they turned to women again and to the ownership of property involved therein. And this is very likely, from the fact that, afterwards, when the great awakening in Conestoga took place, during which similar circumstances arose once more, they always declared that if it were possible to live in such wise, their fathers at Schwarzenau, who for a time had the same zeal, would have succeeded in it. Thus they made their faithlessness the criterion according to which they would judge God's leading, which was the very source whence afterwards arose the division between them and the congregation at Ephrata.

This congregation of Baptists at Schwarzenau increased very much. A branch of it settled in the Marienborn district, but was thrice persecuted there, and finally found a refuge in Creyfeld in the year 1715. Here a division took place. Some say it was with reference to the question whether one might marry out of the congregation. Others maintain that the occasion of it was the marriage, contrary to the teaching of Paul (I COR. 7 :), of a single minister of theirs by the name of Hager. If this be so, there must still have been a considerable measure of awakening among them at that time, and their error consisted only in making a law out of the teaching of Paul, which it was not meant to be. In the year 1719 a party of them arrived in Pennsylvania with Peter Becker, who afterwards became their teacher.

After this necessary excursion, we shall now proceed with our subject itself. The Superintendent first saw the light of the world in the year 1690 at Eberbach, a village on the Neckar, belonging to a sub-bailiwick of the domain of Mossbach in the Palatinate, and bore the family name, John Conrad Beissel. His father carried on the trade of a baker, but was so given to drink that he sank all he owned down his throat, and then died, leaving behind a poor widow with a numerous family. This, his youngest son, was born two months after his death, and was therefore a true *opus posthumum;* by which orphan-birth the Spirit indicated his future lone condition, and that, as one pre-ordained to be a priest after the order of Melchizedek, he should derive little comfort from his natural kindred. His mother was a godly person, and, with the help of his other brothers, raised him until his eighth year, when she also died. From that time on he led a sorry life, after the manner of the country, until he was old enough to learn a trade. With his growth in years he displayed extraordinary natural gifts. He showed a wonderful facility in learning many things without any instruction, merely by his own reflection ; so much so that his oldest brother often said to him : "Your studying will make a fool of you yet." By his orphanlike birth, moreover, he was given so small a person that he often said, if his oldest brother were to have been as small as himself, he would have had to have been born again. At length he was apprenticed to a baker, and as the latter was also a musician, he learned from him to play the violin, and had the opportunity to display his bright disposition at weddings, at which, when exhausted with fiddling, he would betake himself to dancing, and from this again return to the former; so that the wonder was all the greater when afterwards it was said he had become a Pietist.

His conversion took place in the year 1715, therefore in the twenty-fifth year of his age; but ere the spirit of penitence came upon him, his reason became so enlightened that he could easily solve the most intricately involved matters. He turned his attention to mercantile calculation, covering all the walls of his back room with his cipherings, and mastered it without any help. Soon after, however, the awakening-Spirit knocked so loudly at his conscience that his whole being was thrown into the utmost perplexity, and so the foundation was laid for his conversion, which followed after, wherein he attained to such superhuman faithfulness to God that he may well be regarded as a great miracle of our times. The beginning of his conversion was directly from God, without any human instrumentality, and its fame has spread everywhere. It was at this time, too, that George Stiefel, who afterwards shared a hermit's life with him in America for awhile, first became acquainted with him.

At that period, according to the custom of the country, he began his travels as a journeyman at his trade, though he got no further than Strasburg, for the Spirit hindered him. It is a remarkable circumstance that, though he intended, with four hundred other journeymen bakers, to go to Hungary, he was prevented from doing so by God's providence and to his own good fortune, as they were all killed by the Turks. He finally entered the service of a man in Manheim, Kantebecker by name, where he was temporarily brought low in the spirit; for his master, who had marked in him a specially godly simplicity, loved him exceedingly, whereas his mistress was so displeased at this that she broke out into violence. For this he called her a Jezebel, and on that account was obliged to leave the house. At the same time the drawings of the Virgin above were so strong within him, that it was deeply impressed upon his heart that a man who intends to devote himself to the service of God must, at the beginning of his conversion, renounce Adam's generative work, for which reason he bade good-night to earthly woman at the very commencement. On this account also the tribes of the earth expelled him from their fellowship.

From Manheim he turned to Heidelberg and engaged himself to work with a baker by the name of Prior. Here he found greater access in the Spirit; for there was a great awakening going on, and there were many Pietists who were already beginning to be persecuted; yet he was then still so unsophisticated and simple in his awakening, that he made use of the churches, and often said that he never heard the preaching of those two great men, Mieg and Kirchmayer, without being edified thereby; it seems also that the Pietists at another time, afterwards, reported him for church-going. It is to be noticed here, that at this early period of his conversion a blessing descended upon him from God, which was shared by every house that received him, as his master Prior experienced (see the story of Obed-edom, II SAM. 6: 12 comp. GEN. 12: 3). The daughter of the just-mentioned Prior afterwards wrote an edifying letter to him in Pennsylvania, in which she thanked him for the edification which he had wrought in her father's house; from which one can see that his conversion did not run into any mere frivolous babble or fruitless Babel-storming.

At Heidelberg he met a learned scholar named Haller, a strong suitor of the virgin Sophia, and also a correspondent of Gichtel, although at last he for all took to woman. This man made him acquainted with the Pietists in Heidelberg, who all maintained a hidden walk with God. Among them were especially known the wife of Professor Pastoir, a precious soul, who sent her remembrance to him at Ephrata, two brothers Diel, and others, whose names are recorded in the book of life. Haller first introduced him to their meeting, which for fear of men they held in the forest, and he was astonished beyond measure when these dear people the first time called him Brother. He often said that he had passed through three awakenings, in which he always had to deal with newly awakened ones, but he must confess that the greater part of his heart remained at the first awakening at Heidelberg. Therefore his references to these precious souls never passed off without tears, particularly as in after times so much bitterness and gall were served him by his followers.

CHAPTER II.

THE SUPERINTENDENT IS BANISHED FROM THE PALATINATE, AND COMES TO THE INSPIRATIONISTS.

Haller observed a large measure of the Spirit in this new Pietist, and foresaw that their awakening would not be of sufficient import to him. He therefore advised him to betake himself to the friends in Schwarzenau, which was at that time the Pella and rendezvous for all the pious. This advice was re-enforced by the persecution in Heidelberg, which shall now be described. At that time he still was staying with his master Prior, and as by his illumination there was also given him a strange insight into the secrets of nature, he in a short time became the most celebrated baker in the city. His master, too, received a blessing from this; for Christians and Jews ran after him, and the other bakers had little to do; he even sent of his wares to Frankfurt. At this the other master-bakers felt outraged. To this was added yet the circumstance that the guild constituted him Servitor of the Chest. But when at their guild banquets they carried on their usual idle practices, and he reproved them, the masters declared that he ought not have spoken so. "And you," he answered, "ought not act so." In consequence of this the masters managed with the city council to have him put under arrest in the jail. This pained the Pietists very much, for they feared that he might betray them. Haller even wrote to him in jail that he was surprised, and wondered why he had refused to take part in such insignificant matters.

Meanwhile his trial took place, and there it appeared that the charge was not sufficient to have him kept under arrest. His accusers, however, knew how to help themselves, and declared that he was a Pietist. This brought the matter before the ecclesiastical court. The clergy of the three dominant religions took him in charge, and their very first question was concerning his Brethren. But he answered wisely and prudently, that he had no doubt in such a large city there were many pious people. Then they took up the subject of religion, and gave him the choice, either to join one of the three dominant religions, or to leave the country. The above-mentioned Mieg made him the offer, that if he would only go through his church once a year, he would stand by him. But this was against his conscience. Consequently he received his *consilium abeundi*, and had to leave the country. His master Prior had offered the city council 100 Reichsthaler for his employe's freedom ; likewise also a Jewess interceded for him ; but all efforts were in vain. So, after bidding farewell to his Brethren in Heidelberg, whom he never saw again as long as he lived, he departed from Heidelberg, and betook himself to Eberbach to say farewell to his relatives. Before this, while he had worked there, persecutions had already broken out against him, in which the bailiff had been induced to take part. His wife indeed had urged him to leave the innocent man in peace, to which he had replied that he would willingly do so, but that the preachers gave him no rest in the matter. Scarcely had the Superintendent arrived there now, ere his inner guide impelled him to hasten away again, which he obediently did. The very next day his brother came after him, and said that the soldiers had come to seize him immediately after he had left.

Such were the circumstances of his banishment from the country, wherein there is less to be surprised at than if he had been accorded liberty of conscience in the testimony he bore to the destruction of the whole world. In his Discourses, page 326, he described all this under the figure of a restless child whose mother has put it down from her lap, and finally concludes in these words : "Now we see the orphan depart, banished by the mother from city and land." Nevertheless it is sad when a country outrages God's witnesses whom it ought to protect ; for indeed, about the same time many persons were banished from the Palatinate for conscience sake, at Frensheim, Lambsheim, Mutterstadt, Frankenthal, Schriesheim, etc., the most of whom ended their lives in Pennsylvania. It was this that moved the Superintendent thus prophetically to express himself in the 4th *Theosophic Epistle,* page 85 : "*O Land, Land! what will happen unto thee? O Palatinate! what hast thou resting upon thee? How many seasons of gracious visitation from God hast thou allowed to pass over thee? How many of God's witnesses to the truth hast thou consigned to pain and disgrace, and obliged in their misery to sigh and cry out against thee?*"

As to his state of mind, so far as one has been able to gather, it was as follows : He fell into excessive penitence-labors, almost more than his human nature could endure, in which his lively disposition suffered such violence that he contracted consumption, to which was added that the spirit of this world sought to deprive him of every means of making a living, which so deeply affected him that he came near retracting. In this condition he at length came into the region where the Inspirationists lived. There he beheld a worse Babel among the pious who had come out from Babel than he had seen in Babel itself; for while in the latter one religion strove against the other, here persons were opposed one to the other. Each one lived for himself, and regulated his conduct according to his own inclinations, which the Superintendent did not deem possible for truly pious persons. For he has affirmed concerning himself, that from the time of his first conversion he never did anything according to his own ideas, but wherever not under the leading of his inner guide, he subjected himself to the outer authorities. On this point he expressed himself thus in his Discourses : "One has indeed for a long time heard many and various alarm-cries about the fall of Babylon and the judgment of the world ; there has, however, nothing practical come of it, alas! because the vessels and instruments used therefor were of the same material out of which the great Babel itself is built, since they did not attain to the body of Christ, nor were born of water and of the Spirit. Wherefore the work could be no different from what the workman was. And as the vessels were not separated from Adam's body, it was not possible that anything else could result than what had been before ; for ere one was aware of it there arose a worse confusion than in those places where they had spoken scornfully and predicted the fall of Babylon."

There was at that time sojourning in that same region a baker by the name of Schatz, who with his wife feared God, and was a real Gaius, or host, to all the devout. Then they belonged to the Inspired, though they ended their days with the Moravian Brethren. These dear people received him, and together they baked the bread for the devout in that neighborhood, who by their strict life had become spoiled to such a degree that it was a difficult matter to bake for them, so that the Superintendent could bring into play his experience in baking for the saints. He refused, however, to work for wages, as he felt it easier to give his services to any one freely. But Schatz would not agree to this, and said he had had such Brethren before, to whom he always at last had to pay full price for all. In this household he had good opportunity to become acquainted with the Pietists, who found an asylum in this house. Meanwhile he had contracted consumption through his practice of a severe penance, and his strength began palpably to decline ; nor did he know at that time that no spiritual bloom is to be hoped for when once its habitation is destroyed. Everybody felt pity for this young warrior, as for one whose thread of life was about being severed ere yet he had fairly commenced his day's work. But God so ordained it that the renowned Doctor Carl came there ; and then it happened, that while they unitedly engaged in prayer, his spiritual condition was made known to the latter, who accordingly said : "My friend you meditate too much on the world's dark side ;" and after he had given him some instruction as to his condition, he prescribed the use of sheep's-ribs, by which means, through God's grace he became well again. Thereupon his natural liveliness was again awakened in him, and thus he remained until his end ; albeit one could always read in his countenance when he was undergoing sore temptations. At that time, too, he became conscious that for a while his walk in the Spirit had no continuance. He therefore inquired thereof of the mouth of the Lord, when it was revealed to his spirit that he looked too impatiently upon the evil of others—a thing which now is very common among the devout, but not among saints.

He can, however, only be regarded as one of the after-gleanings of that awakening, as there were already two congregations there before him, namely, the Baptists of Schwarzenau, and the Inspirationists of Marienborn. The former seemed to him, as a strict separatist, entirely too sectarian. But among the latter he found entrance through his master, Schatz; they were also nearer to him, wherefore he went with them for a time, although he never became a member of their organization. The head men of the Inspirationists remarked in him a deeply rooted and grounded spirit, which they would not be able to move with all their prophetic exercises; for at his awakening there was entrusted to him a heavenly virginity, so that persons who had the capacity became pregnant thereof if they only came nigh to his person. It once happened that, while he was at one of their meetings, over which Demala, a schoolmaster who had been driven from Worms, had the oversight, beside whom he was kneeling in prayer, two young sisters who knelt opposite them, became violently affected. Demala attributed it to the powers of temptation, and therefore said to him: "Brother Conrad, I advise you to go out." He accordingly did go out, and continued his devotions in another room. After the meeting was over, these sisters were questioned as to their being so strongly moved, when they confessed that they did not know what had caused it, but they did not feel safe themselves. The Inspirationists' displeasure now broke out against him; and it did so in an announcement in which it was said: "Down from thy spiritual high-place; how gladly wouldest thou be called a Brother if," etc. As such announcements were wont to drive men into the fire, he was asked how it had affected him. To this he answered us that it had relieved him, because he had all the while felt a heavier judgment within himself than the one Rock had pronounced. When he noticed, however, that, in order to bring him the more into subjection, they intended to transfer him from the adults' to the children's meeting, he withdrew himself from them. He has, nevertheless, borne favorable testimony concerning the spirit of the Inspiration, namely, that it was a pure, clean, virgin spirit, so that when its instruments went to marrying, it had withdrawn itself again into its chamber; moreover that it was very subtle and skillful to bring to light at the meetings that which was hidden, so that, however anyone behaved at them, none could escape its judgment. At last, however, human powers had mixed in with it, which had subjected everything to themselves ; wherefore, also, they permitted no stranger to attend their meetings oftener than three times.

About this same time he lived with Stiefel, his traveling-companion to America, making a miserable living by spinning wool. For he was poor, and his share of the little which his father had left behind, he had divided among his blood relations. Among his friends was a godly nobleman by the name of Junkerroth, who believed in the transmigration of souls into other bodies, and for this reason never married, as he did not wish to bring up strange spirits. In order to get rid of his wealth he had this custom : when the pious asked him for aid, he gave them the key to his chests and let them take as much as they wished ; and if he heard that anyone had done good on God's account, he paid him therefor. He is known among the learned by his strange translation of the New Testament. Such, then, are the circumstances of the Superintendent's godly calling, wherein he walked for five years in Germany ; now we will examine more closely his divinely-led course in America.

CHAPTER III.

THE SUPERINTENDENT TRAVELS IN PENNSYLVANIA, AND LIVES THERE IN SOLITUDE.

After this latest part of the inhabited earth had lain waste for over 5000 years, it was resolved at a council of the Watchmen to impart unto it a fruitful evening rain, which fell upon Pennsylvania in particular, as shall now be demonstrated. The Superintendent speaks thus of it in his 5th Epistle: "Asia is fallen, and its lamp is gone out. For Europe the sun hath set at bright midday. America sees a lily blooming whose perfume will spread unto the heathen. The evening and the morning will again make a day (GEN. 1). The light of the evening shall send its brightness even unto the morning; and the last promised evening rain shall come to the help of the morning, and bring again the end unto its beginning, whereat Jacob shall be glad, and Israel rejoice." His purpose in this journey really was to spend his life in solitude with God. That in America he should again dive into the ocean of humanity was something of which at that time he probably did not even dream. On the contrary, he was in doubt whether his course was not undertaken in self-will, and therefore wrote to a friend in Manheim : "Know that, since I departed in my self-will from Germany, I have had to pass through many great and bloody trials."

He was, however, induced to undertake this journey by his two intimate friends, Stiefel and Stuntz, who like him were still single and free. Stuntz even offered to pay his way for him. As soon as it became known, the Pietists did their best to dissuade him. Dr. Carl especially advanced the plea of his natural relations, who had become converted through him, and of whom he must render an account if he left them. But a hidden destiny hardened him against all such representations, so that in the year 1720 he entered upon his journey to America. His traveling companions were the afore-mentioned Stiefel and Stuntz, Simon Kœnig, Henry von Bebern, etc. They arrived at Boston that same autumn.

At that time Pennsylvania had a bad name among the neighboring States, and was only known as Quakerland. Its first inhabitants fled for conscience sake into this country, in which they established a peaceful form of government. But after them came differently disposed inhabitants, who took part in the government, though quite opposed to the former. From this there came into being two different kinds of people, who for many years strove for the upper hand, under the names of the Old and the New Assembly, until at last the one party had to yield to the other. Among the then inhabitants is reckoned also a certain religious association, who, under their leader, John Kelpius,[1] settled near Germantown, and for a time were a peculiar light among men because of their holy living; but after their leader died the tempter found occasion to scatter them, as those who had been most zealous against marrying now betook themselves

---

[1] This Kelpius was from Siebenbuergen, of a family of rank; had studied in Helmstadt under Dr. Fabricius; was well versed in the three principal languages, as is to be seen from his letters which still exist among his friends. In London he became acquainted with Pordage, Leade, Deichmann, and Mack, the chaplain of Prince George, and kept up a correspondence with them. In 1694 he arrived in Philadelphia; his traveling companions were Bernhard Kuster, Daniel Falckner, Daniel Lutkins, John Seelig, Lewis Aderman and several others, most of whom were learned men. They were all single, and settled on the Ridge, which then was still a wilderness, on which account they called themselves The Woman in the Wilderness. At that time they numbered about 40 persons, but afterwards increased, for in 1704 Conrad Matthew, a Swiss of rank, joined them, and afterwards Christopher Witt, a celebrated physician and magus, Daniel Geissler and some others.

Kelpius died in the midst of his years, after which their institution went to nothing, although the good name and influence of it have survived even unto the present day. Some betook themselves to women; others had themselves received into the church again; Seelig and Matthews stood fast. The former, in order to escape the society of men, dressed in a coarse habit; the latter, after he had fulfilled righteousness among men by works of love, came to live a life of faith, whereupon God awakened for him a rich merchant, by the name of John Wuester, who served him with his possessions, and also helped to bury him by the side of Kelpius, although he in his humility had not desired to lie beside him, but only at his feet. May God grant him a blessed resurrection!

to women again, which brought such shame on the solitary state that the few who still held to it dared not open their mouths for shame.

In such times the Superintendent arrived at Germantown; but kept very quiet as to his projects for a solitary life, for many, who had maintained a very proper walk in Germany, had here hung up their holy calling on a nail, and, what was worst, would give no one credit for zeal or diligence. Among these were several who in the Palatinate had let themselves be driven from house and home, but here left great wealth behind them after their death. All this caused him much concern; for he everywhere saw the pious sitting at the helm and exercising magisterial offices. As he saw clearly that his trade would not be of much use to him in this country, he determined to learn the weaver's trade, and so put himself under the instruction, for a year, of P. B.,[2] a member of the Baptists. These good people showed him much love, and confessed all their condition to him, namely, how upon the ocean they had lost their love for one another, and now had even become scattered over the country. That the great freedom of this land was one cause of their being thus sold under the spirit of this world, through which all Godly influences had been lost, and each one depended upon himself. "See, dear friend," they further said, "thus it has happened to us; we have become strangers one to the other, and nearly all love and faithfulness have been lost among us." In reply to this he impressively exhorted them not to tarry any longer in so dangerous, loveless, and unregenerate a condition, but to reunite themselves in love to one another, and to drop all contrariness. And then they should make the attempt and see whether they could not call together a meeting; if any good is effected, something will be gained; if not, wait a while longer. This advice was not wholly spoken to the wind, for it is clear from it that he had a hand in the awakening which soon after followed in and about Germantown; for it was through these edifying speeches that these good people were

---

[2] [Peter Becker].

again aroused from their sleepiness. All this occurred in the year 1720, in which year also the rest of the Baptists, under their teacher, Alexander Mack, removed from Schwarzenau to Westervain in West Friesland, whence, after having lived there for nine years, they came to their Brethren in Pennsylvania in the year 1729.

Meanwhile the Superintendent's year of instruction under his master came to an end; and in order to carry out his purpose, he went, in the autumn of the year 1721, into the upper country known as Conestoga, now Lancaster County, which at that time was inhabited by but few Europeans, and there, with the aid of his traveling companion, Stuntz, erected a solitary residence at a place called Muehlbach,[3] where they lived happily for a while. A young Hollander by the name of Isaac von Bebern soon after joined them, with whom he also made a journey to Maryland, probably to visit the remnant of Labadists, who lived there, having left Surinam on account of the climate. These had become so wealthy by their communal life in the latter country that they had owned ships on the sea, all which their descendants had after their death divided among themselves, whereby also many manuscripts of Labadie and Ivonis had come to their hands. Finally a fourth companion came to them in George Stiefel, at the same time that he declared himself to his Brethren that now he would observe the Sabbath and work on Sunday, which did not suit them very well. This strange mode of life aroused much attention among the few settlers, of whom some were continually coming and inquiring what it meant. There is still a person in the Sisters' Convent who in her childhood had gone to school to him, and had become so enamored of his angelic life that she became his steadfast follower, and has now for almost sixty years endured all the hardships of the Solitary and of the communal life.

Before we go any further with this record it will be necessary to call to mind what superstitions at that time disturbed the minds of men. There arose about that time a people in the neighborhood of Oley in Berks County, who called themselves the Newborn, and had one Matthias Baumann as their founder. Their profession was that they could not sin any-

---

[3] [Mill Creek, in what is now Lebanon County].

more. In a pamphlet of 35 pages, 8vo, printed in Germany, and entitled "A Call to the Unregenerate World," it sounds wonderful to hear Baumann say, on page 13 : "Men say that Christ hath taken away sin ; it is true in my case, and of those who are in the same condition in which Adam was before the fall, as I am,"—where he places himself by the side of Adam before his fall. And on page 16 he makes a still bolder leap when he says : "As Adam was before the fall, so have I become, and even firmer." But what provoked people most was what he says on page 12 : "With the body one cannot sin before God but only before men and other creatures, and these the Judge can settle," from which they drew dangerous conclusions. They boasted that they had only been sent by God to confound men, a work which they also diligently carried on during ten years, so that their disputations at market times in Philadelphia were often heard with astonishment, where also Baumann once offered, in order to prove that his doctrine was from God, to walk across the Delaware river.

In their journeys through Conestoga, where they here and there found acceptance, they finally also came to the Superintendent, where Baumann commenced about the new birth. The Superintendent gave him little satisfaction, telling him to smell of his own filth, and then consider whether this belonged to the new birth ; whereupon they called him a crafty spirit full of subtility, and departed. It was observed that from this time on they lost all power to spread their seductions any further, which finally died out with their originators. The Baumann[4] spoken of died about the year 1727.

---

[4]This Matthias Baumann had been a poor day-laborer in the city of Lamsheim in the Palatinate. In the year 1701 he was visited with a severe illness in which he was caught up into heaven and was given revelations for mankind. When he came to himself again, he cried out for hours at a time : "O, men, be converted ! The judgment-day is at hand !" He was caught up again, and then it was told him : Men imagine that they are living in the light of day ; but they are all gone wrong and in the darkness of night. These trances occurred for 14 days, the last one continuing for 24 hours, so that it was thought he had died, and preparations were made for his funeral. When he recovered he went to the minister and told him that God had sent him back into this world to tell men that they should be converted; but the minister, who thought he was out of his mind, sought by means of a worldly book to drive these notions out of his head.

c

He is said otherwise to have been an upright man, and not to have loved the world inordinately; but Kuehlenwein, Jotter, and other followers of his were insatiable in their love of the world.

After this excursion we will return to our main subject. The Superintendent lived very much in privacy at this time, and was held in great straightness by his inner guide; his Brethren knew but little as to where he dwelt. Even when they were provided with means of sustenance, he had no rest in his conscience until he had sent an offering to the hermits on the Ridge. When it was his duty to provide for the table, his Brethren began to complain, and wanted better provisions; to whom he replied that they had not come there to fatten the old Adam. At length Stiefel declared he could not live that way, and took his departure. It was this that broke off their mutual fellowship, so that whatever the Superintendent afterwards did was regarded by Stiefel with displeasure. He ended his life at Bethlehem. God grant him his mercy on the day of judgment! Isaac von Bebern was the next one to desert. He took leave of the Superintendent with much love, and protested that it was not possible for him to live that way. The former gave him the following counsel to take with him: "Know that when you are successful in the world, God has forsaken you; but when all misfortune comes upon you here, then know that God still loves you." After many years he froze both hands and feet in a shipwreck, and was put under the care of Christopher Witt in Germantown. There he remembered this farewell, and sent his last greeting to his old friend.

Stuntz finally even sold their dwelling house and so paid himself back for the traveling expenses which he had loaned him. This breach of faith against God committed by his earliest fellow-warriors, who for the belly's sake forsook the narrow way of the cross, at last brought the Superintendent to the resolve never again to borrow from men on God's account. For he had from the beginning of his conversion been required to walk so rough a road, that he might readily have supposed that hardly one of his followers would remain steadfast in it; and in this skeptical frame of mind he remained for a number of years yet at Ephrata, though here he might have had a better outlook. This was the reason also why so many, who came into too close relations with him, met with misfortune, especially before he yet was connected with any outer communion. For when they beheld the rays of heavenly wisdom that shone forth from him, they fell in love with the heavenly beauty; but as soon as they came nearer to his person, the fire as of a smelting furnace, in which he lived, seized upon them, when straightway they were offended and sought revenge. His circumstances now made it necessary for him to build himself another house, which he did about a mile distant from the former one, at a place called the Swedes' Spring, not knowing what God had further ordained for him. There it came to pass that Michael Wohlfahrt, on his journey to Carolina, visited him for the first time. He was a Pietist, born at Memel on the Baltic Sea, but had grown cool in his faith, and had lost much of it on his many travels. He had come to the Superintendent while Stiefel and Stuntz were still with him, and had so fallen in love with his life that he promised to settle there with him when he should return from Carolina. Meanwhile, when in the year 1724 he came back to him, they had left him. As he laid before him his whole condition, the Superintendent received him in faith. In this man the latter found abundant exercise for his patience, and gained much profit through him in spiritual things. Indeed he fared better with him than he had with his former companions; for, though at times they disagreed, yet Michael Wohlfahrt had such high respect for him that he always confessed himself in the wrong. The next year, however, there joined them J. S., a restless spirit, with unsettled mind, who caused them much trouble. In this solitary state the Superintendent had the desired opportunity to order his life according to his conscience, for then he was not yet overcrowded with men, who delight to empty the lamp of the solitary. In his moderation and abstinence which he then practiced he must be reckoned along with the most approved fathers of the Egyptian wilderness. Frequently, on his visits, he did not eat anything for three days, whereat people took great offence. He has often said, that he did not know to what his great zeal would have brought him, if a visible communion had not been brought into being. And in this solitary state he attained to a blessedness in his communion with God which neither the world nor time can ever outweigh. Wherefore also God afterwards crowned his work with honor and praise, when he had constrained him freely to give this blessedness, which had been gained through so great pains, unto the service of others.

Now also we arrive at the reason why God obliged him to again renounce this seraphic life, and to enter into a communion with others. According to this the life of a hermit is only something granted for a time, but not at all the end itself ; since no solitary person can be fruitful. Accordingly, however innocent his walk before God and man at that time was, it was yet not right in itself ; for with all his renunciations he still had not renounced himself. What was needed was a soil into which he might sow his grain of wheat to die, so that it should spring forth and bear fruit to the glory of God. It has before been mentioned how baptism, as a transplanting into the death of Christ, was again brought to light ; now he had become abundantly convinced on that subject, but at that time he knew neither of a congregation according to his own mind, nor of a man who would have been worthy to baptize him. Once he made an attempt to baptize himself in the waters of Mill Creek ; but his conscience was not satisfied ; nor was the transaction valid, since there were no witnesses present. He was to obtain it through men ; and that was difficult for him. How at last he humbled himself under the ordinance of God, and became a child of the new covenant, this shall be shown forth in the following chapter, although another excursion from the subject will be necessary, in order to trace the matter to its origin.

CHAPTER IV.

THE SUPERINTENDENT IS BAPTIZED IN THE APOSTOLIC MANNER; AND SOON AFTER FOLLOWS THE SEPARATION FROM THE BAPTISTS IN GERMANTOWN.

About the year 1722 many people in Pennsylvania were awakened from their spiritual sleep. The movement first broke out at Germantown, although before this already the Superintendent's solitary life in the wilderness of Conestoga had set the people thereabout to inquiring. In a letter to friend Griess in Manheim he confesses that this awakening had its origin in him; for, after having first spoken of his retired and separate life, he finally says: "In those sorrowful times I purposed to forsake mankind, and with several others betook myself into the forests in the district of Conestoga; but I continued to feel an unchanging heart-yearning to enjoy once more the love of my God before I should die, which also was granted me, and indeed quite suddenly, in an instant, when a ray of light from the divine loving kindness streamed forth, and that too in no other kind of pleasure or enjoyment than that towards which my longing desire had reached forth; then all my misery fell to the ground. Now I thought I had triumphed, and purposed, in the quiet of the spirit, (as separate from all men,) to serve my God continually in his holy temple. But what happened? Ere I was aware, that whole region was illumined by that heavenly light, which in the times following spread over almost all the American provinces, and over various races and tongues of the people. At first, indeed, it tarried for a while in this same region where I dwelt, and in this wise: one heard here and there of one being awakened, and in such places where it was quite unusual, which first of all was the cause for reflection as to what kind of people those must be who lived there solitary in the wilderness (which was myself and another one); at the same time inquiries came to me from inquiring spirits, of a deeply searching kind, as to what were the cause of this quiet and solitary life. Thus it was given me to recommend the mysteries of the kingdom of God by renouncing this world," etc.

Now we must consider the movements of the Baptists at Germantown. Peter Becker, in pursuance of the Superintendent's counsel, with two other Brethren, undertook in the autumn of 1722, a journey to all their Brethren scattered throughout the land, which was their first church visitation in America. They traveled through the regions of Shippack, Falckner's Swamp, Oley, etc., and wherever they came they communicated to their Brethren how they were minded, with their approval, to begin to organize a meeting; also that they were willing to put aside all offences and unpleasant feelings in order that the work might be blessed in its progress. When they came home they began to hold meetings alternately at Peter Becker's and Gomorry's, until the advance of winter prevented them. Next winter, however, they resumed them, weekly, at Peter Becker's.

In August of the year 1723 a rumor was spread through the country that Christ. Libe, a famous Baptist teacher who had long been in the galleys, had arrived in Philadelphia. This moved some newly awakened persons on the Schuylkill to go forth to meet him. The whole thing, however, was a fiction. These persons were persuaded by the Baptists to go with them to their meeting, during and after which they heard so much of the Germans' awakening, that they went home very much edified. Soon after, a second visit was made to Germantown, by which both parties were so much edified that the Germantown Baptists promised them a visit in return, which they also made four weeks afterwards with great blessing. These newly awakened ones were thereby stirred up still more in their love, so that at last they threw themselves at the feet of the Germantown Baptists, and begged to be received into their communion by holy baptism. This was the occasion of important proceedings among the Baptists in Germantown; for they still had in mind the misunderstandings which had arisen between them and their Brethren at Creyfeld. Besides, they were indeed a branch of a congregation, but yet not a congregation that dared to presume to administer the sacraments. The worst was, that they were divided among themselves, and had only lately commenced to draw nigh to one another again. After they had seriously pondered over all these things in the spirit, they finally agreed to consent to the request. Accordingly, after the candidates for baptism had chosen Peter Becker to be their Baptizer, they were baptized in the stream Wiskohikung,[1] near Germantown, on December 25th, of the year 1723. And as these were the firstlings of all baptized from among the high-Germans in America, their names shall here be recorded and given to posterity, namely: Martin Urner and his female house-mate [Hausschwester], Henry Londes and his house-mate, Frederick Lang, and Jan Mayle. The evening following they held the first Lovefeast ever celebrated in America, at John Gomorry's, which created a great stir among the people of that neighborhood; Peter Becker, mentioned before, ministered at the same.

Through such a divine happening the Baptists in Pennsylvania became a congregation, and continued their meetings through that summer with great blessing and edification, until the following winter prevented them. The next spring, of 1724, however, when they resumed their meetings, there was given to them such a blessing that the whole region roundabout was moved thereby. Particularly among their youth was this movement felt, who now, to the great edification of their elders, began to walk in the fear of the Lord and to love the Brethren. And as the fame of this awakening spread abroad, there was such an increase of attendance at their meetings that there was no room to contain the majority.[2] The following summer again many among them were moved, and love-feasts were held, through which many of them were impelled to join them, and so their communion experienced a speedy increase. Under these circumstances

---

[1] [Wissahicken].

[2] It was remarked that the greatest force of this extraordinary awakening did not last longer than seven months; for it commenced in May and began to decline again in the following November, when the awakening in Conestoga took its beginning.

they deemed it well to make a detailed report of this new awakening to their Brethren in Germany. Therefore they prepared in common a writing addressed to them, in which they informed them that they had become reunited in Pennsylvania, and that hereupon a great awakening had resulted in the land, which was still daily increasing; that of the awakened several had joined their communion, to which they had to consent, as they dared not withstand the counsels of God.

Now, after God had so manifestly blessed their labors, they sought to work forward to meet the awakening, and resolved to undertake a general visitation to all their Brethren in the whole country. They fixed upon the twenty-third day of October, of the year 1724, as the time for starting on their visitation from Germantown. They first went to Schippack, thence they traveled to Falckner's Swamp, where a meeting with breaking of bread was held with great blessing, at the house of a Brother named Albertus. From there they journeyed to Oley, where a similar work was done with similar blessing. Finally they came to their newly-baptized Brethren on the Schuylkill, where they held a meeting and bread-breaking, and also baptized two persons. Here they agreed to travel up the country towards Conestoga, for they had heard that there were several awakened persons there. But as some of them were on horseback and some on foot, they divided, and those on foot spent the following night, November 9th, with John Graff, and the riders with Jacob Weber. The following day the party united again at Rudolph Nägele's, at that time a Mennonite teacher, but afterwards a faithful follower of the Superintendent until his death. From there they visited the Superintendent, who at that time lived, a Solitary, with Michael Wohlfahrt. The following night, that is November 10th, they lodged with Stephen Galliond, and thence continued their journey to Henry Höhn, after they had sent two Brethren on before to announce their coming. In this fruitful wilderness there lived at that time part Mennonites, and part Separatists, among which latter the before-mentioned Baumann had spread his doctrine.

A meeting was held at Höhn's on the following day,

November 12th, at which the Superintendent was present. At this meeting extraordinary revival-powers were manifested. The Baptists spoke with such power concerning baptism and the divine purpose concerning fallen man involved therein, that after the close of the meeting five persons applied for baptism, namely, the afore-mentioned Höhn, his house-mate, John Mayer and his house-mate, and Joseph Shäfer, who were at once baptized in Apostolic-wise, by Peter Becker, in the Pequea stream. Soon a sixth one followed these, namely, Veronica, the wife of Isaac Frederick. Now the Superintendent fell into great perplexity. For, to withstand this ordinance of God seemed to him great presumption; at the same time, the calling of these people was not deemed important enough by him, for he had been the recipient of a weighty testimony from God, and feared that, if he associated with them, he might lose all the good he had reached through so much pain. Suddenly, however, his heart was enlightened by a bright ray from the Gospel, in whose light the whole purpose of God was revealed to him, namely, that Christ also had permitted himself to be baptized by one who was less than himself, and had said thereof: "Thus it becometh us to fulfill all righteousness;" and that, in order to make this work easier for us, God himself had thus gone before, and first sought out the field in which he would sow his grain of wheat.

Consequently, after the Sister referred to before came out of the water, he came down from his spiritual pride, humbled himself before his friend Peter Becker, and was baptized by him on the same day in Apostolic-wise, under the water. It was thus that Wisdom brought him into her net: he received the seed of his heavenly virginity at his first awakening; but now a field was prepared for him in America into which he might sow this seed again. Now we will resume our narrative. After the baptism they spent the rest of the day in edifying conversation unto the praise of God, until evening, when a love-feast was held at Höhn's, the first ever held in Conestoga since the country began to be cleansed from its heathenish inhabitants; it was held on November 12th, 1724. The following day they made a visit to Isaac Frederick's mill, when disagreement sprang up among them, because some so vehemently insisted on returning home. Peter Becker and the majority, however, insisted upon holding another meeting, which also was done, on the following Sunday, at Sigmund Landert's. But this meeting was not at all like the previous ones in power and spirit, and it was remarked that from that day on their power declined. First of all, the women began a quarrel; and then Simon König, Michael Wohlfahrt, and others, joined together to assail the Baptists on account of their controversies across the sea. Simon König made the attack, but, as he acted very injudiciously, the rest were ashamed of him and left him in the lurch. Consequently, the meeting passed over fruitlessly, as did also the baptism of Sigmund Landert and his wife, which followed; for they baptized them in such unclean water that they ought to have had a washing afterwards. On this occasion Peter Becker made the following address to the people: "These two persons have applied to us for baptism; but as they are unknown to us in their walk and conversation, we make this announcement of the fact to all men here present, especially to their neighbors. If you can bear favorable witness concerning their lives, it is well, and we can baptize them with the greater assurance; but if you have any complaints to bring against them, we will not do it." It appears from this that he required persons to have led an honorable life before he would baptize them. Whether this is Apostolic we will not stop to discuss; baptism contains in itself the forgiveness of all past sins.

We will now proceed to their departure. Before they left this newly planted congregation, they, especially Peter Becker and Henry Traut, conferred much with the newly baptized with reference to the organization of their household, and said among the rest: "You can now arrange your affairs among yourselves to the best of your ability; the better you do it, the better we will be pleased, since you constitute together a little congregation. You are in no way to be bound to us, as we are at too great a distance from you. We therefore advise you to arrange your affairs among your-

selves, according to your daily circumstances. Neither do we
recognize any pope who would rule over you, but we commend you to the grace of God, which must accomplish everything, etc." Afterwards they were very sorry for these words,
and themselves regarded what they had done as unwise,
because they had let this new congregation pass out of their
hands. They thought one should not have entrusted so
much to beginners, and that now they would have to tolerate
everything, no matter how strangely these newly converted
might act towards them. However, they were entirely mistaken, at least as to the Superintendent, who at that time
had already spent eight years in his calling, and had been
well trained therein. After they had given the kiss of peace to
one another, they betook themselves upon their homeward
journey.

A sensible person, acquainted with the counsels and plans
discussed by them on their homeward journey, as they are
described by a Brother among them, J. M., must soon become
aware that they gave entirely too much room to their suspicion against this new congregation, from which of necessity
such a schism had to follow. They indeed considered it a
blessing that they now already had planted two congregations in the land, namely, one on the Schuylkill and the
other in Conestoga; but concerning the latter they were
in perplexity, and thought they ought to send a Brother
there as Superintendent, for which they proposed one Kemper, as being both edifying and having the gift of prayer.
But what troubled them most was that they had heard that
the Superintendent and two others observed the Sabbath.
Most of them insisted that one should prescribe rules for the
Brethren in Conestoga, that they might observe the Sabbath
for themselves, but should preach its observance to no
one else, so that whoever wished might observe Sunday.
Thereupon another one said: "If they intend to observe the
Sabbath, they must observe also the whole law; for he who
ordained the Sabbath ordained also circumcision." Others
said it was a strange thing that the Brethren in Conestoga
had so firmly settled upon the Sabbath, and yet would not
preach it; for if it was ordained to be observed, it must also

be preached. This they said because the Superintendent had declared that he had received no command to preach it to others, but only to observe it himself. At last, however, they all became agreed that so long as the Brethren in Conestoga were so few in numbers they might grant others their liberty, but that if they should increase they would probably make the attempt to bring others also under this Jewish ordinance. Finally, they charged Peter Becker with having left too much in the hands of these newly converted ones.

All these matters deserve closer investigation. Whoever considers this journey, together with the great blessing accompanying it, must confess that God was with them, at least up to the time when that man was found whom he had destined for a more important work. It is also certain that the Superintendent dealt with them in sincerity, and entered into communion with them with his whole heart. Had they not in the beginning permitted their suspicion against him to overmaster them, but had they condescended to him as he had done to them, he would have been the man through whom they would have recovered again their first vocation received at Schwarzenau; for he had a higher witness than they; such an unpleasant division would not have taken place; but, on the contrary, they might have received into their shelter many virgin spirits in future times. The Superintendent visited Peter Becker yet on his death-bed, and among the rest said to him: "What a pity it is that there were no wise men among you when the awakening in Conestoga commenced; how we could now live under your shelter!" Whereupon the latter wept. Of all this honest Henry Kalckgläser, one of their teachers and originators, who ended his days at Ephrata, may be accepted as a witness; for the same gave as the reason why he left them and joined the new congregation, that at Ephrata he had found again his first revival spirit. However, they had at that time already strayed so far away from the bounds of the Spirit, that they could not live under so sharp a testimony. Defection from God takes place first of all within the heart, even while outwardly there may often still be a great deal of ado made about him, especially in forms of worship; but its fruits at last will be brought to light. Accordingly, as they failed in God's trial of them, his choice passed from them, and with the election all blessing also, unto the person of the Superintendent, of which Peter Becker must have had a consciousness, for he confessed that on the journey to Conestoga they had lost something which they had never afterwards recovered. Even if the Superintendent had been a deceiver, as many of them called him, yet they did not follow the right method to reclaim him; they ought to have come down to him in humble faith, then he would have stood by them, or, if he had not been the right man, God would have released them. This was done by many others who would have had more right to withstand his testimony, since they had been many years under his leadership, which certainly was a stern and strange one; but these made it a matter of conscience to do so, as being convinced of his being divinely sent. Whether or not such trials shall come again, time will show; certain it is that nothing can be overleaped in the divine Providence's leading. The Superintendent, shortly before his end, met some of them on a journey, when he asked a Brother what kind of people they were, being so reserved towards him? The Brother answered, "They are Baptists." "Well, well," said he, "I shall yet become their prince in eternity." These circumstances have a certain likeness to the history of Jacob and Esau; for to these good people belonged indeed, as to the older son, the rights of the first-born; but they lost them through the younger one, and therefore, as Esau against Jacob, they conceived a strong dislike against him, which afterwards they handed down to their descendants.

But O, thou great God! they stumbled at that stumblingstone. O the depth of the riches, both of the wisdom and knowledge of God! how unsearchable are his judgments, and his ways past finding out! Thou dost let us stumble and fall so that in our best efforts we might be confounded, and no man may say to thee, why doest thou thus? For a holy purpose thou didst deliver up to Satan thy servant Job, who faithfully served thee, in order that thy mercy might be magnified in him. Yea, thou didst forsake thy child Jesus himself upon the cross, in order that thy great salvation might be manifested under all the heavens. Therefore spare not us; only lead us not into temptation lest we become vessels of wrath to offend thy saints. And if we must stumble at thee and fall, grant that we may thereby be humbled and brought to a knowledge of ourselves, that the tempter may be confounded in us.

CHAPTER V.

THE NEW CONGREGATION ESTABLISHES ITSELF UPON THE DOCTRINE OF THE HOLY APOSTLES, AND ELECTS THE SUPERINTENDENT AS ITS TEACHER.

After the Superintendent had now ratified his covenant with God in the water, in which he gave himself unconditionally unto him, Providence brought it about that those who had been baptized with him elected him as their Teacher. In this John Mayer was mainly instrumental; and thus without himself seeking it he was thrust into the vineyard. His ordination to this office he received from the same one who had bestowed it upon Elijah, John the Baptist and other reformers, who were awakened specially and directly to come to the help of a church fallen asunder. Experience has shown that, as soon as he assumed the office, a large measure of the Spirit rested upon him; wherefore, as soon as he began to hold meetings, contention arose against him throughout the whole land, which has not ceased even after his death. Many of his former friends, when they became aware of this sudden change in him, declared that he had gone out of his mind; thus Henry Zimmermann once said to him: "Conrad, Conrad! You have taken upon you a sore load; you will get to be a fool; I have known such people in Germany." He conducted all meetings, however, with astonishing strength of spirit, and used so little reflection over it, that even in the beginning he was not suffered to use a Bible; so that the testimony in its delivery might not be weakened by written knowledge. He began his discourse with closed eyes, before a large crowd of hearers; and when he opened his eyes again the most of them were gone, not being able to endure the Spirit's keenness. On such occasions wonderful mysteries of eternity were often revealed through him of which he himself had before been ignorant; but these were soon sealed up again, and then he would say:

"The Spirit retires again into his secret chamber." Whenever he felt that persons were present who sought to catch and confine his discourse in the meshes of reason, he would suddenly be moved to hold a discourse directly contradictory of his former one, and that too with equally strong reasoning, so that his hearers were thrown into a holy confusion. At the same time he was very sensitive to any hidden obstacle that might be present at the meeting, and in such case never ended until everything was right again. On one occasion, while he was engaged in an important discourse at a meeting, a man entered who probably had been living unchastely, whereupon he cried out: "What is that? I smell women——" whereupon the man speedily decamped. He was a born orator, and could carry out a proposition to great lengths, especially if he had rationalistic persons before him, for which his opponents blamed him very much. In his delivery, however, he was too fast, because he had to hurry after the Spirit, when he often concerned himself but little about the rules of language.

To return to the history. The congregation went on, and in December, 1724, held its first love-feast with Brother Sigmund Landert, at which the Superintendent officiated for the first time. At the beginning of the next year he made a journey to the Schuylkill and Germantown to the Baptists, for then they were still united. He had for companions two Judaizing Brethren, who were very burdensome to him and at the places where they lodged; for they had such a fear of pork that they would not eat out of any vessel that was not quite clean. It is true that the Superintendent had a deep insight into the secrets of nature; from the nature of the food he knew how it would affect the unclean members; and from this the suspicion against pork and unclean foods first arose; as the first Christians, it is well known, also avoided them. (Vid. Zozim. Hist. Ecc. Cap. XI). His followers, deeply in love with his pure life, imitated him not only in this, but went still further, and raised scruples against geese also, because these supply man with their feathers for his luxurious indulgence. Consequently both these creatures were banished from the housekeeping of the Sabbatists.

At this circumstance the Baptists were not a little offended, for they had already before suspected the new congregation of intending to revive Judaism. To this was added another circumstance that also pained them much, in that in the year 1725 one of their proselytes, Jan Mayle, went over to the new congregation, whom afterwards many followed.

In the beginning of May, 1725, a meeting was held at John Landes's, where the Superintendent for the first time held a baptism, baptizing seven, of whom the most important were Michael Wohlfahrt and Rudolph Nägele. The first of these had lived with him, and it seems that the Divine Wisdom had given him to the Superintendent that the latter might be exercised in his holy walk, for they were both of choleric disposition. Soon after this man's baptism they two traveled about the country, and announced to men the counsels of God concerning future salvation, whereby many became greatly exercised, and some few were awakened, but the most disregarded it. Several tried to hide themselves from the truth behind the Law of Moses; for soon after, A. W. of Oley, and D. C., circumcised each other after the Jewish manner, and then blasphemed much against Paul because he did away with circumcision. On this account the Superintendent wrote them an emphatic letter, in which he speaks thus: "I counsel you, for the sake of the Mediator Jesus Christ, leave off your folly, lest you lose thereby even the grace and promises of the new Covenant. You have not a single witness among all the Apostles upon going among the Gentiles with the Gospel that circumcision was even so much as thought of at a single place." (See his Theosoph. Epistles, Page 125.)

Circumstances now demanded that they must sacrifice to God their beloved solitude in the wilderness, for the good of their neighbor. Wherefore they moved apart, and a little house was erected for the Superintendent on the land of the afore-mentioned Nägele; and here these spiritual Israelites had their first settlement, after they came out of Egypt, passing through the Red Sea, that is, the water of baptism. Soon others joined themselves to him, and then one could see in their little houses an edifying picture of the huts of the holy Fathers in the Egyptian wilderness. In this region wonderful influences came down upon him from eternity, of which the least ever became known. The afore-mentioned Nägele must have had very minute acquaintance with the same, otherwise he would hardly have been able to endure so strange a leading, in which he manifested greater fidelity to the Superintendent than could have been expected from any man. Wherefore he was often heard to say: "Let Nägele speak and tell what kind of a man I was; so much doth God venture on a man that he may bring him into his net."

Now, however, the time drew nigh when God remembered Rachel in her long barrenness that she became pregnant. For it was resolved in the Council of the Watchers that in the sixth period, as being the Philadelphian church-season, a virgin should be made ready as the bride of the High Priest, and for this Pennsylvania was specially chosen. And now the Spirit awakened many free souls of both sexes, who began to strive for the knightly crown. Among the female sex the first were two natural sisters, A. and M. E.[1] They fled from their father's house in the year 1726, and put themselves under the Superintendent's guidance, which caused much remark in the country, especially since he had to be with them very much. The congregation built them a house on Mill Creek, in which they lived four years. In the same year, at Easter, R. N.[2] held a love-feast, at which two Brethren from the Schuylkill, H. L. and D. E.,[3] were present, and at which a controversy arose between H. L. and the Superintendent. The former asked how it could be consistent with the righteousness of God that so many innocent children had to suffer along with the rest in the general courts of justice. The Superintendent answered: "They have indeed not sinned as yet; but they are not on that account innocent, for the evil nature is in them, which plainly shows itself with increase in years." *Question:* "Do you not believe that they will be saved if they die thus?" *Answer:* "No." *Question:* "Then you consider them to be damned." *Answer:* "That we do not say; but we

---

[1] [Anna and Maria Eicher]. [2] [Rudolph Nägele].
[3] [John Landes and Daniel Eicher.]

hold that they must be purged from their inherited sin by means of a kind of purgatory." Their purpose was to elevate the natural married state into an holy estate, in order thus to give the right to salvation to children; but when they failed in this, they both became offended and did not hold to the congregation any more. One of them afterwards took his child up in his arms, kissed it, and said: "O, thou poor child! art thou to be damned if thou wert now to die? That would be a horrible thing, since thou hast not yet sinned." And because this man afterwards in his offended mood passed into eternity, the rumor was brought to the Baptists that the Superintendent had permitted a Brother to die without being reconciled with him; yes, and that he had spread a new heresy in Conestoga, namely, that innocent children are damned when they die. These people, as is apparent in some of their hymns, agree with the Mennonite Church in this, that they think that infants are born pure and innocent. And because the Superintendent recognized the advantage flesh and blood sought over these people, his opposition caused him to be called a forbidder of wedlock.

Meanwhile, amidst these differences, the work of revival went on. About seven weeks after these occurrences, a Brother on the Schuylkill, by the name of Urner, held a love-feast, on Whitsuntide, to which both congregations were invited, for, apparently at least, they were as yet undivided; and because the regular teacher, P. B.,[4] was not present, the Superintendent was obliged to officiate. On this occasion quite extraordinary powers of eternity manifested themselves, such as were never known before or after, so that it was called the congregation's Pentecost. On the first day of the festival everybody in the meeting was as though drunken with wine, and it was noticed that several, who had engaged in prayer, soon after married, and so dragged the gifts of the Spirit into the flesh. The Superintendent bore himself as calmly in the matter as if it did not concern him at all; for he had then already learned enough in the school of the Spirit to treat the good without any self-assumption, which is the worst of sins. After the meet-

---

[4][Peter Becker].

ting he baptized eleven in the Schuylkill. Through this occurrence the Baptists were confounded in the person of the Superintendent. On the one hand, they had to admire the extraordinary gifts of the man; on the other, they knew that he had the name of being a seducer and a destroyer of wedlock. They put their heads together and took counsel; but knew not what judgment to form. Meanwhile on the following night the love-feast went forward with blessing; at the same it was announced that on the following Whit-Monday another meeting would be held. This meeting finally threw the good Baptists into the greatest amazement; for the powers of the new world were again poured out like a river, the singing was pentacostal and heavenly; yea, some declared that they heard angel-voices mingling with it, of which the reader has liberty to judge for himself. Certain it is that in the times following it pleased the Spirit to bring revivals to men by means of song, so that at length there was developed such singing among the Solitary as has never been equaled by any party in the Christian Church from the days of Ignatius on, to whom first was made known by revelation the antiphonal style of the choral singing of the holy angels. As the suspicion against the Superintendent had notably increased after the close of the meeting, many thought that he must be a sorcerer, and were in fear lest their wives might be seduced. One otherwise upright Brother, M. U., embraced his wife, and exclaimed, "O, my dear wife! I pray you for God's sake do not leave me!" Such is the effect when God reaches forth into the church of Adam.

In August, 1727, a grand visit was made by the Baptists of Germantown to the congregation in Conestoga. On the way Henry Traut and Stephen Koch left the party and visited one named J. S.,[5] who had been with the Superintendent when he was yet a pioneer settler, and his whole house had been drawn to him; at this time, however, he was under a ban for having married too near a relation, and was possessed of satanic powers. Him they loosed from his ban and brought to Henry Höhn, where there was a general gather-

---

[5] [Jacob Stuntz].

ing. There he became raving and imitated the cries of various animals, most however of ducks, so that no one could imitate him. As the two Brethren had loosed him from his ban on their own responsibility, they were put under discipline; wherein the Superintendent had to adapt himself to the circumstances of the time, otherwise the ban was something contrary to his convictions.

CHAPTER VI.

CONCERNING A NEW AWAKENING IN FALCKNER'S SWAMP, AND THE TRANSACTIONS WITH THE BAPTISTS CONNECTED THEREWITH.

At the close of 1727, or the beginning of the next year, Michael Wohlfahrt, with the sanction of the congregation, traveled to Falckner's Swamp, and visited several newly awakened ones there; concerning whom he brought home such good reports that, in March, 1728, the Superintendent with three others made a visit there, and with such effect that, on the eighth of the month, eleven persons were baptized, whom five more followed in May. Over these Andreas Frey[1] was appointed as Elder. Since this awakening not only brought many out of the domestic state to the Superintendent, all of whom now have finished their walk of faith, but also increased the settlement by adding thereto many Solitary ones of both sexes, of whom several are still at their labors; it shall be circumstantially described. After the Baptists at Germantown now received news of this awakening, they were not a little astonished that they of Conestoga still presumed to baptize and break bread, since they stood openly unreconciled with those of Germantown, as they had proved by recently putting two of the Germantown Brethren under the ban. H. L., too, at the Schuylkill, who had had the controversy with them about the salvation of infants, had died unreconciled with them, without their having forgiven him; therefore they considered it their duty to warn these newly awakened ones. Accordingly, they

---

[1] Afterwards, out of opposition to the Superintendent, this A. F. left the congregation and went over to the Moravian Brethren, with whom he traveled to Germany, but afterwards left them also, the circumstances of which he published after his return to America. This awakening produced many false priests, of whom several became the first-born of the devil; all of which was caused by the Superintendent's humility with which he always gave offices to others.

held a meeting at Falckner's Swamp with one Brother John Henry Hagemann, at which they tried to blind the eyes of these newly awakened, and talked much to them of how they loved the Brethren in Conestoga, until they at last stole their hearts, and put their minds into such confusion, that they no longer knew whether they should love or hate the Conestoga Brethren.

When this became known among the congregation at Conestoga the Superintendent sent two Brethren to them with a letter, in which he gave them a stern rebuke for the falseness, deceit, and craftiness which they had practiced upon the newly awakened ones. This letter was an additional cause of the separation that followed. O, how blest these good people would have been, if they could have stopped their self-righteousness and have gone into judgment with themselves! But they missed it. Instead, they made the letter known among the newly awakened, and made them judges concerning the insult (as they called it), to help to condemn its author. Then they held a meeting in the Swamp, with a Brother Albertus, at which it was resolved that in four weeks a meeting should be held there, with William Frey, for trial and judgment, at which both parties, those of Germantown and those of Conestoga, should appear. There the newly awakened should be the judges whether the accusations of the letter against them of Germantown were true or false. To this end they desired them to be neutral, and until then they were to give neither hand nor kiss to anyone. When the Brethren in Conestoga were informed of this proposal they were astonished; first, at its political craftiness; then that inexperienced persons were to be the judges in so important a controversy, and in the third place, at their daring in presuming to invite the congregation at Conestoga to such a mock-proceeding. Therefore, six Brethren from the Conestoga congregation were sent beforehand to Falckner's Swamp, and lodged with Brother John Henry Hagemann, who also received them, contrary to the admonition, with hand and kiss, and whom the other households followed in this, notwithstanding that several took offence, and thought the Conestoga Brethren had no clear conscience, but had come thus early because they did not trust to appear at the trial.

Now let us put aside these quarrels for a while. After A. F.[2] had given up his office among the Brethren, M. W.[3] took his place, who did not fare much better than the former. It was his good fortune that he was a man after God's own heart, who had learned to humble himself when he came into judgment, and besides, had a superhuman fidelity to the Superintendent. He fell from his office with shame and disgrace, and thereupon fell at the feet of the Superintendent, who then revoked the judgment and received him again into spiritual communion. He afterwards filled his place with one J. L.,[4] a novice, who besides was at the time spiritually puffed up. He had his office only six weeks; and how the Superintendent's life was endangered through him will be narrated in the sequel. It would be worth investigating, by the way, as to what was the cause why so many were unfortunate in these offices; for experience has proved that the Order sacrificed its most important persons of both sexes in these offices, some of them having to pay the penalty with their lives, others who fell through them afterwards recovered with great difficulty, and thanked God when they were permitted to spend their days in private life; so that one could hardly get anyone to take the offices any more. On the one hand the cause probably was that subordination to the Superintendent personally was so difficult; but it seems that the Spirit, under whose ordering the Superintendent stood in his work, had chosen him for this important service. Besides, seeing that his whole life was spent in intense pain, as those knew who came into close communion with him,[5] it is a greater wonder that any at all endured under his leading, than that so many were wrecked thereby.

---

[2][Andreas Frey].   [3][Michael Wohlfahrt].   [4][John Landes].

[5]If anyone wishes to know in what straits he spent his life, let him read the 278th hymn of the "Paradisisches Wunderspiel," of which the first verse is as follows:—

"O, eternal glow! what a burning is there among the saints upon earth, who own themselves to God until each is preserved like gold that is purged through incessant smelting in the pot. O, what a wearisome sweating! until one attains the crown of gold."

In this year there were yet several occurrences which deserve to be mentioned. The first is the conversion of the first Prior of the Brotherhood at Ephrata, named Israel Eckerlin, which himself has thus described: "My father, Michael Eckerlin, was a councilman of Strasburg, which office and place he left for conscience sake, and moved to Schwarzenau, where he held to the congregation of Baptists, and stood in good repute on account of his piety. After his death, our mother, with her four sons, moved to Pennsylvania in the year 1725. On the ocean God visited me with sickness, so that I made a vow, that if he would help me to my health again, I would become converted and commence a different life after we would get to land. I thereupon indeed became well again, but my promise I did not fulfill; for when we saw land I remembered my vow, and wished I might always be on the water. As soon as we had landed, vanity again took hold of me. But about the same time M. W.,[6] a Brother of the new congregation, came to my mother, whose words so deeply moved me that I afterwards said to my mother: 'This Brother's words have effected very much for me,' and determined to make a visit to them. Meanwhile I bound myself out to a master who also had a drawing to the good. Once we visited Conrad Matthew at Germantown, who advised us to leave those regions, because the people there lived in vanity, and to move up the country to Conestoga, where the people lived in great simplicity, and which was like a new Switzerland to look upon. This counsel suited us; and in August, 1727, we moved there. For a time we adhered to the Mennonites, because their simplicity of dress pleased us; but to their mode of worship we never could adapt ourselves. Then we inquired about the new congregation and its Superintendent, but heard of nothing but whoredom and lewdness, which were said to prevail there. I said to my master, however, that I could not believe this, as I had a different impression of them. After that we worked for Christopher Saur, who brought us to a meeting of the new congregation, at which I was strengthened in my good resolve to such a degree, by the words of

---

[6] [Michael Wohlfahrt].

the Superintendent, that on Whitsuntide of the year 1728, I was incorporated in this new congregation by holy baptism, together with my master and another Brother, Jacob Gass by name." So far his narrative.

About this time, namely, in the year 1728, the power of God manifested itself palpably in the meetings, witnessing against the old Adam and his many false sanctuaries; whereat many were offended and separated themselves from the congregation. These Separatists, like men sick with a plague, finally banded together, and set up a meeting of their own; so that in those times there were more apostates than there were righteous ones; which, however, by no means confounded the Superintendent; for he had reckoned on all these, and yet worse, quarrelings, when he left his beloved solitary state and waded into the sea of humanity. Since it was known that these apostates were supported by the Baptists of Germantown, M. W. felt himself moved to go into the meeting of these Baptists, and thus spoke to them: "Men and Brethren, thus saith the Lord, ye have gone mad; this is a city that is destroyed! And unto you, Peter Becker, the Lord saith, why dost thou declare my rights and hast my covenant on thy lips, while yet thou hatest order and throwest my words behind thee!" After he had thus done, he went his way again. This occurred in December, 1728.

It is also to be mentioned here that while, during a certain night, the Superintendent was at prayer, and was deeply moved, on behalf of the entire Christian Church, somebody knocked at the door, and asked him to come in haste to a neighbor, Peter Beller. When he came there he found the daughter of the latter about breathing her last, who desired baptism from him. Now although the Superintendent would have had faith to baptize her in flowing water, yet her parents would not allow it; so she was baptized in the house in a tub. Thereupon she asked to have a meeting at her house on the next Sabbath, which the Superintendent granted her; but when the congregation assembled there at the appointed time, they found her lying in her coffin; so the meeting was turned into a funeral. God grant her a blessed resurrection! This so deeply moved the parents that they both had themselves also baptized.

At that time also the Superintendent's Ninety-nine Mystical Sayings became known in print. When a learned scholar, named Gulde, saw them, he traveled to him, and asked him why he had made 99 of them and not 100. His answer was: that as the number 99 was reached he was stopped in the Spirit. Then he asked him why he observed the Sabbath. The answer: That he had experienced that whenever the Sabbath came all his burdens, which rested upon him during the week, were removed, which did not happen to him on Sundays. Against this he had no objections to make, and went his way edified. It was mentioned above that M. W. had borne prophetic witness against the Baptists in Germantown. He did more such work in those days. For on October 19th, 1729, he and another Brother went into a meeting of the Quakers in Philadelphia, and, after he had listened a long while to a female preacher, he finally began to speak: "My friends, I beseech you to hearken unto me, for I have a few words from the Lord to you, therefore I demand that you hear me. For I will not leave this place until I have delivered my message which I am sent to bring, that I may be guiltless before the Lord, and may go my way hence again in peace." The speeches and replies are in print, but are too lengthy to reproduce here. Similarly also he bore witness in the market in Philadelphia, which also was published in English and in German.

CHAPTER VII.

THE SABBATH IS INTRODUCED IN THE CONGREGATION; WHEREFORE THE LATTER IS BROUGHT UNDER THE JUDGMENT OF THE WORLD; BESIDES MANY OTHER DISTURBANCES.

In the year 1728 the Superintendent published a little book on the Sabbath, which was so effective that the congregation now publicly adopted the Sabbath as the day for divine services. Before this the meetings had been held on Sunday, and the Sabbath celebrated in quiet. Neither in this, nor in the consequent disturbances, did the Superintendent have any part. Once the congregation wanted to put him under the ban for working on the Sabbath, whereupon he recognized that the matter was from God. At that time there were among the English people various families who observed the Sabbath, like Abel Noble, Welchs, Ritter, etc., but according to the law of the land they also had to observe Sunday. To this these new Sabbatists did not want by any means to adapt themselves; but they held to the Law, worked six days, and rested the seventh, which occasioned a good deal of commotion in the land. For not only did the mob perpetrate many excesses against them, but at length the civil authorities also interfered, in that they confined the Solitary in prison, and sold the horses of the householders, offering, after deducting the amount of the fine, to pay them back the balance on demand, to which they invariably received the reply that they might keep that also, since it was written, He that taketh from thee that is thine, demand it not of him again. It is worth while to record for posterity the mild conduct of the authorities towards these people, of which several instances are given. Several Brethren, when brought before the justice, who demanded a fine from them, answered thus: that they owed him nothing and still less wanted to give him anything; if he wished to get anything he would have to take it. Others said that they regarded God's law more than England's law. At another time a Brother fell into the hands of a justice who had much to say about the English law with reference to the observance of Sunday, and took up his law-book in order to prove it. The Brother said: that he should lay aside his law-book, as he was subject to a higher, namely God's law-book, so that his English law-book had no authority over him. The justice put away his book, and said he might go home, he would make him a present of his fine if he would not work on Sunday in future. The Brother replied that he would not cease to work on Sunday, and, besides, that he could not make him a present, since he did not owe him anything; but that if he did owe him anything he would pay it, and not accept any present from him; to which the justice said nothing further.

Whoever knew the peaceful disposition of the Superintendent can easily imagine that this behavior of his people was a severe trial for him. To some Brethren who once asked his prayers as they were cited before the authorities, but who were dismissed again in peace, he said that God had given the heart of the authorities into his hand, and he had turned it as he pleased. This had such an effect that afterwards various ones willingly paid their fines; and because they showed such Christian discretion, the authorities relaxed their strictness, and overlooked such people's offences, which is done even to the present day.

Now we will take the new congregation in hand again. The witness of God concerning the judgment against the old Adam, as it was applied by the Superintendent with much severity, was the cause of one revolt after the other among his followers. This continued until his death; yes, some followed him with slander even after his death. No meeting was held at which some did not fall to quarreling, and mostly it was on the subject of the matrimonial estate; for he was accused of seeking to prescribe laws and rules for the same, and this was regarded as a teaching of the devil. It was mentioned above concerning the apostates that they organized an own congregation, in which J. H. and D. E.[1] were

---

[1] [John Hildebrand and Daniel Eicher].

teachers. To these a Brother, Joel by name, went in their meeting, and spoke thus: "To you, J. H., I have a word from the Lord to say. Thus saith ґthe Lord: Thou shalt no longer go forth and preach to others, but first thou and thy house must be converted, then thou canst go forth and convert others. If thou heed not this warning voice, the judgment of the Lord shall come upon thee because thou hast not done according to his Words. Moreover this day it shall be made manifest whether we or you are the congregation of God; for God will to-day perform a wonder and sign in me, in that if I shall fall down before your eyes as one that is dead, and ye will pray for me that I may arise again, then God hath not sent me unto you, and you are the Lord's congregation. But if I do not fall dead before your eyes, but shall go out of the door again well and hearty, then ye shall know that the Lord hath sent me to you this day, and that you are not the Lord's congregation. Eight days ago as I was in your meeting, I said that there were wolves among you;"—and after seizing one of them, Henry Höhn by name, by the arm, he said, "here is a wolf," and then went away with his companion.

Some of the congregation thought as much of this testimony, and also of that of M. W., recorded above, as if the Holy Spirit had dictated it; therefore they had them carefully written out. But another Brother, Amos by name, who looked upon this as idolatry, with the sanction of the Superintendent gained possession of these testimonies by craft and burned them, saying he would try whether they could endure the fire-test. The sensible reader will know how to take the best out of this. About the same time the Superintendent also made a prophetic address against a Brother who used to turn everything good to ridicule, whereby he kept his whole house alienated from God. The address is as follows: "Thou child of man, I have set thee for a watchman over the house of Israel, that, when thou hearest out of my mouth thou mayest warn them on my behalf. If now I say to the ungodly: Thou ungodly one must die the death, and thou dost not tell him so, that the ungodly may be warned from his course, the ungodly shall die because of his ungodliness; but his blood shall be demanded of thy hand. But if thou warn him to repent of his evil ways, and he refuse to repent, then he shall die because of his sin, but thou hast saved thy soul." After he had spoken these words he thought that he was done, but when he awoke the following morning, he was again impelled to speak, and said: "H. H.,[2] thus saith the Lord to thee: Thou ungodly one, thou hast joined thyself to a lot of ungodly ones, to an impious woman, and hast committed adultery against the wife of thy youth. Thy sin and shame shall be uncovered before all people, and thy woes shall be like unto those of a woman in travail, etc." This address he sent to the meeting of the Separatists while the Baptists of Germantown were there, who made it known everywhere.

[2][Henry Höhn].

CHAPTER VIII.

THE TWO BAPTIST CONGREGATIONS SEPARATE ENTIRELY; AND THE BRETHREN AT CONESTOGA GIVE THEIR BAPTISM BACK AGAIN TO THE OTHERS.

It appears that the Superintendent at that time was much beholden in his divine work to the Baptists of Germantown, which came from the fact that he had received his baptism from them. They boasted that they had given birth to the new congregation out of the elements; thus boasting themselves of fleshly things. On this account we must make some allowance for the Superintendent's vehemence against them. They came in the way of that Spirit under whose dominion he stood, so that, in the hymns he made at that time, he used terrible expressions about them. Consequently, when he noticed that their power of opposition was owing to his baptism, the resolve was finally reached to give these people their baptism back again; which also was done in December of the year 1728. For then Brother Amos first rebaptized the Superintendent, who then rebaptized him, another Brother, and four Sisters; so that once more the Sabbatic number seven became the foundation of rebaptism in the congregation. This transaction not only provoked the Baptists anew, but also caused great disturbance in the congregation itself; for some halted between two opinions, and secretly held to the Baptists, because they hankered after such a worship in which flesh and blood could be redeemed.

In the year 1729 Alexander Mack, the founder of the Baptists, with the rest of the congregation mentioned, left Friesland and came to Pennsylvania. This reverend man would have well deserved to be received with arms of love by all the pious in common, after all that he had had to suffer in Germany, especially from his own people. But he was no sooner arrived among his fellow-believers, than they filled his ears with heavy accusations against them of Conestoga, namely, how they had separated from them, had written them abusive letters, and had treated them very unlovingly with judgments and condemnations ; yea, and over and above all this, they had yet done a terrible thing whereby not only they, but even their dead, had been condemned and put under the ban. When he asked what this had been, the reply was, that they had all had themselves rebaptized as separate from the Baptists. Now the good man should, at least until he had made himself thoroughly acquainted with the matter, have suspended his judgment. But prejudices so overpowered his mind, that he was not capable of passing a sound judgment, nor of counteracting the separation. Nevertheless he made an attempt, and in October of the year 1730 undertook a visit to Falckner's Swamp with several of his Brethren. The Superintendent knew nothing of this; but made a journey thither at the same time, and held a meeting at Brother John Senseman's, to which also, quite unexpectedly, the visitors from Germantown came. Alexander Mack made an address and said: "The peace of the Lord be with you!" The Superintendent replied: "We have the same peace." Thereupon Alexander Mack asked why they had put them under the ban ; and proposed that both parties should betake themselves to prayer that God might reveal to them which was guilty of the separation. It would indeed have been better for them to take upon themselves both known and unknown sins than to force the divine righteousness; however, judgment lay so heavily upon them that they had not the grace to do so. They accordingly fell upon their knees, and after making their complaints to God, they arose, and A. M. asked: "Where is Conrad Beissel?" They pointed towards him and said: "There he stands." He answered: "I am a stranger to him; I do not see him; let him speak." It seems that his eyes were holden that he could not see him. This happened several times to the Superintendent, as not less to Christ himself and other holy ones. Thereupon the Superintendent answered thus: "I am the man after whom you ask." A. M. then began asking the reasons why such things had been done. The Superintendent answered : Why they came here in so improper a manner to disturb the meeting; they should have chosen a different time for this matter; and then spoke not a word more. Then things became lively. One Brother of Conestoga said: "A. M., I regard you as a servant of God." Peter Becker replied: "What kind of a servant do you consider him? a servant of his righteousness?" It was remarked that all of those of Conestoga who, at that time and afterwards, became involved with the Baptists in judgment, like Jacob Weiss, Valentine Leslie, David Gemachle, etc., afterwards themselves fell away from their calling. Aye, good M. W. had to suffer for it even on his death-bed, and would certainly have fallen into the hands of the avenger of blood, if the faithfulness of the Superintendent had not saved him, as will be described in its proper place.

With the Superintendent, however, the matter was quite different, for he had to stand up for the charge entrusted to him by God, wherein it was not by any means allowed anyone else to imitate his zeal, and to mix up his own passions with it. Those who know how the affairs stood between the two congregations, know also that a close union between them was impossible; for they were born of diverse causes, since the one had the letter for its foundation, and the other the spirit; and while both had the same Father, they had different mothers. Here it is also to be remarked that, according to law, the standing is always inherited from the mother, so that if a king lies with a slave woman, the child must also be a slave. On the part of God indeed the seed of the new birth is always one and the same; but the great diversity among the awakened arises from their various susceptibility, by reason of which the Word of life penetrates more deeply into one than into another, on which account as great a difference of tribes and families arises under the new covenant as existed under the old, which indeed cannot be changed, and should not diminish their love. As at Schwarzenau the Separatists and others sought to enter the congregation of the Baptists without becoming subject to their ordinances, the good Alexander Mack felt constrained to write a little tract, in which he showed them that each tribe must hold to its own standard. The Superintendent referred to this difference in his letters to P. B. In one of them he also mentions what displeased him in them, where he writes: "I am well disposed toward you all in those matters on which the spirits can unite in God; but in those which concern your mode of divine worship I can take no part." (See his 17th printed epistle). It is easy to understand that in succeeding years this breach must have greatly pained them. And they made several attempts to mend it, but effected nothing, because they would not recognize the fault in themselves. At one time they undertook a visit to him; but before they arrived he was impelled to go out. Then they imagined that he had run away from them, and had no good conscience. At another time both parties met on a visit. The Superintendent saw that something would happen, and called his people aside, where they agreed to offer them peace in Christ, and to forget everything that had happened. But they would not accept this, but wanted to have matters investigated and judgment passed upon them.

As something was said above concerning rebaptism, on account of which the Superintendent had to endure so many accusations, the circumstances demand that a thorough report of it be made, so that it may appear in how far the congregation at Ephrata had a right to introduce such strange customs. Among those who first left the aforementioned Baptists and betook themselves unto the Superintendent's guidance, it was recognized as necessary to give a bill of divorce to their former spiritual wife, in which they had the Superintendent's example. Those who followed after them took the path they had trodden, and why should they not have the right to do so? For in the whole New Testament there is not a word to be found that rebaptism was forbidden. Is it not tyranny then to bind the conscience in matters wherein the Spirit hath set no limits? Moreover there were few under the leading of the Superintendent who were not rebaptized at least three times, according as their zeal for God demanded. That rebaptism was practiced in the time of the Apostles cannot be denied. For even if the passage in ACTS XIX, 5, proves nothing, it is conceded that the most of those whom the Apostles baptized had already been baptized by John. As John's baptism was not the whole, and Christ had a higher witness than he, his disciples had a right to leave him and to receive the baptism of Christ; and thus was it also with the Superintendent. It is settled, however, that such rebaptisms could not be made an article of faith, for the venerable Henry Kalckglässer, one of their first teachers, was left undisturbed at Ephrata until his death in his baptism received from them. Therefore when in later times some of the new congregation went over again to the old, and several hot-heads wanted to have them rebaptized, wise men arose among them and hindered it.

CHAPTER IX.

The New Congregation, Impelled by Holy Zeal, Grows, and the Sweet Savor of Its Walk and Conversation is Spread Abroad.

Let us now again turn to the new congregation and contemplate its growth in grace. First of all we are to be reminded that the Superintendent, who had before his baptism led an angelic life hidden in God, now by baptism had consecrated himself to the lowly humanity of Jesus Christ, in consequence of which, after the example of his Master, he gave up all his acquired possessions in order to win men, and this was the bank wherein he laid up his capital on interest. It is not easy to express what a high degree of self-denial it required, to hazard his own painfully attained sanctification, and again to wade into the ocean of humanity, there to fish for men. Accordingly it was often remarked that he shed many tears, when wearied in his daily labors by the follies of mankind, and led to reflect on his former angelic life. It was easy to see that his own forwardness did not lead him into this work, but that God had plunged him into these circumstances; as also he often said that he knew of a certainty that God would not let him stick ; which the result fully proved. In accordance with his promise to God his house was open day and night to everyone. Whoever was tempted, fled to him as to a city of refuge; and as soon as his threshold was reached, the blood-avenger had to abandon him. At that time it was usual that, when poor people wished to settle in this great wilderness, they applied to the congregation to build them a house, which custom continued until the cloisters at Ephrata were built. In order to be helpful to his neighbors, the Superintendent, together with the Solitary Brethren, after the example of our Master, Jesus Christ, betook themselves to carpentering, and refused no one who desired their assistance; in which work he himself was always foremost. As, however, this labor interfered with his official duties, Christina Höhn, a Sister of the domestic household, ventured to advise him to give up his work, and to devote himself more wholly to the spiritual welfare of mankind. This counsel he obeyed and from that time on did nothing more at his temporal trade; though to be unemployed seemed harder to him than the hardest work.

This Christina Höhn was excessively enamored of the Superintendent's angelic life; she clothed him anew, and with the sanction of her husband early entered upon a life of continence. Partly with and partly without his knowledge she bestowed so many alms that one might have thought the whole household economy must go to nothing. After her husband's death, she followed the Superintendent to Ephrata, and was his next neighbor for more than twenty years, until several years after his death she departed this life. Originally she had been a Quakeress, so that when she engaged in prayer she commonly became contorted, and ended with song; afterwards, however, when she came to herself again, she used to be ashamed of this. She and the other Sisters of the household were always around him and had their delight in this innocent sheep whom God had ordained to become a sacrifice unto his righteousness. They brought his house so full of offerings that the congregation was obliged to elect deacons who had to distribute these offerings to the poor. One saw here a slight likeness of how his Master had kept house among men. They ever paid regard to him, and wanted to be continually about him. Did he go out, they all followed after him. Did he make a visit, old and young went with him, through cold and heat, so that often some were exhausted and had to be carried along, meanwhile engaging in spiritual songs, so that people ran to the street to behold the wonder. If anyone complained to him of poverty, he would advise him to hold a love-feast; and when in order to do this the rest of his means were spent, the power of God so manifested itself, and those present were so restrained, that almost as much was borne from the table as had been put on. Some even noticed that after the ordinance the vessels could not hold all the wine that was left over. It was remarked afterwards that a hidden blessing had rested upon these people in their poverty. Others avowed that they were more blessed in their household affairs than if they had worked half a year for the Community. Once he asked a Brother, who had been wealthy, but had given all his property to the Community, what had made him do this. To which the Brother replied: "I always looked to you." Such fruits are produced where there is a good leader in a Community. All this has purposely been told in detail in order that the reader may with me adore the goodness of God, which in those days so greatly manifested itself again that the portals of grace were reopened to poor mankind.[1]

It is yet to be remarked that these same good people, who were mostly descended from the Mennonites, had, after the manner of that people, a certain simplicity and lowliness of life; and the Superintendent, in spite of the fact that he had had experience in the world of vanity and show, could so thoroughly adapt himself to their ways that his clothing, dwelling, and household were fashioned on the poorest scale. It was not long, however, before persons of social position landed in the Community, among whom the Eckerlins were the first. These took possession of the Superintendent, and dressed him like a Quaker, wherein the rest of the Solitary Brethren followed his example, until the special garb of the Order was introduced; for this reason they were in great favor. Once during his absence a splendid feather-bed was put into his bed-room. Of this he made use for one night; then he had it taken away, and from that time on until his death used nothing but a sleeping-bench; which habit he would not abandon even when dying. At this time also two married women ran away from their husbands and betook themselves under the Superintendent's leading, who also

---

[1] Those who wish to inquire further into these times, should read the 299th hymn of the "*Paradiesisches Wunderspiel*," of which we will give the first two stanzas :

"O, how great a prize my blossom is !— That e'en the old are young with freshest bliss :— The perfume sweet of these good days— Itself both far and near displays.— None is so old but he doth leap :— Youths and maidens come a happy heap :—The heart in love dares all to try— And doth each earthly joy deny."—

received them, notwithstanding it was against the canons of the New Covenant; for at that time the Pentecostal winds still blew so strongly that they dissolved all associations and relations save those entered into directly under the cross of Jesus. The Apostles themselves experienced the same, wherefore they early introduced again the order of nature, and taught that wives should love their husbands. One of the two mentioned was Maria Christiana, the wife of Christopher Saur, who afterwards founded the celebrated high-German printing press at Germantown. She deserted him in the year 1730, and had herself baptized that same autumn. At first she lived alone in the wilderness, and proved by her example that a man's spirit could dwell in a woman's form. Afterwards she held the office of under-prioress in the Sisters' Convent for many years, under the name of Marcella, and did it very edifyingly. At last she was induced by her son to return, in her old age, to her husband; to which the severe mode of life at the Settlement, which she could no longer well endure, may also have conduced. The other one was the wife of Philip Hanselmann, who under the name of Eunice ended her days, at a great age, in the Sisters' Convent.

About this same time, also, two of the first who pledged themselves to a life of spiritual virginity changed their estate, and left the congregation. The one, M. H. by name, married at Germantown; but ere she was aware of it, her husband was seized with the revival spirit of the new congregation, against which she at first set herself with all her might, but at last also yielded, whereupon they removed to the new congregation, and there lived for twenty years in mutual continence, and gained the love of the saints by their holy life. They now are both fallen asleep. God grant them to get through in bliss on the day of judgment! From them a sprout came into the Sisters' Convent by the name of Constantia, who laid aside her mortal tabernacle in the year 1782. The other one was Christina Hill. These two cases were the more noteworthy as at that time the entire congregation had assumed the life of continence, and during the first twenty years there were only two marriages in the congregation, and those were of persons of advanced years.

CHAPTER X.

THE TEMPTER TRIES TO INSTIGATE A PERSECUTION BY RAISING THE CRY OF IMMORALITY.

In the year 1730 the Tempter first began openly to raise an outcry of whoremongering against the Superintendent; for reports of the celibate life now began to spread abroad in the land, and many persons were displeased with it, since one already saw, here and there, solitary ones of both sexes who had renounced the world, living alone in the wilderness. Then a rumor became current among people that the Superintendent had sinned with one of his spiritual daughters, and that she had actually brought into the world a bastard. A justice of the peace, by the name of Samuel Jones, became exercised about it, and had them both summoned before him on a King's Warrant. To the question, Whether they were guilty? the Superintendent demanded the witnesses, and they not being forthcoming, administered a sharp reproof to the justice, and went his way; for he had interfered with his office, as it was the Sabbath. Thereupon the justice sent out the constable after witnesses, who brought together all the old women in the township. Each one of these referred to the other, until at last the accusation was traced back to one. Then the misunderstanding was disclosed; for this one had said it concerning a sister after the flesh of the accused Sister, who had a husband; it had been understood, however, of the latter, who was single. The justice thereupon begged pardon of the accused Sister, and let her go in peace. Afterwards, nevertheless, he levied upon her household goods sufficient to pay the costs of the hearing.

As the divine cause suffered no small affront through this case, it seemed now time to take revenge upon the kingdom of nature for the suffered disgrace; for where the honor of God was concerned the Superintendent was beholden to nobody. Accordingly this same year yet he published in print his Ehebüchlein[1] in which he declares matrimony to be the penitentiary of carnal man, and fully exposes the abominations committed therein under the appearance of right. In the following year 1731, however, another occurrence in the congregation gave the world more right and cause for evil-speaking. One of the oldest Solitary Brethren, Amos by name, fell into the hands of the tempter even while walking on the spiritual heights; he always boasted much of the virgin Sophia, and how he must beget spiritual children with her. The Superintendent faithfully warned him to exercise greater humility; but in vain. He held a bread-breaking service, and wanted unauthorized to officiate at it. He was attacked with erysipelas in the head so that he became possessed, and lost his reason. Thereupon he made himself quite naked during the night, and watching at a man's door, forced himself in and to the man's wife in bed. He was seized, bound, and delivered to a justice of the peace, who sent him to the Poor Directors of the township, who in turn handed him over again to the congregation. The Superintendent took this affair very much to heart, not only on account of the Order of the Solitary, against whom the tempter had designed it, but also on account of the whole household policy; for some did not trust any longer to do without their wives, and contemplated taking up with them again. The following Sabbath the Superintendent held an important discourse on Nadab and Abihu, the sons of Aaron (LEV. I), to whose case this occurrence had a great similarity; for it should be known that God stood by him unto the end against all such as infringed upon his office, of which this circumstance and others bear witness. The fallen Brother, however, in his insanity ran down the country as far as Philadelphia, where he climbed up on the courthouse as high as to the bell, and there commenced to storm so that a great crowd of people was brought together. This was interpreted as an attempt to stir up the people into an uproar against the cause of God. After this he came to himself again and filled the position of baker in the Settlement very acceptably for thirty years, until at last he laid aside his

---

[1] [Book on Matrimony].

earthly tabernacle in 1783, in the 82d year of his age Otherwise he was a very industrious man, useful to the communal life, and charitable, though usually his left hand knew what his right was doing. The Superintendent was wont to say of him that while he could not get other Brethren to work, him he could not get from his work.

The following occurrence is similar to the foregoing both as to time and circumstances. There was a certain housefather who had come pretty close in the Superintendent's fellowship, but who was not cleansed thereby from the false priestly spirit, and who accordingly was appointed as teacher among the awakened in Falckner's Swamp. This man had a wife who was deeply enamored of the good things of God, and therefore tarried more at the house of the Superintendent than was agreeable to her husband, which the Superintendent because of his vows to God had to allow. Meanwhile they lived a life of continence and exercised themselves in godly works, so that it was thought that he would become a useful laborer in the house of God. But after God had touched upon his rights as a husband, the evil in him awoke, so that he turned into evil all the good that he had received from the Superintendent. He said to his wife: "You are my wedded wife. I will not give you up. Your will must be subject to your husband's;" and commanded her to stay at home. And because she could not in all things do his will, he used his power as a husband, and several times took her home by force, and once had her brought by the constable. So likewise on one occasion he attacked the Superintendent in his little home, as one attacks who means to kill, but God rescued him from his hands. At length the tempter impelled him to go to the meeting with the intention of taking his life. It was terrible to behold him as he entered. First he sang the words:

> "Now be prepared, ye heroes true,
> Gird on your trusty swords;
> On Babylon we've war declared,
> Shout out with loudest voice.
> Come, follow then, and trample down
> All Gog and Magog's brethren;
> We'll slay them all and leave them there,
> It is their just reward."

Then he rushed towards the Superintendent, seized him by the throat, and dragged him as far as the door. He would unquestionably have killed him if the people had not come to the rescue, who tied his hands on his back, and chased him home. Meanwhile the Fathers took up the Superintendent's cause, for when the man's wife came to meeting next Sabbath they bade her go home to her husband; and when she asked how long she should stay at home, she was told, until she should be asked to come again; under which heavy ban she resigned herself, and of necessity left the congregation. Through this indeed the man lost his rights over against the Superintendent, but on the other hand sank utterly into the realm of darkness, so that the hellish brimstone was kindled within him, which manifested itself by his presence giving forth a disagreeable smell. Nevertheless he was very insecure in his fortress, for he was in constant dread that his wife might again be seduced from him. Once, when he heard that a love-feast of the congregation was to be held, he took with him another evil fellow and they tied her fast lest she should run away from him again. In him we can see as in a mirror all those who hold to their rights as husbands so rigidly, as if it were an agreeable thing to God, though it is not in agreement with the doctrine of the good Master. Meanwhile the Superintendent, nevertheless, entered into the breach in his behalf, and in one of his printed letters offered him the reconciliation of Jesus Christ, mentioning that their case lay before the great Judge. However the judgment lay so heavily upon the good man that he could not yield; and this is one of the reasons why the Superintendent, even on his death-bed, deplored that he had been the occasion of so many becoming evil men. His wife, however, when she was freed by his death, joined the congregation again; and after leading an edifying life for some years more, she at last laid aside her earthly tabernacle in the year 1779.

CHAPTER XI.

CONCERNING THE SUPERINTENDENT'S OFFICIAL COURSE IN THE CONGREGATION, UNTIL THE FOUNDING OF EPHRATA.

It cannot be expressed with what great care the Superintendent at that time devoted his time to the service of the households; and yet it must be confessed that, at that time at least, he had placed only one foot in the congregation, while the other was still firmly planted in separatism. He did this because he feared that in the ocean of humanity he might lose his crown. For he had in Germany experienced how in this wise several of his fellow-laborers had yielded themselves to women, and he knew also that a teacher was most exposed to such temptations. About this time he said, that if it had happened as God intended, two more orders would have come into being in the congregation, one of Solitary Brethren, and the other of Spiritual Virgins. The sequel proved the truth of this. For, besides the households, he then already had under his guidance various solitary ones, whom in his wisdom he treated differently from the congregation. These he had often warned against the outward church; yes, they once even took counsel whether it were not better, on account of the danger, to leave the household entirely, and after the precept of the holy forefathers, to begin a household in the wilderness. His Solitary Brethren would probably have been quite agreed to this, for they were well aware that with the growth of the congregation their burdens would also increase. But, good God, how weighty are our counsels! The Superintendent was at length necessitated to cast in his fortunes unconditionally with the congregation; whereat his Solitary Brethren became offended at him, and held him in suspicion as though he had deserted his post. Therefore the complaint was afterwards often heard among the Solitary that the church had conformed too much to the spirit of the world, and would have to go forth into the desert again;—which also several afterwards attempted to do, to their own harm.

Now in those days all the divine services for worship were so blessed that no one attended them without having his conscience stirred, or else the evil within him aroused. One may say, indeed, that they were accompanied with special power to crucify the nature of man; particularly the love-feasts, which usually lasted till midnight, sometimes even till the dawn of day, when everyone was so quiet and absorbed that one could easily notice how an unseen power was keeping the whole meeting in such order. From this it is to be presumed that the Superintendent took good heed not to bring his own wares to market; for the Spirit, under whose guardianship he stood, kept so strict a rule over him, that in divine matters he was never permitted to do anything according to his own ideas. Hence at every meeting new wonders of eternity were made manifest, as the Spirit gave utterance, and never was one like the other. This was the cause too why no one could fathom him, and still less find rest and quiet in him. He was so dutiful that he despised no one's poverty, and often held the most important meetings at the houses of the worst people. When taken to task for this, he would answer thus: that with such people David had won his kingdom. How from himself the congregation was born he himself has described, as follows: "When my ecclesiastical dignity was taken from me, and I no longer took pleasure in myself, this came upon others, without my knowing how it happened. Indeed I saw to my greatest astonishment that so many people became enamored of my works of love, on account of which I before had to endure such harsh judgments. This wonderful spectacle made the beginning of a Christian church according to the gospel, wherein I was forced to be a leader. This indeed seemed hard to me, once more to begin to live with others, whereby my diligence and faithfulness had to endure so severe a judgment. Meantime matters made desirable progress, and my painfully sown seed appeared in some places to yield fruit an hundred-fold. Whereupon I resigned myself, with all the sorrow and care I had within myself, and let self-denial be my spiritual staff in the whole affair. At the same time I did not neglect to think what would become of the whole matter if it should be tried as my heart had been. Nevertheless the affair made a noise before the world, as though the second temple of the Christian church were about to appear in its might. Since the matter looked thus, I cast aside the doubts and mistrusts which I had felt, took hold, and became desirous to bind sheaves in this field. Then I became aware, however, of the piercing of so poisonous a thorn, and that, too, among the very best wheat, that horror seized upon me."—*Vide Delicias Ephratenses. Pars I. Page 195. Discourse XXXI.*

In the meantime, after he had been at the head of the meeting with great blessing for several years, he was finally driven in upon himself, and called the congregation together. After speaking many things concerning the kingdom of God, he appointed Elders, and handed them the New Testament, to govern the congregation in accordance therewith. Then he laid down his office, and moved eight miles away, to a barren spot where Ephrata now stands. Here he settled himself anew. What induced him to make so sudden a change is hard to surmise; neither did he ever make it known. It may be that he wanted to test the matter in this way, whether it were of God or of man's intention. For one can well imagine what temptations there must have been, when he, a Solitary, who had but recently left his angelic life in the desert, was now run after by so many people. This seems probable, that an unseen hand drove him on to find the place which afterwards attracted so great attention in North America. Meanwhile this sudden change threw the new congregation into the utmost consternation; and about this time Casper Walter, an earnest housefather, went out of time to eternity in deep sorrow of heart on account of the sad schisms in Zion. With this we will close this chapter, as we will begin in the next the description of the Economy at Ephrata. The time of the congregation's existence, from the Superintendent's baptism until the building of Ephrata, was seven years and four months.

CHAPTER XII.

How Ephrata Was Founded, and Ordained for the Settlement of the Solitary.

Ephrata is situated in Lancaster County, thirteen miles from Lancaster, eighteen from Reading, and sixty-five from Philadelphia, in an angle where two great highways intersect each other, the one from Philadelphia to Paxton, the other from Reading to Lancaster. The Delaware Indians, who inhabited this region, named it and the stream that flows past Ephrata, *Koch-Halekung*, that is Serpents' Den, on account of the many snakes found there. The Europeans kept the word, but pronounced it Cocalico, which is also the name of the township. The inhabitants did not value the land, as being unfruitful. A Solitary Brother, Elimalech[1] by name, was the first one to build on this barren spot; and he gave his little house to the Superintendent when the latter fled thither. Thus it appears that the founding of Ephrata sprang entirely from a providential occurrence, and not from the premeditated will of man. After the foundation of this wonderful household, which made fools of so many both in and outside of its limits, had been thus laid, the further building up of the place was not permitted otherwise than with the severest self-denial on the part of the builders; wherefore also so many strange events happened. This is the reason, too, why the tempter prevailed against it in nothing, although the enterprise was often delivered up to him by God that he might sift it; for he could find in it nothing of man's will, even as the Superintendent frankly said to one who asked him whether he had built up the work: No, for the whole thing was against his conscience. In a certain place he speaks further on the subject thus: "So then Ephrata is now built up out of this soil of suffering, endured in the conscience for the sake of God's kingdom."

---

[1] [Emanuel Eckerle].

Here in this wilderness he fixed himself as though he intended to live apart from men to the end of his days. He cleared himself a tract of land, and cultivated it with the hoe, and in general made such arrangements that, in case men should again deliver him up, it would not be any loss to him. It is easy of belief that in the short period of his seclusion, during which men left him in peace for awhile, his addresses to the virgin Sophia were redoubled, for it was then he composed the beautiful hymn, "O blessed life of loneliness when all creation silence keeps." He often told what pains it cost him in the beginning to free this region from the evil spirits which hold dominion over the whole earth. If this seems strange to anyone, let him read Otto Clusing's Life of the Fathers in the Desert; there he will find more about such things.

The congregation now, after having been robbed of its teacher, held its meetings with a housefather named Sealthiel.[2] But so many legal quarrels took place that they were called the "court meetings." Meanwhile the Superintendent found an opportunity, and summoned the heads of the congregation to his new dwelling place, where they took counsel with reference to the general matter, and finally opened another meeting, after the Superintendent had been withdrawn for seven months. It was held for the first time on September 4th 1732. About this same time the Solitary Brethren also made up their minds, and moved after their spiritual leader, and built, in the winter of 1732, the second house in the Settlement. Their names were Jethro, Jephune,[3] and Martin Bremer, the last of whom was the firstling of those who fell asleep in Ephrata. This was not the end of it, however. Soon after two of the Sisters who had earliest been devoted to virginity, A. and M. E.,[4] also came and asked to be taken in. The Brethren, who went according to the Fathers in the Desert, of whom it was known that they did not tolerate such a thing among themselves, protested against it to the Superintendent as being improper and per-

---

[2] [Simon Landes].
[3] [Jethro—Jacob Gast. Jephune—Sam. Eckerlin].
[4] [Anna and Maria Eicher].

haps a cause of offence. But he was not of their mind. It seems that he foresaw in the spirit what would be the outcome of the matter. The result was that a house was built for them on the other side of the stream, into which they moved in May, 1733, and where they lived until the Sisters' Convent was founded. In the following year another house was built, for two brothers, Onesimus and Jotham,[5] otherwise called Eckerlin. This was followed by the common bake-house, and a magazine for the supply of the poor; with these building stopped for a while.

These matters created a terrible stir in the land, especially among the neighbors, who were partly degenerate Mennonites and partly spoiled church-people. They did all against these newcomers that one could expect from that kind of people devoid of all fear of God. Once they, without warning, set fire to the forest, in the hope of burning down the Settlement; but the fire turned, and laid in ashes the barn of a householder with all its contents. Then they began everywhere to warn one another against seduction, parents warned their children, and husbands their wives. This was among the common people; but the great ones of the land harbored the suspicion that the Jesuits had something to do with it, so that the Brethren were often asked, when they were seen to have gold, whether they had brought it from Mexico. Such were the sorrowful times wherein the foundations of Ephrata were laid; they were specially like unto the times of Nehemiah and Ezra.

About the same time, in the year 1734, the awakened in Falckner's Swamp, it being the seventh year of their awakening, began to break up and move towards the Settlement, which increased the alarm in the country. They bought up from the spirit of this world the regions around Ephrata, so that in a few years the country for from three to four miles around the Settlement was occupied by this kind of people. Wherever there was a spring of water, no matter how unfertile the soil might be, there lived some household that was waiting for the Lord's salvation. Afterwards these regions were divided up, and each one received its own

---

[5] [Israel and Gabriel Eckerlin].

particular name; one was called Massa, another Zoar, the third Hebron, and the fourth Kadesh. After these, the awakened from the Schuylkill also came and settled down around the Settlement. From them the Sisters' Convent gained a number of members; but only two, natural sisters, endured to the end. These have finished their course, under the names of Drusiana and Basilla. The rest were gathered in again by the spirit of the world. How the Superintendent must have felt through all this, can well be imagined. He knew well that it all would be reckoned to his account and to that of the good that had been entrusted to him. He was so little proud of it that, on the contrary, he used to say that God had sent all these people to him to humble him; wherein many of them spared no pains. He was to each that which each one sought in him—to this one a savour of life unto life, to that one a savour of death unto death.

Before I close this chapter what happened in the country with a Frenchman named John Reignier must yet be reported. He was a native of Vivres in Switzerland, and professed to have been awakened in his seventh year; but he was not completely rid of the upspringing flames of masculinity within him. He came into the Settlement just at a time when the Solitary Brethren were in deepest earnest; but they had not the gift of discerning the spirits, so that he could insinuate himself among them through false powers of light. The Superintendent, to whom this person's true condition was manifest, warned them against his seduction. But they were already so taken up with the man by reason of his semblance of holiness, that these warnings did not impress them. As in everything he avoided the middle path, he at length led them into strange extravagances, so that they bound themselves with him not to eat any more bread. Accordingly they gathered a great store of acorns. But judgment followed them, so that their store of provisions was devoured by worms. He even went further, and taught them that it belonged to holiness, after the example of Elijah and other saints, not to dwell in any house. The Superintendent finally determined to bring the affair to an end, and prevailed upon the Brethren to build a hut for the

man, hard by the Settlement, where he was maintained at
the general expense. At last, however, he lost his reason,
whereupon the Brethren rid themselves of him. Afterwards
he joined himself to one Gemaehle by name, by whom he
had himself baptized. The two then went through the
country as Apostles. As such they aroused much attention
everywhere, especially in New York in the Jew-school.
Such is the power of perversion. At length he made a
journey of 600 miles, with bare head and feet, through the
great wilderness to Georgia, where he joined himself to the
Moravian Brethren, who took him to Herrenhaag, where the
Ordinarius Fratrum[6] wedded him to a wife, with the following
wedding discourse: "See, dear Brethren, here is a proud
saint from America, whom God hath cast down so that he
must now celebrate a marriage with a public harlot." This
would have been a good opportunity for him to humble
himself; but instead he repaid these kind offices with evil,
which was published to his shame in Frankfurt. Nevertheless
for a while all went according to his wishes; for they
sent him as a laborer[7] to St. Thomas. But when from there
he came to Bethlehem, and they were going to bring him
under the strict regulations of the congregation, he left their
communion again. Thereupon he came to the Superintendent
a second time, who took his Delilah from him and put
her into the Sisters' Convent, at which he rejoiced and had
himself received into the Brothers' Convent. But his wife
became regretful and demanded her husband again, to which
he was forced to yield against his will; this gave him such a
shock that, for the second time in the Settlement, he lost his
reason. When he came to himself once more, the old
brother-hatred towards the Superintendent again became
alive in him, so that he uttered many slanders against him
and his about whoremongering. But, as the name of Brother
was therefore taken from him, he and his wife moved away,
and at length he ended his restless life at Savannah in
Georgia. God be merciful to him on the day of judgment!

To this time it yet belongs that the Superintendent with

---

[6] [Count Nicholas Lewis von Zinzendorf].
[7] [Minister or Assistant].

several Solitary Brethren made a visit to Oley, where the powers of eternity were remarkably manifested. They came into a house where the daughter was a bride, who at first sight let herself be so overpowered with these forces that her earthly bridal love fell dead before them. Without the bridegroom's knowledge she followed the visitors, and in the Settlement took her vows of eternal virginity among the original Sisters. Whereupon her parents followed her; but she continued to shine among her sex by her virtuous walk, until at last, under the name of Berenice, she finished her course, which is recorded in heaven, because for her future glory's sake she denied herself her carnal bridal-couch here below.

CHAPTER XIII.

Concerning a New Awakening in Tulpehocken.

It is again necessary to make an excursion from our main subject, in order to trace matters to their origin; which may also serve as an introduction to the church history of Pennsylvania. For since those whom God appointed for this work were chosen out of all denominations, we are necessarily led to touch upon the church history of the land. About the year 1726 the first high-German Reformed preacher, Weiss by name, arrived in Pennsylvania. He was born at Stebbach, a Palatine place in the Neckar valley; studied at Heidelberg, and finished his course in Koschehoppen[1] in the county of Philadelphia. The second, P. M.[2] by name, followed him in 1730. He was born in the Upper Domain of Lautern in the Palatine Electorate, and studied at Heidelberg with the preceding. In the year 1731 Bartholomew Rieger also came. He was born at Upper Ingleheim in the Palatine Electorate; studied at Basle and Heidelberg, and was gathered to his fathers at Lancaster where he was stationed. About this time there were great disturbances in church circles in Pennsylvania, so that many were made so confused that they no longer knew what to believe. At that time the region of Dulpehakin[3] was settled entirely by Protestants. These had agreed among themselves not to suffer among them any who were differently minded; so that many who were of like persuasion came to them. But shrewdly as they contrived it, God yet at last set up his candle on a candlestick in that then dark region, as will soon be narrated. These now had called the afore-mentioned P. M. to be their teacher, which office he served among them and in other places during four years. The Superintendent, after he had heard that two young preachers had come into the country, who stood in good

---

[1][Conshohocken].   [2][Peter Miller].
[3][Tulpehocken].

repute as to their character, and also thought well of his work, aware of his own inability in view of the important work before him, thought in his foolishness that this work would be better carried out if God would provide one of these young preachers for him, for which also he often bowed his knees before God. This led to important matters. For the Superintendent soon after found occasion to make a visit to Tulpehocken with several of his disciples, where he was received by the teacher and elders with the consideration due to him as an ambassador of God; while on his return the teacher and C. W.,[4] an elder, accompanied him over the mountains for six miles. The result of their visit in Tulpehocken was that the teacher, the elders, and several others withdrew from the church; whereupon a venerable Pietist, by the name of Casper Leibbecker, took the teacher's place in the church.

Among these seceders was C. W., an elder of the Lutheran faith, a man who had received from God remarkable natural gifts and sound judgment, and therefore carried great weight with him into whatever sphere he might turn, whether that of nature or of the church. He was the teacher's main stay, for they were on intimate terms together, which death itself did not destroy. But now the question was, what to do further. For where was there a church that had greater spiritual strength than the mother-church which they had left? And to enter into a fruitless separatism, or even to join hands with the Ishmaelites, Laodiceans, Naturalists, or yet Atheists, of whom the country was full, and who all had forsaken their mother-church—this was not according to their mind.

In the meantime C. W. visited the Superintendent in his solitude in the Settlement. During this visit he was so enmeshed by the Philadelphian "little strength"[5] that Wisdom finally drew him into her net. Among other things the Superintendent asked him, what the young preachers were doing; and when he heard that B. R. had taken a wife, he sighed deeply and said, "Good God! they are spoiling in one's very hands. But," he continued, "what is the other

---

[4] [Conrad Weisser].   [5] [*Vide* Rev. III, 8].

one doing?" He was told that he was engaged in building. "Ay, ay," he replied, "let him build on; he has but little more time left." That he spoke this in a prophetic spirit, was shown by the result that soon followed. On retiring, the Superintendent promised him a visit, which also followed soon after, though then taking in only his house and the teacher. Not long afterwards, however, he made another extended visit thither, on which the spirit of revival spread itself over that entire region, so that all doors were opened unto him; though it was remarked that this awakening was confined within certain limits. As everybody hoped from its failures and mistakes that the new awakening in Conestoga would come to nothing, so many were now concerned as to what would come out of this movement in Tulpehocken; for it was well known that, wherever these people might land, they would bring great weight with them. But, good God! a great hill had yet to be surmounted ere that disgrace was overcome which distinguished God's people from the children of this world. And this rested so heavily upon the Settlement at that time that superhuman power was needed to break through it.

In this whole matter, however, God made use of the faithfulness of the afore-mentioned C. W. For through his prudence it was that a great visitation, in which the heads of the revival were engaged, came to the Settlement. Now it was that the Superintendent had the wished-for opportunity to spread his net and catch men for the virgin Sophia; especially did he hope that his prayers with reference to the teacher would now be fulfilled. Accordingly he took him into his house, and after he had spoken various things with him concerning the counsels of God towards fallen man, he at last came to the point, and said he should let himself be baptized. To this the answer was difficult; for since holy baptism is a transplanting into the death of Christ, it was easy to suppose that it was done not only for the good name's sake, but also for that of the right of citizenship in the world, and of all the privileges derived from Adam onward. But here it was. Nothing ventured, nothing won. After they had settled this important point, all difficulty about the others was soon overcome. Accordingly they were baptized together under the water, after the teaching of Christ; which was done on a Sabbath in May of the year 1735. Thus the teacher, schoolmaster, three elders, besides various other households, went over from the Protestants to this new awakening; while for some time after the door was kept open for the Babylonian refugees. The Solitary Brethren harvested two Brethren in this awakening, of whom one, Jemini by name, has finished his course; while the other is still engaged in his daily labors. The Sisters also had an addition, but only one of them, under the name of Thekla, remained faithful to the end. Soon after the Brethren erected a solitary residence for the teacher at the foot of a high hill in Tulpehocken, where however he lived no longer than till the next November. At the time the work of God was much oppressed, and it was dangerous for a Brother to travel on the highways. The report of this great conversion filled not only this and neighboring countries, but penetrated even into Germany. The Doctores warned their candidates against this country; and wrote to the preachers here that they should not concern themselves about the matter as it was only a fire of straw; yet there might come from it a new "Evische Rotte."

Soon after this important event, the Superintendent made another visit to Tulpehocken, on which, after treating much of the work of God, he handed this new congregation over to the teacher again, with the announcement that now he would have an addition to his charge, even though he should wish to resume the office where he had left it. This he said to try him; for he was very much concerned that this awakening should remain under the Spirit's power, and not be sold under his spirit. The teacher requested a night's time for reflection; and it was his great good fortune that next day he declined the offer, for there were already others waiting for it. Now the matter stood thus under the Government Above: that besides the altar in the Settlement none other could be erected; but these good people were not yet emancipated from the calf-worship, and therefore hungered after a priest, and he must be the good M. W. But when he again had to retire in shame and disgrace, as formerly at Falckner's Swamp, a Solitary Brother, Elimelech, was given them, a born priest, who possessed all the endowments for spiritual perversion. But as these people were too good for perversion, he fared even worse than the former. It must be remembered that the false priest-spirit is inherent in all flesh, but becomes manifest only at an awakening. It is more difficult to overcome than the devil of whoredom; for as the true priest receives his power from the Virgin above, this one derives his from woman. After the priestly chair was now empty again among the awakened, C. W. incautiously seated himself in it, and thereby opened the door for the tempter to try him. For while according to the manner of those times matrimonial bonds were considerably weakened through baptism, there were spiritual courtings through which the void in his side might easily have been filled again; although the temptation thereto lay only in the conditions, while the will for it was not there. The Superintendent once washed his feet, and as he noticed from the feeling of the feet to what temptations he was most exposed, he said to him: "The Brother must take heed against the female sex." Nevertheless the blood-avenger meanwhile got him into his power and tried to destroy him. (Mark, dear reader, this account agrees with that of Zipporah;[6] for she did not belong to Moses' people, wherefore also Moses sent her home again. That she saved her son from the destroying angel through the blood of the covenant, showed great wisdom in her). He hurriedly notified the Superintendent and sought his aid, who paid him a visit, when they opened their hearts to each other in private; whereupon the Superintendent took his burden upon himself, so that the good Brother was freed from all temptation. The traveling-companions of the Superintendent knew nothing of this; but on the way home they noticed that he seemed heavy-laden, like a woman in travail, while his countenance was pale and shining. No one, however, ventured to speak to him, until at length a Brother took the liberty to ask him whether God required him to enter so far into domestic

---

[6] [*Vide* Exod. II, 21; IV, 25].

matters and to assume such burdens? To which he only made reply with kindly looks. Such labors the Superintendent frequently had in those days, but as few ever knew his secrets, it all remained hidden. Once a Sister of the household confessed to him an act of adultery, committed before her conversion, which he faithfully kept to himself as a secret of the confessional, until she fell away again from the testimony, when he revealed the whole affair.

In this severe trial this Brother [C. W.] in his God-enamored condition found himself, and because he did not take sufficient heed to himself the tempter assailed him anew, and would probably have overcome him, had not God put it into the heart of the Sister to seek out the covenant and have herself rebaptized by the Superintendent. Then the cords of the tempter were torn, and they again became as strangers to each other.

CHAPTER XIV.

EPHRATA IS OCCUPIED BY THE SOLITARY OF BOTH SEXES; DIVINE WORSHIP IS INSTITUTED; AND THE COMMUNAL LIFE INTRODUCED.

After the Superintendent through this awakening in Tulpehocken had received valuable re-inforcements for his divine work, and thereby was made aware that God was with him, he took advantage thereof, and instituted measures for building a meeting-house to God's glory; for hitherto the meetings had been held in private houses. For its erection both the Solitary and householders willingly contributed their share. The structure contained, besides the hall for meetings, also large halls fully furnished for holding the *Agapæ*, or lovefeasts, besides which there were also cells built for the Solitary, after the manner of the old Greek church. At that time it happened that a housefather handed over his daughter, a young lass, to the Superintendent, with the request that he should bring her up to the glory of God. Anyone else would probably have declined such a present; but he regarded the matter as a providential leading, received her, and had her serve him for a purpose, namely, to found the Order of Spiritual Virgins. She with two others were given a residence in the second story of the church-building just mentioned; which latter was named Kedar. These four Sisters were the first who bound themselves by a pledge to a communal life; but the one who gave the first occasion to it, at last forsook again the narrow way of the cross, and joined herself to a man, after having lived in their convent many years, under the name of Abigail. Soon after this the Superintendent quartered four Solitary Brethren in the lower story of this house; which increased the suspicion against them, for no one would believe that matters could go on properly thus. The Superintendent, however, cared more to have an essential separateness, than that there should be an outward appearance thereof which might not be real. Consequently there finally came to be as unrestrained a life in the Settlement as though all were of the same sex. It must be granted the Superintendent that in this respect he went further than some before him in the conventual or celibate life; for where others went out of the way of danger, he plunged his followers into the midst of it.

When the house Kedar was finished, a general love-feast was held in it, contributed by the households to the glory of God who had made known his wonders in these heathen lands. Messengers were sent out into the country to invite to it all friends and well-wishers. How greatly this displeased the Prince of Darkness may be judged from the fact that, at this very time, at midnight, the Superintendent was so severely belabored with blows from an invisible power that he was forced to take refuge with the nearest Brethren; upon whose authority it is here mentioned. After this, although the love-feast was held, only a few of the invited guests came; and these were more offended than edified thereby, because they saw how a Brother during the feet-washing kissed the Superintendent's feet, and said: "These feet have made many a step for our welfare." Soon after this the Superintendent instituted a visitation through the country as far as New Jersey. It consisted of twelve fathers of the congregation, and everywhere occasioned great wonder, partly because so many respectable men permitted themselves to be governed by so humble and despised an instrument, and also because they saw among them a man so famous in the land as C. W. For the latter was so far brought down by works of penance, and had let his beard grow, that hardly anybody recognized him; besides which he had voluntarily offered up, for the glory of God, a part of his possessions towards the upbuilding of this new economy.

Even before Kedar was quite completed, the nightly divine services among the Solitary in the Settlement had been commenced. They were called Night Watches, and were held at midnight, because at that hour the advent of the Judge was expected. At first they lasted four hours, so that from this severe spiritual exercise one had to go at once to one's physical work, which was a sore crucifixion of the flesh; afterwards, however, the time was fixed at two hours. At first the Superintendent himself presided at them, particularly when both sexes met together; and he did so with such power of the Spirit that he never let them come to the bending of the knee so long as he noticed that a ban was on them and there had been quarrels, when he had to have recourse to scolding until finally their eyes became wet with tears. Moreover he taught them on both sides, as a priestly generation, to lift up hands unto God on behalf of the domestic household, which was so sorely bound under the yoke of the world; and that this was the continual service of God. In succeeding times he withdrew from this service, out of consideration for the work, lest it might become constrained on his account, and waited upon God in his own house of watching. Then each meeting had to help itself as well as it could; though whenever quarrels arose at the service, and he was asked for help, he never failed to give it. .

This record would be imperfect if here were not inserted also an account of the zeal of the congregation. For after it had taken the Superintendent as its priest, the worship of the congregation lay nearest his heart. The confidence which every household at that time yet felt towards him (for as yet there was no one who doubted his divine mission,) was such that all their real and personal possessions were in his hands, and they would not have refused, at a mere wink from him, to give up all for the glory of God. At that time every house in the congregation stood open to the poor. Accordingly when such persons applied to the Superintendent, as was common, he would ask one housefather after the other, during meeting, whether he had any money; and he was seldom disappointed in his confidence in them. Was there any charitable work to be done, then an investigation was made after meeting, and his work for the following week appointed for each member who was able, when often many an one devoted his own share to the use of the poor. This method continued for many years, but has now been abrogated by death.

In autumn of the year 1735 all the Solitary, of both sexes,

who had dwelt as settlers scattered through the country, moved to the Settlement. Thus this holy mode of life, over which God had poured out the powers of the new world, was brought to its end in Pennsylvania, and will hardly be revived again; for other schools afterwards arose, and when God wants to transfer any one to a higher duty, he makes his former estate to be sinful for him, otherwise would no one be brought to renounce it. In this same movement the afore-mentioned teacher of Tulpehocken in a letter to the Superintendent asked to be taken up in the Settlement. The Brethren did not think that such an one would be able to endure the severe mode of life, and advised against his reception. But the Superintendent had greater faith, and through his mediation he moved into the Settlement that autumn yet, and several of his household followed him. The rest fell away again from their testimony.

After the meetings had been held for a short time in Kedar, the following changes took place: A widower of property in the congregation, Sigmund Landert by name, felt himself obligated in his conscience to offer up his possessions to the glory of God; wherefore he asked the Superintendent's advice, who counseled him not to do it. But he soon came again, full of sorrow, and made this proposition, namely: that if he and his two daughters would be received into the Settlement, he would build out of his means another house of prayer adjoining Kedar, besides a dwelling-house for the Superintendent; then Kedar might be changed into a Sisters' Convent. This, the Superintendent saw, was from God, and accordingly agreed to his request. Here one can see how in those days the Spirit reigned and manfully urged them on, with the power of apostolic times, to a communal life. More such cases occurred in those times. Among the rest, a housefather sold his property, and, in apostolic wise, laid the price thereof at the Superintendent's feet; who used it for God's glory, and incorporated him and his family in the household at Ephrata, where, after much faithfulness in God's work, he ended his course under the name of Macarius. The erection of the church now went forward without hindrance; for the housefather before referred to brought all his possessions into the Settlement, besides his two daughters, who entered the Sisters' Convent. The younger of them had recourse to the world again; but the older entered into her rest, at this same Convent, in November of the year 1773. Their father, however, who was a skillful mechanic, rendered good service in building up the Settlement; and after a holy poverty and abnegation of all things had become his portion, he went home to his eternal fatherland under the name of Sealthiel; he had proved by his example that a domestic household may be dissolved through the heavenly call.

This house was a sightly structure, furnished with a hall for love-feasts, and one for meetings, which had two "portkirchen" for the use of the Solitary, besides a gallery occupied by gray-haired fathers; here and there, moreover, texts in black-letter were hung. This beautiful building, after having stood about four years, was razed to the ground again, the cause of which can scarcely be comprehended by human reason; the standard is too limited. The Superintendent's followers were confounded in him, and knew not whether the erection or the destruction of this house, or both were from God. Other persons held him to be a sorcerer, and said he had made fools of his people. It is probable that a hidden Hand made use of him, in this wise symbolically to represent the wonders of eternity, after which the veil was again drawn over the affair; for there is a likeness in its history to that of the temple at Jerusalem, which, after it was scarcely finished, was plundered by the king of Egypt. Since a dwelling had been erected for him adjoining this building, he was now for the second time obliged to abandon his seclusion and therefore removed into the confines of the Sisterhood. Here God made use of him to found their Order; whereupon he devoted himself wholly unto them. For it is to be known that at his first awakening at Heidelberg he came unto the Virgin above, through whom the whole creation is restored again to God, and who was enamored of his *limbum* beyond measure, which was one cause of his many sufferings, for she wished to have him feminine and quite subject unto herself, whereas he was still possessed of the ardor of rising manhood. Now however the graft of the upper virginhood was through him to be

implanted in others for the spread of God's kingdom.
Wherefore his spiritual daughters were sent unto him in the
bloom of youth; all of whom, without distinction, he
received. Whoever came to him at that time saw with
astonishment his whole house filled with his spiritual
daughters; and as he then had reached his fortieth year, it
is easy to imagine what temptations he had to endure in his
natural body, in reference to which he once declared that he
had really first learned to know his Father in his fortieth
year. Before his death also, he placed among the many
blessings God had shown him this, that he had preserved
him from the allurements of the female sex.

At this same time when the female part was incorporated
in his household, and while the Brothers' Convent was being
built, the Superintendent was impelled to lay the foundations of the communal life. Accordingly all provisions were
delivered to the Sisters in their kitchen, who daily prepared
a supper for the entire Settlement in a large dining-hall,
they being separated from them by a dividing screen.
Everything, withal, was done in order and reverently according to the leading of the Holy Ghost, and under the supervision of the Superintendent, so that the powers of the new
world were markedly manifested. After this had continued
for half a year, and the common household of the Sisters
had been dedicated, the Brethren were again dismissed in
peace, and the Superintendent restored to them their prescribed rations.

At this time the *Lectiones* were first instituted in the
Settlement; namely, the Superintendent ordered that weekly,
on the evening of the sixth day, every one should examine
his heart before God, in his own cell, and then hand in to
the Superintendent a written statement of his spiritual condition, which he read at the meeting of the congregation on
the following Sabbath. These confessional papers were
called *Lectiones*, and several hundred of them were afterwards published in printed form. It is remarkable that the
most unlearned and simple-minded stated their condition so
artlessly, unreservedly, and simply that one cannot but be
astonished at their simplicity.

G

CHAPTER XV.

NEW PERSECUTIONS ARE COMMENCED; IN PART BY THE MEMBERS OF THE CONGREGATION.

There are some things in the Superintendent's course which are specially remarkable and scarcely can be understood. Such is this, that people who at first exalted him to the heavens, afterwards became his worst opponents. In the preceding chapter we described the earnest conversion of a Brother, C. W. But as he did not keep watch over himself, there grew from the root of enmity to God within him, which had not been killed, an antagonism against the Superintendent, which was the cause of his renouncing the testimony of God again, and allowing himself to be taken up by the world. Since, however, God finally vindicated his glory in him, and through many circuitous by-ways brought him back to his first love and the wife of his youth, we do not hesitate to incorporate in this history so much as belongs here of the mistakes and circumstances of this remarkable man. As he possessed great natural talents in matters pertaining to the government of the land, and, besides, was Indian interpreter, having been adopted into their tribes, so that the country could neither wage war nor make peace with the Indians without him, everybody was sorry that so useful a man should have allowed himself to be fooled so. Wherefore Governor Th. who then was ruler, and who well understood the art of dissimulation, took measures to bring him over to his side again, to cope with which the good Brother was by no means competent. The former took hold of the matter very shrewdly, spoke in praise of the organization at Ephrata, and that he was not disinclined to come into closer relations with such a people. This he could well say, for he went to the trouble to visit the Settlement with a following of twenty horses and accompanied by many people of quality from Virginia and Maryland. He was worthily received by the Brethren, though the Superintendent and the Mother Superior of the Sisters held themselves aloof. He declared himself well pleased with the institution. But when he saw that the families also had an own household in the Settlement, he wanted to know what the object of this was; and on being told that they too had entered the celibate state, he regarded it as something curious. Having made a favorable impression on the Brother [C. W.], he now tendered him the office of a justice of the peace, which the Brother would no doubt have gladly accepted if it were not against the principles of his people; he did so, however, only on condition that the congregation would permit it. Thereupon at his request a council was held to decide the question whether a Brother of this confession might be allowed to hold a governmental office. The fathers were of opinion that this could not be done. But the Superintendent thought differently, and asked them whether they had a right to restrict a Brother's conscience. And when he [C. W.] was asked about it, he declared that his conscience did not forbid him to accept; upon which full liberty was granted him. The Governor also gave him the privilege to withdraw from court whenever such matters should happen to come up as were against his conscience.

For a time favorable winds blew for him after this, and he could soon be seen as chief justice of court seated beneath the crown wearing his accustomed beard. At length, however, his office came to occupy him so much that he became estranged from his Brethren. He first and most severely took offence at his tried friend the Superintendent himself, of which the latter was himself the cause, for he loved the good Brother more than he could bear. He was indeed more than once repaid for his love in such coin, so that he used to say, that he trusted no one until he had been aggrieved by him. The occasion for his being offended C. W. took from a remark of the Superintendent, who told him that once, when he stood in the breach for a deceased Brother, the blood was forced from his finger nails; from which he inferred that the Superintendent must think himself to be Christ. Moreover, because the Superintendent on account of his office had to be in the Sisters' Convent a great deal, he forbade him this under penalty of severe punishment; because he took for granted that things were not as they should be. At length he was given an opportunity to carry out his purpose. It was thus: One of the first spiritual virgins took the liberty to propose marriage to the Superintendent. And when he told her that if he were to do that he would have to deny God, she insisted on it no more; but still she thought he should allow her to assume his name. And when he declined this also, and when furthermore her younger sister after the flesh was preferred before her and appointed Mother Superior of the Sisters' Convent, her love changed to hatred, and she sought the Superintendent's life at the risk of her own. For she testified to the afore-mentioned C. W. that she and the Superintendent had made away with a bastard child. This he at once reported to the Governor. Just at the time when this was made known in the Settlement the Superintendent was in a sad condition, as the powers of darkness, whose lords rule in the air, lay heavily upon him, in addition to which sickness came from without. For, though he lived an innocent life before God and men, yet this did not protect him against the tempter; in whose domain his natural body had grown up. Meanwhile two Solitary Brethren were sent to him [C. W.], who implored him for God's sake not to imbrue himself in innocent blood; to whom he also promised, if it were possible, to withdraw the matter. But the Governor wrote to him that he should give the witness another hearing, and then bring the case before the court at Lancaster. Thereupon he had another hearing of the witness in presence of a housefather, when she again confessed the whole thing; though soon after, when she heard that her own life was endangered, she took it all back, and confessed that her temptations had brought her to make the charge. And since she no longer had any guardian, she married. But just after she was wedded, and was about to retire to the bridal bed of the old Adam, she was suddenly called into eternity; which we consider to have been a divine favor rather than a judgment.

As this attempt failed, he [C. W] again sought out those who had been his acquaintances before his conversion, who rejoiced over him exceedingly, and in all things put him at the head; although there was little cause for rejoicing over one whose conversion had been such a failure. He may have formed many plans at that time to bring to naught the judgment of God against fallen man. Once he tried to prove in a writing that Adam had been created for nothing higher than the natural life; that God had offered him a higher destiny under certain conditions, which was to be attained if these latter were fulfilled, but if not, then he would remain as he had been created. This effort, however, never saw the light of day, as no one gave any countenance to it.

Another incident concerning him must be mentioned. When he saw how heavily burdened the household of the congregation was, it did not seem right to him, and therefore he wrote the following letter to the organization:—"C. W., your former Brother, has the following to say to you in this writing, on behalf of the poor, sighing souls, of whom there are not a few among you, who are groaning day and night unto God because of the heavy Pharaohic and Egyptian bond-service with which the congregation is so heavily laden and burdened that it scarcely can endure it any longer. Besides which, this bond-service is much worse than the Egyptian; for the latter was for the payment of debts, but with that under which the congregation is in bondage no debts can be paid. Yea, what am I saying? Pay? The more one lets oneself come under this service, the more one sinks into debt. But they who withdraw from it, because they see that no debts can be paid with this bond-service, and that one cannot fulfill it so long as one lives, are refused fellowship as though they were evil-doers, and are even expelled from the congregation, etc." Moreover he advised that a reformation be commenced in the church which was very necessary, and said that if he were given word of it, he would come and help reform the church. The Superintendent made this letter known, but it was not taken into consideration, for every one knew that it had been written during temptation and with no good purpose.

After this all remembrance of him ceased in the Settlement, though various offices in the worldly life were heaped upon him. Meanwhile, however, God, in view of his earlier faithfulness in the work of God, bore him in mind, and opened the door of his long spiritual captivity, so that he visited first of all his old friend P. M. at the Settlement. And when he noticed that no one passed severe judgment upon him, he also hunted up the Superintendent, who soon became aware that the good once done for him had not been in vain, and received him with open arms of love, taking him into the Sisters' house, where his old acquaintances rejoiced with him that he had found again his piece of silver that had been lost. Soon after the congregation assembled for a lovefeast, at which he by partaking of the holy sacraments, was re-incorporated in the spiritual communion; although we willingly yield to his mother-church the honor of having garnered in his body.

Now we will take up again the regular course of our story. The fathers in the Egyptian deserts practiced works of love to such an extent that with the earnings of the harvest they supplied with bread the poor and captive; wherefore Theodosius and other Christian emperors absolved them from all taxes. The Solitary at the Settlement were an Order equally useful to the human race, because of the many services they rendered to the poor of their neighborhood; wherefore also they insisted that similar privileges should be accorded them. But there was no statute to that effect in the laws of the land. Six Brethren however joined themselves together to try their fortune (more did not venture to make the attempt). These refused to pay tax, so that their neighbors had to deliver them up to prison, which they did very willingly, mingling their malice with it; for they hoped that it would become a cause for persecuting them. Hardly were they in prison, however, ere the rumor went forth that the Sabbatists in Lancaster County were being persecuted, so that crowds stood all day before the prison bars, although the authorities were quite innocent, and had no hand in the matter. But in the congregation there was great fear lest a persecution might arise in which all one's possessions might be lost. The Superintendent, however, stood up for them; for the more strange the circumstances the more fully he rose to meet them. After they had been prisoners for ten days, the justices of the county held a council, and gave them a hearing, when a venerable justice, Tobias Hendricks by name, offered to go security for them if they would promise him to appear at the next court, which they did, and therefore were released from captivity. May God recompense him for this act of love on the day of judgment.

At the following May Court of the year 1737 they were brought up for a hearing before the Commissioners and Assessors of Taxes, over whom, when they saw before them the men who in the bloom of youth had raised such a warfare against the world, the fear of the Lord came so that they did not speak to them otherwise than friendly, and offered them every favor. The first question was, Whether they would be loyal subjects of the king? To which they answered respectfully, that they had already pledged allegiance to another King, and therefore could obey the King only in so far as his rights agreed with those of their king. The other question was, Whether they would pay the taxes? Answer: "Not the head-tax; because they acknowledged no worldly authority's right over their bodies, since they had been redeemed from the world and men." Moreover, they considered it unjust that, as they were pledged to spend their lives in their present condition, they should be measured by the same standard as vagabonds, and be made to pay the same tax as these. If they would consider them as a spiritual family, however, they would be willing to pay of their earthly possessions according to what was just. All this was granted them, and remains unchanged to the present day. This was the last time that the Solitary came in conflict with the civil authorities. . The latter had always shown themselves of a mild and Christian character. When these Brethren returned to their own, during one of the midnight services, they were welcomed with the hymn: "A mighty fortress is our God, etc," after which the Superintendent made an impressive address on the power of the Beast upon earth. Upon those neighbors, however, who had gloated over the misfortune of the Brethren, there fell the terror of the Lord, so that they hurriedly left this region.

CHAPTER XVI.

The Household of the Solitary is so Constituted as to Oppose the World in Everything. A Visitation from the Baptists Arrives at the Settlement.

It is maintained, not without reason, that the Solitary in the Settlement would have been happy people if it had been granted to them to end their days in the Settlement in the spirit of self-denial which God had put into their hearts. Certainly there would not have been revealed in them so much of what was evil. But afterwards through the guidance of the Holy Spirit there was established such a household, in which were to be found all the instrumentalities belonging to a spiritual martyrdom. For the Spirit sought to restore, even externally, that unity in all things, which was destroyed by the fall of man, and transformed into diversity. Accordingly the condition of the Solitary Brethren was first taken up; for since the dress of the male sex is designed so as to please the female, it was resolved in council to muffle the mortal body in such a style of garment, for its humiliation, that but little of it should be visible. Even before this matter was taken up, and when the garments of the world had already been laid aside, all sorts of strange garbs were donned by the Solitary, whereby the world was much offended; so that necessity demanded a uniformity of dress. The garb of the Order of the Brotherhood was designed with particular care in the council, and was intended to represent a spiritual man. It consisted of a *Thalar* [surplice] reaching down to the feet; over this was a garment having an apron in front and a veil behind which covered the back, and to which was fastened a pointed monk's hood, which could be put on or allowed to hang down the back as one pleased; the whole was provided with a girdle around the waist. During services they wore a cloak besides, reaching down to the girdle, to which also a hood was fastened. Upon contemplating this garb it was found

that they who had designed it for the Order had, without
knowing it, borrowed the style from the Order of Capuchins;
and as said Order prided itself that its habit had been the
dress of the first Christians, the Solitary at Ephrata felt flat-
tered that they should have the honor to dip water from the
same well with so venerable, famous and ancient an Order.
This costume of the Order all the Solitary Brethren at that
time adopted without any objections; and have kept it this
long time; nor did they permit it to be worn either by a
widower who might be among them, nor by a novice until
after the close of his year of trial.

Soon afterwards the Sisters undertook a similar work in
their convent, with the co-operation of the Superintendent.
Their costume, like that of the Brethren, was designed so
that but little was visible of that humiliating image revealed
by sin. They wore hoods like the Brethren, but rounded
instead of pointed, which while they were at work hung
down the back; whenever they noticed anyone coming,
however, they drew the same up over the head and face, so
that one could see little of the latter. The distinguishing
mark of their spiritual betrothal, however, was a large veil,
which covered them entirely in front, and down to the girdle
behind; of this members of Roman Catholic Orders, who
saw it, said that it was known among them as the *Scapula*.
This costume of the Order the Sisterhood has retained with
particular care in its establishment, called Sharon, for now
nigh unto fifty years.

As the Solitary of both sexes in the Settlement had now
firmly established themselves in their newly formed Orders,
the domestic households did the same, in view of the fact
that at all awakenings a change of dress has ever followed
upon a change in forms of worship (*vide* Gen. xxxv, 2).
They therefore applied to the Superintendent for a reformation; for at that time there still flourished the first love and
unity of spirit, and as the Solitary followed the Superintendent, so the domestic households ordered themselves according to the Solitary. Accordingly the households at that
time also laid aside the worldly dress of their members, and
both sexes adopted a new garb which differed from that of

the Solitary (besides some unimportant details) only in this, that the Solitary appeared at divine services in white garments, but the married in gray ones. Thus whenever there was a public procession, as commonly was the case at baptisms, one saw the host of God stand by the water divided into four regiments. The households, however, afterwards changed about again, and conformed themselves to the world in dress as in other respects.

About this same time the Settlement together with the surrounding district took a new form; for it appeared as if Joel's prophecy would again be fulfilled, and the last temple be built up as the temple of the Holy Ghost. Prophecies streamed forth from the Superintendent at all the meetings, witnesses whereof are still to be found in the hymns then composed by him. But this power of the Spirit in the Settlement at that time was like fuller's soap and a refiner's fire, whereby men's natures were tamed to such a degree that, although both sexes were in the very bloom of youth, they nevertheless led an angelic and separate walk. Whoso will compare these circumstances with those of the holy fathers of old in the desert, will confess that the Superintendent, at least in some respects, surpassed them in his course; for while the former were wont to shun danger, he on the contrary plunged his followers into the very midst of it. The Superintendent stood high in the esteem of the Sisterhood and house-wives, they being so firmly convinced of his divine mission, that the former would rather have laid down their lives than submit to a man. The latter, with the consent of the house-fathers, their husbands, committed themselves to his leading, for both were convinced that the married state had originated in sin, and therefore would have to come to an end. He frequently also submitted to their counsel. It has already been mentioned that they were the first to clothe him, and gave him the advice for the sake of God's work to renounce other labors. On one occasion, too, they would have ejected a Swedish preacher, who had caused a disturbance in meeting, if the Superintendent had not interfered in his behalf.

A matter, the like of which one does not find in church

histories, is worthy of special notice here. He held love-feasts with the female portion, no Brethren participating, at which the Sisters were his *Diaconae*, and officiated in all things. At the same time there was in the Settlement a special band of holy Matrons and Virgins who acknowledged no headship but that of Christ, and no guardianship but that of the Christian Church. The reader will learn in the sequel how this glorious state at last ended in a strange tragedy. As it would seem, God made use of him to manifest forth the wonders of eternity, and after this was accomplished he was divested of this ecclesiastical dignity, and clothed again with his former orphaned condition, in which also he ended his life, and which perhaps was better for him than if he had died as a famous saint; since his Master too, notwithstanding that he had excelled in great miracles, yet at last, hanging on the cross, naked between two murderers, had to vanquish the evil one, and then first was enabled to speak of the entrance into paradise. Remarkable it is that neither did the gifts vouchsafed to him distort his mind, nor did his frequent contact with the other sex leave a stain upon his character, although he was not exempt from slanderous misrepresentations. Now we proceed to the order of our narration.

About this same time, namely, in the year 1736, the Baptists of Germantown undertook a visitation to the Settlement. When the Superintendent heard of this, he made preparations to receive them. But when they did not arrive at the appointed time, he was invited to make a visit to Tulpehocken, where he had to tarry longer than he had anticipated. They arrived during his absence, and when they did not find him at home, they concluded that he had purposely avoided them. This was ordained by God as a test for the congregation, whether they would enter upon the mode of worship of these people and unite with them. Had they done so, the Superintendent would have been released from his vow, and would have been free to take up again his former way of life. For it was not unknown to him that some were already tired of his leading, and hungered after an easier way of serving God. Meanwhile the householders opened their doors unto the Baptist visitors and received them well; but they could not tarry long in the Settlement, the weight of the Spirit was too heavy upon them. Among the visitors was an old and venerable teacher, who had but recently come from Germany; his name was Naass, and when he saw the beautiful way of child-training, and the quiet life in the houses, he was so much edified thereby that he declared, that while he had lived through many awakenings in Germany, he had never seen the like of this; and that he would not rest until he had seen the man who had instituted this awakening. In this indeed he was not successful at that time; but later he met the Superintendent, and had the latter not prevented it, the strong attraction of love would have caused him to come over into membership with the congregation, as was done by the good Kalkglässer. When the Superintendent returned home he soon noticed that something was wrong with the divine clockwork here; for there had been spiritual adultery committed, according to the teaching of Christ "Whosoever looketh upon a woman to lust after her," etc. This circumstance caused him on the following Sabbath to make an address on Spiritual Whoredom and Adultery, which on account of its importance is herewith reproduced, as follows:—

"I have something important to remark, partly as a warning, partly as instruction; namely, about spiritual whoredom and adultery, which so beset us on our way to God. There are in the natural realm whoremongers and adulterers, who are alike in this, that both follow after their lusts, and seek to avoid the burdens of matrimonial life. They are unlike, however, in that the one shuns the bonds of matrimony, while the other breaks them. Now it cannot be denied that matrimony is an ordinance of God in the natural realm. But that whereby God still maintains his hold on this estate is the cross, through whose severity married people still can be brought right and to God. So is it also in the Christian Church. For although the gospel is glad tidings which attracts to it the free will of man, there yet is always something more behind the hill, which man at the beginning of his conversion, when he enters into the covenant with Christ, does not yet understand, namely, the cross, and the severe disciplinary training by which he is to be humbled and brought right. When God then brings a person to that point where the old man of sin is to be condemned and he to be refined in the furnace of tribulation, it often happens that one transgresses the bonds of one's spiritual married estate; and as there are plenty of people who live in a hypocritical semblance of piety even while they hate the spiritual matrimony and are unwilling to bear its burdens, (even as whoremongers and adulterers despise the outer, physical estate of matrimony,) one allows oneself to associate with such people, carries on coquetry with them, and so cools oneself off again, by which the mind has secretly sown in it deceit and suspicion against the good, of which it is difficult afterwards to be cured again.

"For man is thereby made spiritually reckless, so that he tries to tread under foot that which is put over him in spirit and through which he is meant to be made better; and, as Lucifer did, so he puts himself above everything that is of God. To this end he takes opportunity also to use the instruments of the congregation, whence proceeds the Word of life, who usually are bad, insignificant and despised people; even as also the Jews made the person of Christ a ground for belittling his miracles. Such conduct brings heavy judgments with it, and is more wicked than physical whoredom; for the latter is judged of men, but the former is spiritual and awaits the great universal judgment to come. Such illicit courtship, however, is not made manifest except where there is a Christian organization with matrimonial vows and birth apparatus, where children are born. From long experience one could mention several things on this subject; but this is not the time for it. We can only wish that the spirit of Phinehas might awaken again, and pierce such damnable whoremongery through the belly. It is not without significance that the Apostles had so much trouble with whoremongers and adulterers, all which belongs in this connection. As such whoremongers we designate all fortune-tellers, star-gazers, and interpreters of omens, who have not come over in their calling to the simplicity of Christ, but who, because the secrets of the starry *magia* are disclosed in them, have taken this instead of their heavenly inheritance. For this reason they are at pains to destroy the innocent child-life wherever it shines forth, and to ascribe everything to the stars. Remarkable it is that such persons always have done great injury to the kingdom of Christ. Already in Moses' time the sorcerers took pains to imitate him; and they succeeded till it came to the lice, there they came to a standstill. Consequently the Jews had a severe law according to which all soothsayers must be punished with death. When Christ came with his miracles, the Jewish star-gazers, the Pharisees, also came, and knew how to explain it all, and to attribute it to Beelzebub. And when the truth rose highest with the apostles the powers of sorcery also rose highest in Simon the sorcerer, who wished to overcome the mysteries of God by violence. Therefore we close with the teaching of the precious John: 'If there come any unto you, and bring not this doctrine, receive him not into your house.'"

At the conclusion of this address, which was held on Nov. 20th, 1736, a Brother named John Roland arose and said: "This is a hard saying." Thereupon he went away, and no longer dwelt with the congregation.

CHAPTER XVII.

AN AWAKENING TAKES PLACE IN THE CONGREGATION OF BAP-
TISTS AT GERMANTOWN, THE MOST OF WHOSE MEMBERS JOIN
THE AWAKENING AT EPHRATA.

Chronologically there follows now this important awakening at Germantown, an account of which shall now be given, together with various other circumstances which belong to this period. A holy impulse to have a share in the great store of hymns which the awakened in Germany brought to light, induced the Solitary to make a collection of said hymns, which also was published through the celebrated high-German printing press there, under the title of Zionitischer Weyrauch's Hügel.[1] Now it may also be that the Community, which at that time had an open door of access at Germantown, contributed something from without to this awakening. It is made clear, however, by certain facts which shall now be related, that the same was a work of the Spirit. At that time there was among the Baptists at Germantown an old experienced Solitary Brother, Stephen Koch by name, who stood in good repute because of his piety, and who ended his holy walk in the Settlement. This person gives the following account of the awakening referred to.

"It is known," he says, "that the Schwarzenau Baptists at first were an awakened people, among whom the spirit of virginity had his abode, and the way of holiness was walked. It was noticed, however, that after they became a people by covenant and thereby were joined together into an external brotherhood, the revival spirit gradually was extinguished among them, and they instead fell back upon mere external forms of divine worship as that upon which flesh and blood depended for redemption. Though these were instituted by God himself, they yet were never meant to be the end itself, as though everything were fulfilled if one meets once every

---

[1] The Zionitic Hill of Incense.

week and hears something talked about, which after all no one intends to carry out, and then devotes the remaining days of the week to the world. For this cause God kept the worship of the Jews in constant disturbance, and often destroyed their temple, so that it might not become the essential thing for them.

"In this, however, they did not succeed any better than the other parties in the Christian church; for each one has inculcated a form of service peculiar to its own people whereby it is distinguished from every other people, until so many religious hedges have come into being that it is hardly possible to count them any longer. Thus among these good people the outer forms of service, which should have helped them in their awakening, became their lord and master, and they all became bondsmen to them. It is consequently no wonder that the spirit of awakening, in its virgin strictness had to leave them, and place their ordering into the hands of that man who everywhere builds up again the church of Adam. Wherefore among them as among other parties the claim is made: Come hither! We have the true Church here one baptizes into the faith in Jesus, etc.

"As they have been sold into bonds under their forms of worship, so also with their water baptism; for they recognize no one as a Brother who has not been baptized, even though he should surpass them in knowledge and experience; such an one has to be satisfied with the title of friend. They went still further in this literal and narrow manner, and committed the teaching office mostly into the hands of married men. Thereby they brought matrimony into high favor, and finally cast off the estate of virginity, which before their baptism they had rated so high. Young people, when they saw that the married state was so highly honored, lusted after it; but as long as they were unbaptized they were regarded as heathen, for according to their principles marriage is consummated only between two believers. If therefore they wished to marry, they first had to have themselves baptized; which at last opened a wide door for carnal presumption.

"Under such circumstances, when there were still many

who had witnessed the awakening at Schwarzenau, it is no wonder that the fire yet smouldering under the ashes should have been rekindled. About this same time, however, an important Brother, Henry Traut by name, passed out of time into eternity, on Jan. 4th, 1733. When with sorrowful heart and deeply grieved I saw him pass into eternity, it made so deep an impression on me that I continually sighed unto God whether it were not possible that in this life yet I might attain unto health of conscience. For I might do what I would, yet I always lacked that which was best, because it appeared to me that I had never in my heart been converted to God, which indeed also I experienced to be the case. The deeper I searched, the more I became aware that in my deepest nature I was still lacking that true change of heart, without which the peace of God, which passeth all understanding, could not reveal itself in me. From this I could well see that there was nothing else for me to do than to repent anew and be heartily converted unto God. Wherefore I constantly prayed to God that for Jesus Christ's sake he would graciously regard me, and cleanse me from all my transgressions.

[1] "For this repentance and conversion, however, I had no power within me. A long while I went about in grief and with sighing, and I was even as it is written: 'The children are come to the birth and there is no strength to bear them.' But at length the power of Darkness so revolted within me, that for the life of me I had no resource left; and I now could realize in what grievous condition the deceased Brother, Henry Traut, had been when at times he had so sorely wept, for I was in like condition. But I did not feel free to tell any man of it. To God, however, I often said: 'Must I then forever be cast off from Thee? Alas, must I now become the prey of unclean spirits! Was it in vain that so many years I have shed so many tears, and poured out unto Thee, my God,

---

[1] His temptations were the following: He was a wooer of the Virgin ["Sophia," the heavenly Wisdom, i. e. saving faith], but because he incautiously forsook his stronghold [celibacy], and betrothed himself to a widow, his Virgin left him, and he fell into earthly ways, until, finally, after many tears of penitence, she again took him up. See Matt. XIX: 10, 11 and 12.

so many heart-sighings? Have mercy upon me, or I perish, for my uncleanness is become so great that it ever hangs over my head, and my enemies rejoice over me, and say, aha! aha! this we gladly see! when once he is down, he shall not rise again!' (Ps. XXXV.) And this I had to hear continually.

"But with all this I found no salvation; but it grew ever worse, so that at last I became very fearful, and thought, Now it will continue until my poor life is consumed, and what will happen after that, God knows. In this way I spent several years, and had, besides, great pain from stones in the bladder, so that I often lay two or three days in the greatest extremity, and had death ever before me, until I was again relieved from it for a time. But God finally regarded my misery, and came to my help in a wonderful manner. On the 3d of May, 1735, at Germantown, as late at night I went behind the house into the orchard, it being bright moonlight, there came to me a delightful odor, partly from the blossoms of the trees, partly from the flowers in the garden, whereat I sobbing spoke to God: 'O, my God, everything is in its order and contributes to Thy glory and honor, save I alone! For I am created and called by a holy calling to love Thee above everything, and to become a pleasant savor unto the glorifying of Thy name. Now, however, I behold the contradiction; for I not only do not love Thee as I ought, but am also become an evil smell in Thy nostrils. Alas, unfortunate that I am! Must I then pass my days in such misery? I gladly would love God, the highest Good, but I cannot. The world with all its glories cannot satisfy my sad spirit, for I ever see before my eyes spiritual and bodily death.'

"While I lamented thus to God it seemed to me as though suddenly a flame of God's love struck into me, which entirely illumined me inside, and I heard a voice say to me: 'Yet one thing thou lackest.' I asked, 'What is it then?' The answer was, 'You do not know God, and never have really known him.' I said, 'Yes, that is so; but how shall I attain to it?' Then it seemed as though I were beside myself. But when I came to myself again, I felt an inexpressibly pleasing love to God in my heart; and on the other hand all anxiety, with all the temptations of the unclean spirits, had vanished. Yea, it seemed as if all my transgressions were pardoned and sealed, and day and night there was nothing else in my heart but joy, love, and praise to God. After several days I came to my intimate Brother, the young Alexander Mack, who told me that he was in so sorrowful a state that he believed he would soon die. Therefore he had made his last testament, wherein he had made several whom he mentioned to me by name his heirs. I told him how I too had made a testament that I would belong wholly to my God. He asked me how that had happened. I said that he probably had noticed that for several years already I had been in a sorrowful condition. Thereupon I recounted the whole matter to him, what had happened to me, and how God had saved me from all my misery in a wonderful manner, and that I now felt in my heart such a love to God that I could not express it. He said: 'O, if you really are such as you say, then are you happy indeed! I believe you will remain thus, and will come to quite a different estate from what you were before. I feel from what you say that something marvelous has happened to you, and I rejoice greatly thereat.' We often had similar conversations with each other, and it was not long before he also came to an awakened condition. As he was a ready speaker, he began to speak in the meeting so powerfully that it was a marvel to hear him, and aroused much notice in the congregation. Some were well pleased at it; but others could not comprehend it. At that time we had a meeting for the unmarried every Sunday afternoon, where we also spoke together as narrated above. At last the spirit of revival came upon all who were assembled together, so that one often heard with astonishment how they praised God; however with many it did not last long.

"In the meantime it happened that the people in the house in which I had lived so long were no longer satisfied with me; for the life that I now led was a witness against their life. Accordingly the afore-mentioned A. Mack received me into his house; but he lived together with another

Brother, Henry Hœcker, in half the house, while the other half was occupied by his brother after the flesh, Valentine Mack. At this time Henry Kalckglässer, then the oldest teacher of the congregation at Germantown, who afterwards ended his course at Ephrata, came to us in the house, and said: 'I hear so much said about you among the people, Brother Stephen Koch; tell me the truth: In what condition were you? how did you come to another condition? and how are you now?' I told him first of all in what a sad state I had been; how marvelously God had brought me out of it; and that I now day and night felt such a love to God in my heart that no tongue could express it. Thereupon he answered, 'O, I know your condition very well, for I was in the same state a long while; but through the various occurrences one meets therein, I fell away from it again. Now I will learn anew to walk before God.' He rejoiced greatly that the good old way shown him at the beginning of his conversion was again revealed to him; in everything of which we had spoken he agreed with us. For we spoke yet much more concerning the celibate estate, and a life of virginity, of which he said, that all this had been revealed to him at his first conversion. Thus this old Brother was quickened again, and spake openly at the meeting concerning such things with much impressiveness, remarking also that he believed that if he had died in the condition in which he had been he would have been found to be a foolish virgin. Many of the congregation, however, took this amiss of him, and said that he had been a teacher so long already, and had baptized so many, and yet now spoke of himself thus doubtfully. But he insisted that such had been his experience.

"At another time the other teacher, Peter Becker, also came to us. During the night we spoke much together, so that in the morning he tearfully bade us farewell. He said to us, that he also would begin anew to walk before God; but this was so far reversed in him again, that he at last declared himself against us.

"Before I came to live with Brother A. Mack I saw in a vision a beautiful virgin come into our meeting, who preached wonderfully concerning sanctification and a life of virginity.

At this I was so glad that in the morning I said to the Brethren that I had seen a most beautiful virgin come into our meeting, who had held an extraordinary address concerning purity and the life of virginity; whereat they rejoiced with me. At the time when I saw this vision, V. Mack saw me go to his brother Alexander very often, and said to me: 'You come into the house so often, yet never come to see me.' I answered, 'Perhaps your house-sister [wife] would not like it.' From that time on I frequently visited them, and spoke with them of the way of holiness, when she always listened with devout attention (of her edifying life and blessed departure mention will be made at the proper place).

"On April 12th, 1736, therefore, I moved to Brother A. Mack, when for a time we three lived together. In the year 1737 we built a house, in a valley, a mile from Germantown, into which we moved on October 14th of said year. There another Solitary Brother, named John Riesmann, besides a pious married couple, came to live with us. But on March 21st, 1738, my three Brethren, Alexander Mack, Henry Hœcker, and John Riesmann, removed to the Solitary at Ephrata, and the housefather, before mentioned, went back to his own piece of land. Thereupon another pious housefather, Lewis Hœcker by name, came to live with me; but we did not live together any longer than until March 27th, 1739, when I also removed to the Solitary at Ephrata. Thus my first call came back to me again, and thus I found again the piece of silver I had lost, whereat I exceedingly rejoice. May God comfort all the sorrowing in Zion, and redeem Israel from the rod of the oppressor, Amen."

This tried warrior of Jesus Christ lived many years more among the Solitary in the Settlement, and finally entered upon his rest on the 7th of June, 1763.

From this small beginning there finally arose a great awakening in and about Germantown, which so many young people joined that, if persons of experience had been connected with it, something very useful might have been the outcome. The fame of it soon resounded through the whole land; for they held their meetings in the woods, and then walked through Germantown hand in hand, which attracted much attention. Besides, they had frequent meetings at night. The teachers of the Baptists themselves went astray in this movement. Some of them, like Henry Kalckglässer, Valentine Mack, John Hildebrand, supported it; while others, like P. Becker, Naass, etc, who had had a similar experience in Germany, opposed it. Yes, Peter Becker often said to them: "Dear children, it is the seventh-day-spirit of Conestoga!" At length the affair came to another separation, in which the Baptists a second time were made naked, and the flower of the congregation was lost. The separatists went together to the Settlement of the Solitary, while the rest of this awakening gradually became extinguished like a straw fire. It must be known that this Baptist removal to Ephrata was wholly unexpected to the Superintendent and the congregation. Indeed they had resolved not long before, because those of the Baptists who had gone over to them had turned out so badly, that they would not receive any more of this people: but who can withstand the counsels of God? and who can set bounds to his Spirit? It was indeed a great marvel to the Superintendent, that those who, according to their spiritual age, could have been his fathers, now became as children unto him, and put themselves under his leading. It appears also that these occurrences gave him an insight into his own circumstances, whereof he knew nothing before, or wished to know nothing, because of his own self-depreciation. For I consider it unquestionable that this occurrence gave occasion to him to compose that hymn, whereof as a specimen I have given the first three verses, and in which he clearly shows that all these awakenings were in their spirit dependent on him.

Before I lay aside this matter, however, I will here mention for hallowed remembrance the names of all those who in this awakening came to the congregation at Ephrata, from among whom arose some of the most trusty Solitary ones. The married ones were Henry Kalckglässer, Valentine Mack, John Hildebrand, Lewis Hœcker, Pettikofer, the widow Gorgas, and their children; to the Solitary belonged Henry Hœcker, Alexander Mack, John Riesmann, Christian

Eckstein, Elizabeth Eckstein, Martha Kinsing, Miriam Gorgas.

The printing of the above-mentioned hymn-book now went forward. But towards the end there happened a matter which caused a great stir in the land, and which shall now be communicated. The printer Saur had already in Germany become acquainted with the Superintendent during the awakening there. He considered him indeed to be a God-fearing man; but when Providence placed him at the head of a great awakening in Conestoga, the good man held him in suspicion of seeking to become a pope, to which there came yet a secret dislike for the Superintendent because the latter received his wife, who had separated from him, under his leading, and even made her sub-superintendent of the Sisters' House. At that time opinions concerning the Superintendent varied in the country. The greater and coarser part of the people regarded him as a great wizard, whereto certain things that had happened gave an appearance of plausibility. As has been mentioned above, the spirit under whose guidance he was, at times made him invisible, concerning which the following is yet to be mentioned in passing. A justice of the peace sent a constable after him with a warrant; he took an assistant with him, named Martin Graff. As they came towards the house, they saw him go in with a pitcher of water. They followed him, and while one stationed himself at the door, the other searched the house from top to bottom; but no Superintendent was to be found. As they departed, however, and were quite a distance from the house, they saw him come out again.

His Brethren, however, who were daily with him, and may have seen much of this kind of thing, fell into the opposite extreme, and like the Jews concerning John, thought whether he might not be Christ. Even Brother Prior Onesimus said that such thoughts often came to him. Of all this the printer was aware. Wherefore when in printing the hymn-book he came upon the hymn: [2]"Since the pillar of cloud

---

[2] The fact that the printer took such violent offence at this hymn, as did also not a few others, merits closer examination. In a congregation in which the way of holiness is pursued, the stone of stumbling and rock of

dissolveth," etc., he wanted to force out of the 37th verse a meaning as if the Superintendent intended himself thereby. He accordingly took the *corrector* to task about it, who however, asked him, whether he then believed only in one Christ? This so outraged him that he wrote a sharp letter to the Superintendent, in which he reproached him for his spiritual pride. The Superintendent, who in such things never remained anyone's debtor, sent back to him a short reply to the following intent : "Answer not a fool according to his folly, etc." "As vinegar upon nitre, so is he that singeth songs to an heavy heart." (PROV. XXV, 20.) This aroused the good man to a fiery heat, and he resolved to avenge himself for this affront. Therefore he published a document against the Superintendent in which he told under how strange a conjunction of the stars the Superintendent was, and how each planet manifested in him its own character-

offence is set up. Whoso goes beyond him becomes Anti-Christ, and whoso comes under him is crushed and ground to dust; to such an object of contention did God ordain him among his people, nor did it cease with the close of his life. For, when the glories of paradise were revealed in him prophetically, everybody ran after him; but when it became known what was behind this, the cross of Christ, many took so great offence thereat that they tried every means to overthrow him, although they never accomplished anything. For he himself had experienced such opposition in his own private inner life far more powerfully, so that he said at times that there was no harder work under the sun than to serve God, for do what one please it was never right, and that he wondered what would happen if his fellow-laborers were tried as sorely as he. His followers, however, were not aware of these circumstances, and by their mistaken zeal made the life of this witness of God so bitter, that judgment finally overtook them, and then, so long as there was a possibility of saving, he had to step into the breach, and redeem that which he had never robbed.

Accordingly it is no wonder that there were so many strange happenings at the Settlement during his superintendency, which will yet be mentioned. Certain it is that he spent his life in such a fervor that but few of his followers were able to keep up with him. Since, therefore, he was a saviour of his people, whose transgressions were bound upon his back, no one need be surprised that he permitted something of his difficult priesthood to enter into this hymn, though he was constrained for reason's sake to represent it in so flowery and ambiguous a wise that one could not know of whom he spoke. The printer, however, had him in suspicion before already, and hence was all the more able to kindle such a fire. One can surely conclude, then, that a congregation which has not produced Anti-Christ is not a congregation of Christ.

istics: from Mars he had his great severity, from Jupiter his friendliness, from Venus that the female sex ran after him, Mercury had taught him the art of a comedian, etc. He even found in his name, *Conradus Beusselus*, the numbers of the Beast, 666. By this occurrence the good understanding between the printer and the Community at Ephrata was interrupted for many years, and was not restored until the printer's wife, who had hitherto lived at Ephrata, went back to him again. From that time on until his death, he lived on good terms with the Superintendent and all the Solitary in the Settlement, and won for himself an everlasting remembrance among them by many deeds of love. May the Lord grant him to enjoy the fruits of this good seed in the resurrection of the righteous !

Before I close this chapter it is yet to be remarked that about this same time the first Moravian Brethren arrived in Pennsylvania, viz: Spangenberg and Nitschmann, whom three Solitary Brethren soon visited at Shippack, in a family by the name of Wügner. At first sight there was felt by both parties a magnetic attraction between their spirits; for both were yet in their first love. Therefore also they resolved to journey with the afore-mentioned Solitary Brethren and to pay a visit to the Settlement; which also was done with great blessing. On their return, the Brethren accompanied them part of the way, formed a circle, and after having praised God in a hymn, they embraced and commended one another to God. It has been reported concerning them that in St. Thomas, whither they went from Ephrata, they baptized the blacks whom they converted there, by baptizing them under the water, according to the Ephrata manner; which I give as reported. It is to be desired that this good feeling and confidence might not so soon have been lost on both sides, as much offence might thus have been avoided in succeeding times. All these things happened about the year 1739.

CHAPTER XVIII.

THE BROTHERS' CONVENT, NAMED ZION, IS BUILT.

In Chap. XIV we mentioned how the first meeting-house in the Settlement, named Kedar, fell into the hands of the Sisters, and was constituted a convent; and how a housefather of means had a chapel for them added to it. At that time the Brethren still dwelt scattered here and there in the Settlement, while each one was allowed a small possession in land, because it was not considered right to constrain anyone to self-denial against his will. Among the Brethren there were four who lived together in a house, viz: Brother Onesimus, who afterwards became Prior, Brother Jotham, his brother according to the flesh, Brother Nehemiah and Brother Jabez; these because of their superior excellence were regarded as the choicest of the Brethren. Their house was built half against the hill, and therefore was called the Hill House. Moreover they were well furnished for the entertainment of guests, had cleared a goodly tract of land, and established a right pleasant settlement, where they thought to maintain themselves even though all else should go to nothing; but these were mere men's thoughts. With them the Superintendent was on confidential terms; all love-feasts in the Settlement were held in their house; and all guests were harbored there; on which account the rest of the Brethren harbored ill-will against them. But what would be the final outcome no one knew at that time; God had hidden it from their eyes, otherwise none would have gone into the net.

As now so many wooers of the Virgin continually announced themselves at the Settlement, the Superintendent was at a loss what should be done with these numerous young people, and whether it were not better to teach them to renounce their self-will in convents under spiritual authority, than to let them raise up their own altars of selfhood in corners; in this matter a certain occurrence brought him to a decision. At that time a very rich young Swiss had himself received in the Settlement, Benedict Yuchly[1] by name, from Kilchery-turnen in the district of Berne. Inflamed by the love of God he resolved to devote his fortune to the erection of a convent; which was accepted as coming by divine direction, and his proposition granted. There was in the Settlement a pleasant elevation from which one had a beautiful view of the fertile valley and the mountains lying opposite; of this height the Brethren in the Hill House at that time held possession. When now it came to the selection of a site, the most held that the valley along the Cocalico creek was the most desirable, on account of the water; the Superintendent, however, went up the hill until he came within

[1] This Benedict Yuchly, after having lived in this new convent several years, became very much disgusted with this narrowly circumscribed life, and sought some good excuse again to become free. As he still had large possessions in Switzerland, he asked permission to go and get this fortune, promising to hand it over to the Community. In reality, however, his intention was again to take up his residence in his native land, though at first only as an immigrant settler. This request was granted in a brotherly council, and his traveling expenses advanced out of the treasury, in return for which he made the Brethren his heirs in his will, if he should die on the journey. But who can understand the wonderful ways of God ; for, in his covenant with God sealed in the water, he had pledged himself not to love his life unto death, which could not be broken. Therefore, as long as there still was some good to be found in him, and that his transgressions might not multiply, the judgment overtook him even before he had arrived outside the boundaries of God's people, and severed the thread of his life in Philadelphia, just as he was ready to go on board the ship.

If this had been the only one in the Settlement who shortened his life by his heedlessness, one might perhaps regard it as a mere coincidence. But since there were probably more than twenty, of both sexes in the Settlement, who similarly paid the penalty with their lives, it must be acknowledged that the hand of Providence was concerned therein, for they would after all have gained no more than to make their offence against the Lord greater.

Thereupon two Brethren were sent to Philadelphia. But they came too late for his funeral, and therefore were going to disinter his remains and bring them here to his Brethren, which however caused a great tumult of the people, and caused them to be ill thought of after their return home. This deceased Brother's memory will be hallowed so long as the Settlement of the Solitary remains inhabited ; for although he departed out of time as one prematurely born, yet he left his Brethren so much by his will, that they bought a mill therewith, which for this long while has furnished the bread for the entire Settlement.

the limits of the property of the Brethren of the Hill House, and there was the site chosen. By this the spirit of wonders indicated at the very beginning that the Brotherhood would at first build its structure on the heights of reason, and thus soar aloft, until at length by a great storm they would be cast down into the valley; all which was afterwards fulfilled in minutest detail. But the good Brethren of the Hill House were moved to sensitiveness by this, for they realized that this convent would be at their expense. This hill was called Zion, and from it the society afterwards went by the name of the Zionitic Brotherhood, which name clung to them in all their doings. At this time, too, the name Ephrata was given to the Settlement by the Superintendent, of which he said, that here his Rachel, for whom he had served so many years, was buried, after she had borne to him Benoni, the child of anguish; whereby he pointed to the history of the patriarch Jacob.

Work on this great house went forward rapidly. Its frame was erected in May, 1738, and in the following October the first Brethren moved into it; they were, with a few exceptions, all novices, and had but little experience in the spiritual life. Soon after they moved in there were certain happenings from which one could infer that this house would be a source of many sorrows for its inmates; for each one brought with him his inflammable passions, while the divine fount by which all acerbity is softened, had not yet been opened in them; besides this, the older Brethren had not yet put their interest in this house. The house was not entirely finished nor fully occupied until five years after this.

The Superintendent spoke much with the older Brethren concerning this new institution, how it demanded a man who would be its sole head, without whom the institution would not be able to be maintained. But when he noticed that his words did not make any impression on them, he made use of a trick, and pretended that he would place the two Brethren Nehemiah and Jabez in authority at Zion; which when the Eckerlins heard, they regarded it as an insult that Brethren who were younger than they in their calling should be preferred before them. Therefore the youngest among them, Jotham by name, went off, and moved to Zion with the two Brethren named; but his elder brother, Onesimus, who was intended for the office, at that time yet held back. As now the Brethren in Zion were obliged to accept this authority, they came into great temptations, and thought their freedom was lost forever; for although they were very earnest, they had not yet learned that obedience by which the Son of God overcame the evil one; nor was it any wonder, because their superiors also lacked the same. Consequently their natural characteristics came into collision, so that often, if the Superintendent had not come into the breach, the name of God would have been brought into dishonor among them. Now it became apparent what the Superintendent had intended when he said that the house demanded a man; there was no one of dignity enough among them to be chosen. For notwithstanding that the same Brother used every effort to bring the house into subjection, in which also he in a measure succeeded, it yet was only a government of selfishness; wherefore also it broke up again the following year, 1740.

Thus at length the hermit Order in the Settlement was converted, amid many temptations, to a conventual life. Our predecessors of both sexes followed this angelic life in the forests of Conestoga for ten years before Ephrata was built, and it was spread abroad in different parts of the land. And that God first practices his saints in a separate and solitary life ere he hires them for his vineyard, is shown by the example of John the Baptist, as well as by that of Moses in the wilderness where he tended sheep for forty years. The Superintendent was able to adapt himself pretty well to these peculiar conditions, though it cost him a thousand tears to renounce his angelic way of life and again to plunge into the ocean of humanity; for he clearly saw that the hermit life, however innocent it be, could yet contribute nothing to the fruitfulness of the house of God, because, as he says in his discourses, no hermit enters the kingdom of God. Therefore when afterwards every spring the cry arose that the Brethren in Zion would go forth into the wilderness, it did not move him, since he foresaw that the sons of

Ephraim, who clad in armor were bearing the bow, would yet fall away in the time of battle, which the Eckerlins ventured to do when they wanted to revive the hermit-life on New River, where the storm of the Almighty Lord then overthrew their structure, erected in selfishness, so that several lost their lives, and others fell away and afterwards multiplied in the flesh.

With the other Solitary ones, however, it was different; for their longing was always after solitariness, so that, when the Superintendent installed the first Mother over the Sisters, their house was so violently moved that several ran away; yet they came back again after the storm had passed. So hard it is to learn to fight orderly under command. The Brethren had so thoroughly prepared everything for their solitary life that, when they brought their household furniture together to Zion, it was a matter of astonishment how they were furnished in every detail. That God must have specially blessed this Order is known to those who at that time visited the Solitary saints in their huts; yes, even long after their departure one could notice something attractive in said huts. O, how many fiery trials these warriors might have avoided, if it had been permitted them to end their lives in this angelic existence! But since its course was run, the Order will probably not again be restored to its former estate; the light has risen higher, wherefore also we wished to speak their eulogy at its funeral. Remarkable it is that the holy fathers in the desert made their disciples first learn obedience in convents, and afterwards sent them into the desert for higher schooling; here it was turned around, they went from solitude to convent life. And although then already everyone was convinced that this was the leading of God, there nevertheless were some who even thus early ran off the track, among whom Peter Gehr was one of the first, whose biography, since it was a remarkable one, we will add here.[2]

---

[2] He was born at Seckenheim near Heidelberg in the Palatinate, and was brought to his conversion early in life under the Superintendent's ministry in Pennsylvania. And as his walk shone forth with special brilliance he was also employed by the latter to baptize others; but as it happened that

the Superintendent rebaptized several of those baptized by him, this young warrior came to harbor suspicions against his spiritual leader, which at length resulted in a root of bitterness. Soon after his conversion he became intimate with a young Sister, Rebecca by name, who had been consecrated to God, and married her in presence of the congregation; which indeed was imputed to him as a mistaken act; but as he led an angelic life with her he began to exalt his estate above that of the Solitary Brethren, because he was able to do more than they did. Finally the Solitary Sisters took his helpmate up in their Convent, wherefore he gave her a bill of divorce, and as mentioned above, betook himself to the Brethren in Zion whom, however, he also soon left again. On January 9th, 1740, he made another attempt to live with the Brethren in Zion, when the Superintendent with much love offered him in spirit the hand of fellowship. Notwithstanding this, his temptations overcame him. so that he soon went away again, which happened in October of the year mentioned.

Since he was not capable of living in subjection to a spiritual Order, on account of his strong spirit of selfhood, he spent the remainder of the time in separatism. There he outwardly led a quiet and retiring life, though within himself he may have been very much exercised, as one who had missed God's purpose, in trying to bring God's testimony under his feet, a testimony which so marvellously makes a fool of one. Certain it is that on his death-bed he ordered a whole ream of paper, which he had written full, to be torn up and thrown into the water; wherein, perchance, his counsels and plans against the simplicity of God may have been contained. In this state he lived about twenty years without expressing any accusations against the community which he had left, although he associated with those who were dissatisfied with God's leading in the organization, which also caused him severe trials at his departure into eternity.

Finally he came to die; whereupon, instead of passing away in peace, stern justice delivered him over to the powers of darkness, who delayed his end so that for twenty-four hours he was dying and lying in the midst of the severest temptations. The relatives noticed that heavy stones of offence lay at the bottom of this, and therefore asked him whether he were reconciled with his former Brethren. This hit the mark; for at his request a messenger quickly had to go and bring three of his former most intimate Brethren. They found him in a state of struggling with despair, like another Spira, and this was his constant lamentation: "I am fallen among murderers!" The presence of his Brethren, however, gave him more confidence, and he expressed to them his condition in the following wise: "You are my Brethren! Unto you will I live, and unto you will I die, and you shall also bury me." Thereupon he reverted to the Sisterhood, and as he was made aware that these still held him in some favor, his desire was that the Brethren should hasten home, and in fellowship with these Sisters should bow their knees in their chapel in prayer to God on his behalf. Meanwhile the door opened, and there entered one of his fellow-separatists, who greeted him in a friendly way, but which, as was remarked with astonishment, renewed his temptations, wherefore he turned his back to him, and faced the wall. May God preserve his saints from falling into folly! For persons who are joined together against the Divine counsels, and thereby have embittered the life of the laborers in the vineyard, will have a heavy responsibility to answer for in eternity.

The Brother's condition was not yet relieved, however, for there still lay a heavy weight upon him in reference to the Superintendent, from whose authority, under which he should have wrought out his salvation, he had withdrawn himself in willful manner. At last he drew to himself a Brother who he knew availed much with the Superin tendent, and whispered in his ear that he should take his cordial greeting to the Superintendent. That settled it. The brotherly balsam flowed forth and entered his soul, especially when the Brother mentioned laid his hands upon him and blessed him; whereupon, to the amazement of all who were gathered about him, most of whom were of the Lutheran church, he was relieved of all his temptations, and entered upon a divine peacefulness. Soon after the departure of the Brethren he died, as we hope, happily. This threw into great terror all those who had cast under foot the testimony of God, forasmuch as such a person even, who had lived so irreproachable a life, at last, at the end of his life, again had to subject himself humbly under that very cause above which he had impiously tried to set himself. But the Solitary at the Settlement took fresh courage therefrom, so that next day they hastened to dress the deceased in the garb of their Order, and thus at the same time raised over him the standard of victory, as a sign that by the grace of God they had snatched his prey from the hellish blood-avenger; whereat surely all the saints in heaven and on earth will rejoice. The tragedy aroused much commotion in that region. Some said to the deceased: "Poor Gehr! must you now again be that against which during life you strove so earnestly?" Others declared that it was wonderful that so strict an organization existed among the Solitary at Ephrata. But no one ventured to deny that the hand of God was in the affair; for everyone well knew that all these changes had wrought themselves out in him freely, and that no one had persuaded him. He was committed to the earth among the Solitary at Ephrata, where may God grant him his portion in the first resurrection! I have purposely gone into details in this narrative. The reader will notice therefrom that God has his eye specially upon the footsteps of such persons as have once come to his hand. Had this warrior gone over into eternity in his unreconciled condition, how hard would it have been to redeem him out of the same, because his freedom of will would have been gone. It appears, however, that in the days of his innocence he had wrought much good, whereby God had become his debtor to stand faithfully by him in the time of need; which also the good God did, whose name be praised!

CHAPTER XIX.

THE TITLE OF FATHER IS GIVEN TO THE SUPERINTENDENT; AND CONCERNING THE QUARRELS THAT AROSE ON ACCOUNT OF IT.

It early came to be the custom in the Settlement to lay aside one's common name, and take a new one, which was called the church-name. The common name of the Superintendent was Conrad Beissel, wherefore he was usually called Brother Conrad. Finally, however, he assumed another name, either because the old one had made him seem too familiar [alletägisch], or because a new epoch in his life had begun. That pride should have impelled him to do so no one can believe who was acquainted with his circumstances. He expressed his wish to several house-fathers, who went to great trouble to find a name for him that should be suitable; but none of all those suggested seemed to harmonize with his estate. Thereupon he proposed to them the name Brother Friedsam, which met with their approval; and when they had adopted it, it was at once made known to the congregation.

When the Solitary Brethren at the Settlement heard it, it appeared a bad thing to them simply to call him a Brother, since to many of them he had been, next to God, the cause of their salvation. Therefore they resolved in their council to call him a Father, of which they notified him through two deputies, and which also he accepted without contradiction; for he was so instructed from above that he would not readily have refused the good intentions of anyone, even though he might therefor reap the greatest reproach, as happened in this case. When it was made known at a lovefeast, it offended the house-fathers, particularly because the Eckerlins were movers in the matter, against whom they had a grudge as it was, for trying to exalt the Superintendent beyond measure. This occasioned various conferences, where it was decided that the Solitary should call him Father, while those of the domestic households should call him Brother; though this was never strictly observed.

'Thus the matter stood until the year 1741, when a housefather of the congregation, John Hildebrand by name, was moved to draw up a great document, and to present it to the Superintendent, wherein he proved from many Scripture passages that strictly speaking the title of Father belonged to no one but God. It came to us from the times of apostasy and the Roman church, when one had placed himself upon a chair whom they called Holy Father. The Superintendent did not permit himself to quarrel about it, but received the Brother's work, and said he believed there was good contained in it. At the same time he told him that he felt that people had put him into an evil situation, in which, he feared, harm might come to the testimony of God; wherefore also he had asked for another name, upon which the Solitary Brethren had imposed this name upon him. When the Superintendent showed this condescension to the Brother, he went home apparently quite satisfied and happy. Soon after, however, he brought the Superintendent a long letter of similar purport with the preceding document. The Superintendent had him read his letter in the presence of two of the house-fathers themselves. In it he went so far as almost to deny the incarnation of Christ. Then the Superintendent declared that it would be easier for him to give up this title entirely if by the same he would be obligated to stand for something which he would not have to do if this name were taken from him. It was difficult to discern from the Superintendent's conduct whether he was in favor of or against the title. Those who regarded his action only superficially and from the outside were indeed tempted to think that he coveted titles of honor, as also the good Hildebrand thought. But those who had an insight into his spiritual condition, knew very well that for conscience sake he might not avoid any reproach, such as also this Father-title was. And surely this title would not have been set for a stone of stumbling to these men wise in their own conceits by God's providence. Why then did men, even after his death, rave so violently, since it is not their wont to be so zealous against evil, else they would have had occasion enough, even without this title, to kindle their wild natural passions by their zeal.

After Brother Hildebrand had now read his letter, as was mentioned, the Superintendent called into the council three Solitary Brethren, namely, Jephune, Jotham and Jethro, besides two house-fathers, and thus addressed them: "Brother Hildebrand has been moved within himself on account of me with regard to the title Father, which the Solitary Brethren and some house-fathers applied to me, and says that it belongs to no creature, but to God alone, whereupon a controversy has arisen." The Solitary Brethren, who first had manufactured the title, were soon ready, and cast aside at once the great things of Brother Hildebrand. But the two house-fathers held back, and only said that they had lost the Superintendent after he had assumed this title. It appears from this how, from the beginning of the Community, the Solitary Brethren and the householders quarreled about the person of the Superintendent, even like Judah and Israel about King David.

This strife continued throughout the Superintendent's life-time, and became a bitter cross unto them who were involved in it. It was commonly spoken of as the strife between Judah and Ephraim, of which Isaiah makes frequent mention. It surely is a difficult matter to keep in unity a church composed of such unequal estates; for the solitary estate would not stand under the domestic, nor the latter under the former; but with the Superintendent as head they all hung together, and whichever had him was usually on top. Of this our Protestants know nothing, for among them everything is shorn over one comb. In church history we find that this strife was often brought up before the councils; whereupon canons were enacted that the solitary should not exalt itself over the domestic estate. Now in this organization too, as still is the case in the Romish church, the church government was wholly in the hands of the Solitary, so that even the domestic estate would not receive a married man or widower as priest. But in order that the domestic estate, as being the weaker part, might not be oppressed by the Solitary, God had given the balance into the hands of the Superintendent, so that they to whom he gave his fellowship, rose up, and they from whom he withdrew it sank down, by which means he kept the work in continual motion. He never gave his favor too long to the one or to the other, thereby preventing anyone from getting undue advantage. But as I am going to describe the spiritual government of the Settlement in another chapter, I will save until then the rest of this subject.

After the council mentioned, the Superintendent censured the two house-fathers, Joiada and Lamech, for not having defended Brother Hildebrand better against the Brethren in Zion, for at that time this Brotherhood was strong and had the preponderance in the Settlement. Thereupon next day the two house-fathers went to the convent of Zion, and told the Brethren how greatly concerned they were about the Father-title. "For," said they, "if this name is not made more general, the Superintendent is as good as taken from the congregation, and you have brought him over to your side by means of this title." But they effected nothing by this; for the Zion's Brethren had two principal accusations against them: 1. That they had made common cause with the Brother Hildebrand in his affairs against the Superintendent. 2. That they had not maintained a close enough fellowship with the Zion's Brethren; if they had done so, they would also have found again the Superintendent.

Soon after this the Superintendent went to the Zion's Brethren and gave them to know that he would now no longer be responsible for the title of Father; but that if the Brethren would stand for it, it would have to be settled at a general council. Thereupon the Brethren agreed upon the following resolutions in their council, which also they handed to him in writing, namely: That they recognized and acknowledged the Superintendent to be their spiritual father, since he bore the testimony out of which the Solitary in the Settlement as well as the congregation had sprung, and that they would defend this title for the Superintendent against all objectors. Because of this the Superintendent also bore the Brethren in Zion in special remembrance before God. This is now the second time that the Brethren in Zion defended the Father-title against the adversaries, wherefore it was adopted at both the convents, though it was not yet approved by the congregation. All this happened on a sixth day of the week. On the following Sabbath, however, the Superintendent declared himself as follows before the entire congregation: "Brother John Hildebrand this week testified against me, both in writing and by word of mouth, that it was not right that I allowed myself to be called a Father, because that title belonged to God alone." He desired to bring this before the congregation. Now they would have to choose one or the other, namely, either to stand by the title, or not to do so.

At this the congregation was greatly surprised. But Brother John Hildebrand began to justify his course, and to call upon God as the one at whose command he had borne this testimony. With many other words also he disclosed his motives. Upon this the Superintendent expressed himself thus: That henceforth he would have nothing more to do with the Father-title; the congregation should decide what was to be done. And that it might feel freer in its judgment, he would withdraw; whereupon he betook himself to the upper hall. Now the votes of the congregation were gathered, when it was found that all, with a few exceptions, were of opinion that he should be confirmed in the title by common consent. This they announced to him, with the added condition, that, if the title were burdensome to him, he should not be obliged to take it. This offer of the congregation the Superintendent respectfully accepted, and so the matter was concluded thus: that the two Solitary Orders, and all in the congregation who thought well of it, should call him Father; while the rest should be free to do as they pleased. Thus Brother Hildebrand, with his testimony, came to nought.

I have deemed it necessary to trace this affair to its source, in order to convince the reader that the Superintendent did not arbitrarily assume this title, as was charged by many. It were to be wished that the entire congregation had remained steadfast in its original simplicity; but it was here even as in the time of the Apostles. As soon as the Superintendent had fallen asleep in the Lord many betrayed themselves that they were not satisfied with this title. Therefore when seven years after the Superintendent's death a monument was erected to him, and counsel was taken with reference to the inscription to be put thereon, it was resolved, in order not to give offence to any, to leave off the two names of Father and Gottrecht. Upon others, who are unworthy, the title is freely bestowed; but from this one, because he was worthy, it was taken away even after his death; so everything in this world must be mixed with hypocrisy if it is to be acceptable. The above mentioned Brother Hildebrand was one of the first awakened in Germany during this century, and lived with such ascetic rigor that at the beginning he even ate his bread by weight. He was a man of peculiar gifts, and had a deep insight into the writings of Jacob Boehme. Nevertheless he had become pretty well cooled off; but when the fires of the awakening in Conestoga burned so brightly, it warmed him up too, so that he joined the congregation. His oldest daughter was the first virgin to be consecrated, and also the first one to exchange her angelic estate for matrimony, being wedded to the middle son of Alexander Mack. Because her father became sorely offended at the rock of offence in the congregation, he separated from it again, and for a time took up with the opposing party in Conestoga. Afterwards he followed his daughter and moved to Germantown, where the Baptists made him one of their teachers. But when the awakening referred to made itself felt at Germantown, he again removed to the congregation at Ephrata, with his son-in-law and daughter. From that time on he stood in the way of the Superintendent, which caused many quarrels; for because he was older in his spiritual calling than the Superintendent, he was unable to subject himself to the latter; besides which he also was very wise in his own conceit. Yet the Superintendent rose above his opposition in the spirit of love, and after his death committed him to the earth with expressions of high esteem.

CHAPTER XX.

A House of Prayer is Built in Zion; Besides Other Occurrences Which Took Place in the Congregation and Settlement About the Year 1740.

In October of the year 1739 the sons of two of the housefathers adopted the solitary life, and were received by the Brotherhood in Zion. After their year of probation was over, they were invested with the dress of the Order, and the one received the name of Zephaniah, the other Obadiah. Both endured their trial, and are now in eternity. May God give them grace on the day of doom! Hitherto divine service had been held in the chapel of the Sisters; but now the fathers of the two mentioned Brethren, named Nägele and Funck, offered in the name of their sons to build a prayer and school house, which it was granted them to do. They furnished all the material for it, and the Brethren did the work. The mason-work was done in six weeks, in which time it neither snowed nor rained, and was raised up in December of the year 1739. At that time things were done as in the days of the restoration of Jerusalem; all the Brethren were masons, builders, carpenters, etc., for God gave them wisdom and great patience in their daily work; moreover they were greatly concerned that none of the show of the world-spirit should be introduced. This house of prayer[1] was a large and sightly structure. Below was a large room furnished with chairs, and adorned with texts in Gothic letters, for the congregation. Here the Superintendent had his seat; behind him a choir-gallery was built, in the lower part of which sat the Solitary Brethren, and in the upper, the Sisters. In the second story there was another large hall, furnished with everything needed for holding the

---

[1] This handsome Prayer-house, in which were manifested forth many wonders of God, did not stand more than 38 years, being converted into a hospital during the war of the Americans, after which it was never restored again.

Agapæ. In the third story were dwelling rooms for eight Solitary persons. In this house many wonders of God were manifested forth, so that its future fate was much lamented.

In August of the year 1740 the rest of the Brethren in the Settlement also left their solitary dwellings and moved into the convent Zion; among these was the later so well known Prior Onesimus. Him the Superintendent, as his first-born son, not only appointed to be Prior in Zion, but also, together with two other Brethren, Enoch and Jabez, solemnly consecrated to the work of the Lord by the laying on of hands in presence of the congregation. But great difficulties arose in Zion upon his entrance there, for his brother after the flesh, Jotham, held the authority there, and had all the Brethren on his side. In hallowed commemoration we will here give the names of all the Brethren who at that time dwelt in Zion, as also of all belonging to the Order of the Sisters. At the present time, 1785, there are seven of the former, and nine of the latter, still living.

BROTHER ONESIMUS, Prior of the Convent.

BR. AGONIUS,	BR. JONATHAN,	BR. BENJAMIN,
BR. JOTHAM,	BR. PHILEMON,	BR. NATHANAEL,
BR. ELIMELECH,	BR. AGABUS,	BR. ENOCH,
BR. JABEZ,	BR. ZEPHANIAH,	BR. ABEL,
BR. JEPHUNE,	BR. OBADIAH,	BR. SIMEON,
BR. OBED,	BR. NEHEMIAH,	BR. GOTTLIEB,
BR. TIMOTHEUS,	BR. GIDEON,	BR. JEMINI,
BR. JOEL,	BR. WILLIAM,	BR. BENEDICT,
BR. THEONIS,	BR. JUST,	BR. ISAI.
BR. BENO,	BR. JOSEPH,	BR. SEALTHIEL.
BR. EPHRAIM,	BR. AMOS,	
BR. JONADAB,	BR. SOLOMON,	

SISTER MARIA, Mother of the Sisters.

SR. JAEL,	SR. EUGENIA,	SR. PAULINA,
SR. IPHIGENIA,	SR. PHOEBE,	SR. SYNCLETICA,
SR. HANNAH,	SR. ARMELLA,	SR. KETURAH,
SR. EUPHROSINA,	SR. REBECCA,	SR. BERNICE,
SR. ANNA,	SR. MARIA CHRISTIANA,	SR. CATHARINE,
SR. EUNICE,	SR. PERSIDA,	SR. ESTHER,
SR. DEBORAH,	SR. LOUISA,	SR. RACHEL,

Sr. Naemi,	Sr. Thekla,	Sr. Naema,
Sr. Prisca,	Sr. Theresia,	Sr. Anastasia,
Sr. Miriam,	Sr. Basila,	Sr. Drusianna,
Sr. Flavia,	Sr. Barbara,	Sr. Martha.

Now they began to order their life in every respect in monastic wise. First of all, property was declared sinful, and everything was brought together in common, in support of a fund, out of which everything needed for the sustenance of the Brethren was bought; the same was also done in the Sisters' Convent. It was therefore a great reproach for anyone to be accused of ownership. This lasted many years, namely, that no one owned anything, until at last necessity forced a return to ownership; although to this day everything in the main work is held in common. And in order that no one who had contributed anything might even in the future claim it, as for example, if he should leave the convent, it was resolved that anyone who should leave it, should forfeit whatever he had contributed; to which all agreed without any objections. When, owing to an absurd separation which then was mutually observed, the Sisters had been obliged to cut their own fire-wood, there was afterwards a contract made with them, agreed to by the Superintendent, that the Brethren should supply the Settlement with wood, while the Sisters, on their part, should look after the Brethren's wash. A common table was also introduced in both convents, during the first hour of the evening. Now they also began to tear down the separate hermit houses in the Settlement, out of which several work-shops were built.

On the 21st of September of this year the two societies separated from each other in divine worship, and the Brethren held their first midnight prayer meeting in their new house of prayer. As at this time a bell was sent as a present to one of the Brethren in the convent by his father in Germany, the Brethren prevailed upon the Superintendent, after much begging, to let them hang it in their prayer-house. When this was rung at midnight, not only did all the Settlement arise, but as one could hear it for four English miles around the Settlement, all the families also rose and held their home worship at the same time; for in those days the fires of the first love still burned everywhere. The Brethren attended their services clothed in the garb of the Order, wearing in addition also a mantle with a hood like that of the Capuchins. I shall speak of the spirit and power of this worship at another place.

There is another circumstance that belongs here, though it happened in the year 1738. About that time the custom came into vogue to have one's self baptized for the dead, as it was supposed from the words of Paul that the first Christians did the same. Two Brethren first originated this at the Settlement, Elimelech[2] and Timotheus,[3] the first of whom had himself baptized for his deceased mother, and the other for his deceased father, although it was known that both their parents had been baptized in Germany. This custom was practiced for many years in the households, and has not yet wholly died out, there always being some who became substitutes and pledges for their parents, or other relatives, though these had in their life time received their divine calling, but had not attained unto the covenant of God.

In December of the year mentioned the Superintendent, with many of the Solitary, made a considerable visit to the Baptists at Amwell, in Jersey. These people, from the time of their first awakening, had a great love for the work of the Lord in the Settlement; whereupon this visit opened the door for the breaking of bread together, which otherwise, because they were united with a congregation of Baptists in Germantown, would not have been looked upon with approval. When the Superintendent returned home, he called together a church-council, and announced with what love they had been received in those regions by the children of God (may this be recorded in their favor in the book of holy remembrance before God!). At the same time he announced how concerned he was for those poor people, and that they would have to be helped out with a Brother from Ephrata. These good people in Amwell specially availed themselves of this open Philadelphian church door, and made many a visit of more than a hundred English miles to the Settlement, and

---

[2][Emmanuel Eckerlin].   [3][Alexander Mack].

built themselves up in the unity of the Spirit on the death of Jesus Christ. Thereby the Superintendent was induced to undertake another visit, on which he was accompanied only by Solitary Brethren. As many of the Baptists there stood in judgment against the work of God in the Settlement, some feared that the two parties might get into each other's wool, whereby the general edification might be hindered. Yea, some sought to bring the visitors to the then Baptist teacher, Bechtelsheimer by name, in the hope that then matters might occur over which they might gloat; but they were disappointed in this hope. The Superintendent, who bore in his heart the seal of the redemption of the whole world, started on his visit, and was received with all affection by the teacher referred to and his helpmate. They sat down with him and listened to him for more than an hour, during which there flowed from him in a flood all that the Spirit gave him. And as everybody thought the visitors might now be dismissed in peace, these good people first showed forth their particular love by treating them to a rich collation. May God reward them on the day of reckoning! So likewise the whole organization helped the visitors across the water again at its own expense. This is mentioned here with the intent that, if any of these dear people should still be living and should read this, they may know that their faithfulness shown towards the work of God has been held in hallowed remembrance.

Meanwhile some among them longed that there might be established among them a household, such as they had seen at the Settlement, for they had well brought up young people, and hoped something useful might be accomplished among them. It would indeed have been easy to introduce the form among them, but to fill this effigy with the Spirit was not a human work. At that time there was among the Brethren at the Settlement one by the name of Elimelech, one of the Eckerlins, whom the stars had formed for a priest and redeemer of the bodily life, so that while other Brethren, spent their time in hard labor, he sought his own pastures and imposed his priesthood upon people. And though he was a great opponent of the Germantown Baptists, so that at their meetings he often preached them all out of the room; he nevertheless finally left the convent, and removed to them, when Peter Bëcker received him on condition that he must suspend his priesthood. But he did not carry this out; but established a large congregation in South Carolina under their auspices, where also he ended his life under the following circumstances. Latterly there arose in the congregation some young people by the name of Martin, who by their powers of speech drew the people to themselves. When he noticed this, he openly declared that he must be better received or he would die. And when he afterwards repeated these words, albeit with poor results, he soon after did die, which may well cause thoughtful persons to reflect. May God grant him a blessed resurrection! The Superintendent, who knew how to use all manner of instruments in the upbuilding of his church, made use of this Brother in all revivals. This he did in holy simplicity and self-depreciation, wherefore God treated him so sorely, since it gave occasion to many to elevate themselves above him, who afterwards had such severe falls; as he sings in a hymn: "Our mistakes the cause have been, That we oft our aim have missed, And have others raised up seen; Though we always want the best."

After the Superintendent had ordained Brother Elimelech to be teacher at Amwell, he publicly consecrated him to this office by the laying on of hands, on account of which many maintained that he would become the Superintendent's successor in his office, as he was already his right hand. About this same time also church-books were introduced, in which the congregation and the Solitary had to pledge themselves, by subscribing their names, to recognize a head of the church, which was the Elimelech referred to. The Superintendent, however, was so cautious that he never bound anyone formally to himself. This affair therefore caused so much offence to some that they left the congregation. Among the Superintendent's printed Letters, the 54th was written to Elimelech at that time, and is full of priestly unction; therein he speaks thus: "Continue steadfast in prayer and with watchfulness of spirit for the flock of Christ, that thou mayest rightly divide the Word of Truth which hath been sown in you."

This letter he took with him to Amwell, where he showed it to everyone as his credentials which he had received from the Superintendent. His people indeed sought to sustain him in his office, but when they noticed that it was an imitated affair and not inborn, they lost courage, so that when he wanted to institute midnight meetings, like those in the Settlement, and invited their daughters to the same, they feared that offences might arise, and dismissed him; whereupon he returned again to the Settlement in disgrace. Thereupon several families in Amwell left, and removed to the Settlement, namely, Dietrich Fahnstick, Conrad Boldhausen, John Mohr, Bernhard Gitter, etc., which added several Solitary ones to the Sisters' House, though none of them remained steadfast save one, Armella by name, who ended her course among them.

In this year, too, the ordinary Tonsure, or head-shearing, was introduced in the convents, which deserves to be mentioned here, as it contributed not a little to the vicissitudes of the Settlement. Two Brethren[4] engaged in an intimate conversation with the Superintendent with reference to their spiritual course, and confided to him that something was still wanting in their consecration; they were indeed baptized in the name of Christ, but they could still marry and have intercourse with the world; there was still wanting some special pledge for their particular estate, otherwise there was no difference between them and the domestic households. On this they were agreed; but they could come to no decision as to the nature of the covenant desired, until at last they unanimously chose the Virgin Mary as the Patroness of their Order. After they had arrived at this conclusion they sought to propagate the same secretly, for they supposed that it would cause a great stir in the Settlement. But the Brethren discovered their secret, and consulted one of their private counsellors, who opposed their project for three hours. They, however, did not care for this, but the Superintendent ordered the Prior to kneel down, and after the latter had made a vow of perpetual chastity, he cut a

---

[4][Israel Eckerlin and Alexander Mack].

large bald spot on his head; after which he and the other Brethren had the same done to themselves by the Prior. Thereupon a day was ordained as a festival on which the Order of the Solitary should take their vows of perpetual chastity. And notwithstanding that secretly many objections were made to it, because the Scriptures expressly forbid the shaving of the head, and because it was nothing but the warming up again of a custom that had originated in the Popish church, yet at the time set, in holy obedience, the entire Brotherhood appeared in its chapel; for they knew that the Superintendent stood under God, and that whoever opposed him struck at the very apple of God's eye. After the pledges were openly read, one Brother after the other kneeled down, and had his hair cut and afterwards his crown shorn. Then the Superintendent went over to the Sisters, who were awaiting him in their chapel, and after their hair had been cut, after the manner of virgins in the primitive church, they all took the vow, and then had their crowns likewise shorn. Since this ordinance was instituted in the face of such strong opposition of the reason, it is fair to conclude that the Holy Ghost was in the work, for He shall sit as a refiner, and shall purify the sons of Levi. But Thou, good God, hast drawn us, Thy servants and handmaidens, into the holy net, where indeed a large measure of the sufferings of Christ fell to our share, until we have become the offscouring of the tribes of the earth, and our mothers' children know us no more; but the times of refreshing from before Thy presence Thou hast hidden from us till this hour. Therefore do we pray to Thee, Give unto us, Thy servants and handmaidens, courage and strength in our weakness, that we may carry on Thy work, and that we may not, besides all this, through our negligence, become a cause of delaying Thy appearance.

After the consecration of the Sisters was done, the Superintendent returned to the Brethren, bringing with him the hair of the Sisters, which he laid on the table with the wish that he might live until their heads were gray; which God granted him, for he did not enter upon his rest until the year 1768. Afterwards it was ordained that the memorial of this consecration should be celebrated every quarter of a year, when their hair should be cut again and their tonsures renewed; in the meantime no one was allowed to put a shear to his head.

On the 5th of July, 1740, the last divine service of the congregation was held in the prayer-house of the Sisters, named Kedar. Thereafter the entire house fell to the use of the Sisters alone, a thing which no one had thought of when it was built; for at that time one lived without plans for the future, but allowed oneself to be governed by the spirit of the Community, without knowing what would be the outcome of the matter. Then a house-father, Henry Miller, paid the expenses for dedicating the prayer-house on Zion, which took place on the 16th of the same month; and now the congregation began to hold its services in this house. But it was not long before the Superintendent declared himself thus: That it was not yet a settled thing for the congregation to hold its meetings in this house, and it would only be to its disadvantage if this should continue for any length of time. The congregation must build itself an own house of prayer; thus is it ordained in the divine order of the work, and I will render aid thereto in the spirit. In this way God kept the household in the Settlement in continual straits, in which all human reason was turned into folly. After this speech, however, a house-father named John Mayer arose and said: That if these words were truth, then he did not yet know what truth was; therefore he would go home, and do penance for himself. In his footsteps another one, John Mergel by name, followed, and soon after two more house-fathers, namely Henry Gut and Abraham Paul, likewise went away. Thus God ever purged the fold of such persons as loved their own life better than the leading of God. But neither the congregation nor the Superintendent cared about such matters; for in the winter of 1740, which is still remembered for its severe cold, the Brethren in Zion and in the congregation joined together and provided a great supply of building lumber with which, the following summer, a large prayer-house was built and named Peniel. Whoever beholds the various large edifices which the Brethren, aided by the congregation, erected inside of four years, must be astonished and marvel whence they received the strength and courage to accomplish such great things. And herewith we will close this chapter.

CHAPTER XXI.

CONCERNING THE SPIRITUAL COURSE OF THE CHURCH IN THE SETTLEMENT; AND THE VARIOUS PROPHETIC GIFTS.

As introductory to this chapter it is to be remarked that all the mysteries of eternity, in order to be manifested in time, must clothe themselves in a body, otherwise they cannot impart themselves to man; and everything divine that does not become human, remains unfruitful, for fruitfulness lies in the body; and therein is contained the mystery of the incarnation of Christ. As has been remarked, there was intrusted to the Superintendent, at his conversion, a good thing, which he in general calls the fundamental good. Note well, reader, it is the goodness of God, which ruled before the fall, whereby the fallen angel became the devil, and over which Adam stumbled too, which therefore will also become a cause of restoration. Now, the fall might perhaps have been prevented if the cherub had sooner been placed as guardian over man, as was afterwards done. But the pure simplicity of God did not permit him to know this, otherwise he would have become impure. Now, Adam was created to repair the evil, and he should have taken the Virgin into his domicile. It happened with him, however, as with the fallen angel, he wanted to have the good in his own peculiar possession, and therefore God was obliged to construct a helpmate for him out of his own body, so that he might by all means have something over which to rule.

With this good the Superintendent was loaded at his first awakening at Heidelberg; for in conversion everything depends upon the first impregnation. Hence his portion, and that of all who came nigh him, was such a bitter one. When he was obliged to enter the world of men with this good, he foresaw the danger of losing it, and that if he would maintain his post, he would call down upon his head the hatred of all the children of Adam; and this was also the case. For many of his followers, who seemed to have much love for him, when they noticed that they could not possess themselves of his good, but rather that it sought to possess them, exchanged their love for a deadly hatred. It was noticed that his first followers, who entered the work with him before the schools of the solitary life had been opened, either suffered shipwreck, or had to pass through seasons of sore trial, because they pocketed too much of the good into their natural life. Among the first belong John Landes and A. E.,[1] who have been mentioned before, and of whom the first became a thistle on the road, and the other, one of his spiritual daughters, became offended, and ended her life in that state. At this dangerous post all the Eckerlins were wrecked, especially that one of them who was Brethren's Prior; for in spite of the fact that he was an ardent wooer of the Virgin, his efforts only resulted in bringing her under his man-power. The Superintendent once warned him not to presume too much upon the good, when he wrote to him, in the 66th of his printed Letters: "If you should find that the body seems heavier than the feet and ankles can bear, remember that this may be because of the superfluous breast-milk which you drank so abundantly on the mother's lap, and that the difficulty will be helped of itself by your merely weaning yourself from the mother's lap and breast."

After the Solitary in the Settlement, however, were lodged in their convents, the schools of the solitary life began, where such lessons had to be learned that one often almost lost sight and hearing, and to which the oldest Solitary ones had become as little used in their hermit-life as the novice who had been received only the day before. And now the cause became known why the hermit-life came to be changed into the communal; and that the holy fathers in the desert had erred when they maintained that the foundations of the Solitary life were to be laid in the convent, but that its perfection would be reached only in the desert. The Superintendent now so managed with the good, that while everyone might partake of it, yet no one could gain selfish possession of it. He was on his feet day and night, and whoso wanted to be rid of him had to lock his door at night;

---

[1] [Anna Eicher].

for he was in the service of the four living creatures which have no rest by day or night, so that he was often accused by his calumniators of being under the spur of his natural spirit. There was accordingly a constant stir in the Settlement, so that, if anyone were absent but for three days, he became a stranger, and had much trouble afterwards again to work his way into the order of affairs. No one would have been able, even though he had lived in the Settlement for many years, to give a correct description of the course of events there; it was inconceivable, and at the same time highly offensive to the mere reason. Falling and rising alternated continually; he who to-day was exalted on spiritual heights, to-morrow was laid low; and this was unavoidable. He whom the Superintendent took into his confidence, was elevated on high; he from whom he withdrew it, sank down again, sometimes even into the darkest depths, where then he was nailed to the cross; which things happened frequently. Here was the post of danger, where many of his followers were offended in him, and afterwards closed themselves against him, some of whom, through God's grace, were loosed again upon their death-beds, as the Brother Peter Gehr mentioned above; others bore the offence with them into eternity, in spite of the fact that he offered them the peace of God in Christ Jesus; wherefore it may well be said: Blessed are they who are not offended in me. Others combined themselves against him, and though they accomplished nothing, they yet often drew deep furrows across his back. In the bestowal and withdrawal of his confidence he was immoderate. When he imposed himself upon one, the sharpness of his spirit pierced such an one through bone and marrow, so that he soon was too much for him. But if he withdrew himself, he did not show himself for a long time, for he had no need of men since he had his power from above. In his intercourse he was not natural, and they who were nigh to him had to adapt themselves accordingly; wherefore no one could lay hold on him with his personality. Divine worship he appointed for the most inconvenient time, at midnight, and took special delight in the spirit if he could carry it on until daylight. If anyone offered him refreshment, he often said, "It gives me none," for his emaciated body was nourished by the Word that proceeded out of the mouth of God, otherwise he could not have endured such severity. When, constrained by love, he was often seen to eat during the day, it nevertheless made no change either in his body or his spirit, for he was a living skeleton until his death. Whenever he went into the Sisters' convent the whole house was moved; and when out of every corner they called to him, he was pleased with this open-heartedness, and said: "The young birds have the same simplicity when their provider comes to feed them." He was most careful to maintain the equilibrium of the Settlement, for God had placed the balances in his hand; and although, during the revolt of Korah, he was for a time deposed from the government, still finally it all fell into his hands again. His house was an asylum and city of refuge for all widows, orphans, and destitute ones; and whoso could reach its borders was safe against the avenger of blood.

As such discipline, so unpleasant to the flesh, was imposed upon the good Brethren of the Settlement, the passion of the body of Christ increased among them; whoever beheld them was amazed at their lean and pale appearance. This was indeed made known to the world by writings, but no one entered into the secret of it, because they were reticent and silent about it.

Now we again come to the Brethren in Zion. After Brother Onesimus had been made Prior of the convent of Zion by the Superintendent, the latter gave him his intimate confidence and fellowship, by reason of which the Prior ruled the Brethren with such severity that, if anyone lifted but a hand against him, it was an understood thing that such an one sinned against God, and jeopardized his eternal salvation; and though they often intended to rebel against him, yet they feared the Superintendent, whom they held to be an ambassador of God. Thus the Prior brought the Brotherhood into such thralldom that the only difference between a Brother of Zion and a negro was that the latter was a black and involuntary slave, while the former was a white and voluntary one. Yet one must bear witness of the Prior that he never ordered another one to do anything that he would not himself have been willing to do; for he was the first to go to work, and the last to leave it. It was, however, soon evident that it would cost the Prior dearly to maintain this intimacy; for the Superintendent was exceedingly watchful lest his fellowship should be misappropriated, and if any did do so, he was excluded by him. Now the Prior had three brothers after the flesh, who indeed were continually striving with him for the priesthood, but who nevertheless always stood up for him when he was attacked by others. It was also correctly supposed that the Mother of the Sisters was another cause of his fall and of his later tearing himself away from his spiritual Father, in that she brought to him much sympathy from the Sisters' House; for she sought to further her own profit by stirring up differences between the Superintendent and the Prior.

In spite of all this, however, everything went on all right for awhile. The Prior showed all conceivable honor to his spiritual Father. He wrote several books in praise of him; and in his letters to him he always called him a Holy Father, and although such eulogies did not blind the Superintendent's eyes, it yet kept the Prior in his good graces, which also was very needful, for there were already various ones in the Settlement who would have liked to have him overthrown. The Superintendent, moreover, had a superhuman fidelity to him, and gave him every protection, even though the entire Brotherhood was against him. Once it was proposed to elect a new Prior, which the Superintendent granted. The votes were gathered, and it was found that the Prior lacked two votes of being elected. Then the Superintendent, who, by virtue of his office, was entitled to two votes, cast these for the Prior, and so again secured the office for him. The greatest difficulties at that time were caused by the Night-Watches of the Brethren in Zion; for despite the fact that at that time several of the Brethren had already for ten years lived a Solitary life, there yet was no commingling of spirits among them, still less anything priestly, that might have filled in the breach and closed up the fissures. The Prior, however, was seized by the spirit of office, so that he considered himself bound to bring the Brethren under; if he had not done so, his conscience would have smitten him. This occasioned much quarrelling at the divine worship, which at times was kept up for several hours. But whenever they called in the Superintendent, he soon had everything adjusted to everyone's satisfaction. In those days many an one may have cried unto God for release from this spiritual tyranny, but the answer to their prayers was postponed for yet greater trials. Meanwhile the Prior was diligent in his office. He employed two Brethren who had to transcribe his writings; and if he was tired of preaching at the matins, he had his Lectors who had to read from his writings the rest of the time, wherefore many an one in his vexation exclaimed: "He preached us to death again!"

Unedifying as these things may seem, it must yet be confessed that there was no lack of that essential of true service of God, the crucifying of the flesh; hence we make remembrance of those blessed times when, beside these sorrows, the spirit of prophecy also manifested itself so strongly. The Superintendent in those days was lifted above the world of sense, and had surmounted time with its changes. His hymns composed then are full of prophecy, and belong to the evening of the sixth time-period, that is, to the holy Ante-Sabbath. They represent the mysteries of the last times so impressively, that it seems as though the kingdom were already dawning. It appears that it was the intention to set upon a candlestick the wonders of the last times through the revelation of the heavenly Virgin-estate and of the Melchizedekian priesthood in America; for that these hymns were given unto him in visions he at times betrays, when he adds, "This did we see in the spirit," while ordinarily under similar circumstances he is very self-reliant. All these hymns are to be found in a new collection under the title "*Paradiesisches Wunderspiel.*" Soon after he undertook an important work in the spirit, namely, he investigated what must have moved God to have so many animals slaughtered in his service for the redemption of man, which his righteousness would not have permitted if animals had not guilt resting upon them because of the fall of man. About this he became spiritually exercised, and produced a singular writing which he called "*Wunder Schrifft.*" Because he thereby disregarded nature too much, he contracted a severe illness. On account of its excellence it was printed in English with the title: "Dissertation on Man's Fall." Unless, however, the reader is versed in the spirit of the Virgin-estate, it is somewhat unclear in its expressions. In it, however, he has opened up a far outlook into eternity, and has gone further than even the holy Apostles in their revelations, bringing glorious things to light concerning the Mother Church, and how the Father finally shall deliver his office to the Mother; similarly concerning the Sabbatic Church in the time of the bound dragon; what God's purposes are with this Church; and why he permitted her to be so severely tried by Gog and Magog.

His followers had their part also in all this. Through their heavenly calling they were instructed thoroughly to plow up their human nature as being the soil into which are to be sown the seeds of the new manhood; and because thus their humanity was under the sword of the Cherub, God opened unto them again an entrance unto the tree of life, so that they again ate of the *Verbo Domini*, and so satisfied themselves with unceasing prayer as though they had been at some sumptuous banquet; all which Adam forfeited when he descended to earthly things. How otherwise would it have been possible for them, amidst their severe labors, to live in such abstemiousness? The attractions of the angelic life had overcome all mercy towards the body, so that the Superintendent was obliged to restrain many an one in his too great zeal. It was now no secret among them any more how Adam before the fall had eaten; also how it was still possible to live without animal food and without evacuation of the bowels. Clem. Alex., Lib. III, left a glorious witness of this, where he says: "Jesus ate and drank in ordinary fashion, and did not expel the food from him;" so great power of abstinence had he, that the food within him was not consumed, because there was no corruptibility in him.

It was remarked that afterwards the spirit of prophecy descended upon the offices, and therefore hit also the Prior of the Brethren and the Mother of the Sisters; even as among the Jews, when the spirit of prophecy entered into the room, the high-priest began to prophecy. The Prior wrote so much at this time, that he employed two Brethren in copying; but as he was then himself but only rising, his witness also was confused and unclear. His writings were kept hidden by his admirers long after his death; but now no one knows anything of them. After the prophetic spirit had withdrawn again into his chamber, an echo of it yet remained from the time of the bound dragon or the Sabbatic Church, with which the meeting was entertained for years. Herewith we will close this chapter.

CHAPTER XXII.

CONCERNING THE TEMPORAL COURSE OF EVENTS AMONG THE BRETHREN IN ZION, AND HOW THEY LAPSED INTO THE WORLD. ITEM, THE SUPERINTENDENT'S CO-WORKER DIES.

Before the government among the Solitary was systematized a certain simplicity reigned among all; the Superintendent was the father of all of them, and they all were his children; and when they travelled, it looked like a hen going with her brood of chicks. He held the funds, and whoever had any money, handed it over to him; and he appropriated it in such wise that the Settlement always remained poor. Not till after his death was it revealed that the most of it was carried away by beggars. But after the Brethren and Sisters were established in their convents, they were so abundantly supplied with spiritual officials that no one could stir a step without them; and the hours of day and night were so apportioned that no one had any time left for recreation except the holy Sabbath. Now everyone was diligent in a blind obedience, which was indeed the easiest but not the most excellent way of procedure; for it was this that hastened the fall of their rulers, who, as it was, had already assumed too much authority. It was remarked that those Brethren fared best who kept on good terms with the Superintendent and maintained a constant strife with the Prior. The Superintendent was much concerned about this singular economy, for he was obliged to give up his best beloved sons and daughters, since he ever impressed upon the Solitary that they must be obedient to their superiors; such was his innocence. This one thing yet remained to him, that at the same time the Prior still clung to him as a son to his father, wherefore also he favored him with all fidelity. For this, one may refer to the 65th, 66th and 67th of his printed Letters, in one of which he writes thus: "I think, indeed, that my resources would be sufficient to supply all your deficiencies; for when I consider the state of your mind, I feel that at this time you may be helped by courage coupled with fear and trembling. Exercise yourself in a right childlike boldness in your walk, regardless of the falls that may happen." The Superintendent at that time also occasionally visited the Brethren in their sad condition at their matins, when their miserable state deeply moved him so that he often was melted to overflowing. But the Prior hedged the Brethren in against any approach to intimacy with the Superintendent, for fear they might become too exalted; so that many an one did not enter his spiritual Father's house for a whole year at a time, which was probably a Nicolaitan teaching.

The domestic households at that time still had a high regard for the work of God in the Settlement. Their daily offerings were the main sustenance of the Solitary; yes, they brought tithes of their crops into the Settlement, although these were not placed upon the altar according to their sense of it, but were used in trade, on which account no one wanted to make any more offerings. Meanwhile God's work went forward rightly in the two convents of Zion and Sharon (which was the name of the Sisters' convent), which caused a great stir in the land; for the people again fell into the old suspicion that there must be Jesuits from Mexico concerned in the matter. The simplicity which the Brethren in Zion had learned from their spiritual father prevailed among them for quite a time. They drew their cart themselves, and were their own horses; when they travelled, they went heavily laden like camels, and sometimes the whole Brotherhood might be seen trooping around the hill of Zion. The communal life was now formally instituted, and all private ownership was declared to be an Ananias-sin; this was a matter which the Prior was continually impressing upon the Brethren, from which it was apparent that it was artificial rather than inspired by the Spirit. Nevertheless the Superintendent supported him herein, for he writes in a letter to the Brethren thus: "If one could not deny oneself of this stale and childish I and Mine, how would it be if one would have to deny oneself of life itself? I for my part could not live so, and would rather die than disappoint God and cause men to be deceived in me." (See Del. Ephr. P. 2, page 247).

After the number of the Brethren increased, it was asked how so many young people should be kept employed, outside of the work of divine worship, and preserved from idleness. Circumstances, too, demanded this, for the convent was poor, because the good Brethren cared for others more than for themselves. And since at this time also the offerings did not come in very plentifully anymore, the Prior was seized with unbelief, and sank into purely temporal prospects. And as the Mother of the Sisters also fell into this faithlessness, they secretly took counsel together how they might organize the economy so as to provide a living without having to depend upon the favor of the domestic households upon which dependence could no longer be placed. All this took place behind the Superintendent's back, who had ever been solicitous that the things of this world might not find entrance in the Settlement; although the Mother herself complained of the Brethren to the Superintendent when they carried it to extremes; for she sought her own interest in arousing differences between the Superintendent and the Prior. Now therefore there was instituted in the Settlement a worldly economy for the sustenance of the natural life, which represented a ducal court-economy, wherein the Brethren and Sisters were made men servants and women servants. Through this much of the primitive simplicity was lost, wherein God had manifested his wonders; and in its stead was opened a wide outlook into the world, for the Brethren, whose intelligence had been widened at their conversion, set up various mechanical trades, which brought in great profits, and which they handed over to the Prior, so that in a short time the treasury became so rich that money began to be loaned out; yes, it is likely that if God had not destroyed this economy, the Brethren would by this time have ships upon the sea.

Besides this, the possessions of those who entered the Order were taken from them without considering whether or not these would find their benefit in the Order; and if they left the Order again, they received nothing back, and this by virtue of a rule that anyone who should leave the

Order would lose whatever he had contributed to the same. Not even the Courts could prevent this, for it was always claimed that there were no laws covering such cases. One by the name of Henry Bone moved into Zion and surrendered his possessions; but because he did not have any pleasure in the house, he left the Order, and demanded the return of his property. But this was refused him; whereupon in despair he took his own life. This and other acts of injustice might have redounded to the disadvantage of the Brotherhood, if in after times amends had not been made therefor as far as possible. Soon after this the Brethren purchased a mill near by, where they afterwards set up the seat of their worldly realm. Sad it is that so many otherwise earnest Brethren fortified their calling there. For market was held there every day, and everybody wished to deal with these pious people, not only because of their honesty, but because there was erected an altar for a spurious atonement. This was the reason, too, that whenever his quarters became too narrow for a Brother at the Settlement, he betook himself to the mill, for there he could live according to his natural inclinations.

At this time Brother Agonius[1] died, who had been a great restraint upon the Prior in his worldly tendencies. His death

---

[1] This remarkable man, otherwise called Michael Wohlfahrt, was born at the fortress of Memel, on the Baltic sea. How he first became acquainted with the Superintendent, when the latter yet lived in solitude, has already been recounted. All his life he was a faithful assistant of the Superintendent, and not only was his companion on all his travels when he declared to the people in Pennsylvania the counsels of God concerning their salvation, but also sat by his side at all meetings, and followed him in speaking. Otherwise, according to the manner of the time, he was in pretty close agreement with the Inspirationists, and at Philadelphia spoke prophetically both in the market-place and at the Quaker meetings; so also at other places, though he never received therefor more than a prophet's reward. In the difficulty between the Superintendent and the Baptists he incautiously proceeded too far in judgment with those people, which rose up against him severely on his death-bed This was expressed by the Superintendent as follows in the last verse of his funeral hymn:

"This in time my error was,
Wherefore it must be the cause
Why so sore my strife must be,
Ere by death I was set free."

secured to the Prior and his three brothers after the flesh the preponderance in the Settlement, and they were enabled to perform great things, because the Brethren lived in blind obedience. The Prior was really pregnant with important projects; three wagons were kept, on which a great deal of lumber was brought, for it was intended to add another wing to the convent, also to build the mill and all the bridges

His great merit, which stood by him in every temptation, was this, that he was a man after God's own heart, like David, who knew how to humble himself when brought into judgment. For, especially in the beginning, he often stood in the way of the Superintendent's spiritual work; and because a hidden hand always protected the Superintendent, the good Brother was often thereby brought into severe condemnation, when he might, like others did, have parted from him in anger; but as he walked in David's footsteps he humbled himself, and accepted the judgment, even as his hymns bear witness. When, contrary to his and others' supposition, the large houses were built in the Settlement, he was sore confounded, especially when he saw that great churches with bells were being procured, abuses against which he and others had so earnestly striven. This tempted him not a little to mistrust whether the Superintendent had not perhaps forsaken his post. And although he never broke the bond of brotherly love between them, these temptations yet brought him so far that he again became a hermit, though without withdrawing from fellowship. To this end the Brethren built him a solitary dwelling in the mountains of Zoar, some five miles from the Settlement. Finally, however, he was especially strengthened in the faith that God's hand was in the work, by considering that there were already seventy persons, of both sexes, and mostly young people, dwelling together in the Settlement, who had renounced all their earthly happiness for the sake of the kingdom of God. Wherefore he again renounced his seclusion and removed to the convent of Zion, where he led a very edifying life until its close, being subject to all the rules of the Order. His decease was greatly deplored, because, as has already been mentioned, he brought about great changes.

His departure into eternity fell into the year 1741. The circumstances thereof are as follows: This important change was made known to him some time before, though he did not think it was so near. Though a weakness overcame him a short time before, he yet recovered so far that on the Sabbath before his death he was at meeting, and the following evening at the Brethren's table, so that there were good hopes of his entire recovery. But his malady returned with such violence that, when the Brethren came from their midnight devotions they found him in such a condition that they saw that now his eager desire to depart would soon be fulfilled. His illness was brief and very severe, lasting only four days; in which time God's hand lay heavily upon him, and fulfilled the remainder of his sufferings until his sacrifice on the cross was complete, wherefore also he said: that he did not know whether any saint had ever endured such martyrdom. On the fol-

of stone; besides a vault was to be built in Zion wherein the deceased were to be entombed. The old Brethren he wanted to exempt from all work; for it was his way to throw suspicion upon the worldly life of the domestic households; and had he succeeded, all plantations for about two miles around the Settlement would have been convent-land, and he would have received the families into the Settlement, and laid the

lowing second day, at night, just as the Brethren were at their service and were singing the hymn, "The time is not yet come," &c., their intercessions were asked for that God might open to him his prison door.

All his words during his severe conflicts were weighty, and flowed from him in streams, as the anguish of his heart wrung them from him. Being concerned lest his words might be burdensome to the Brethren, he finally said: "I am not yet such a saint as to be able to keep silence in my suffering." He was wont especially to repeat such words as these: "The arrows of the Almighty are within me. He hath reckoned me with the godless, and hath become cruel towards me. Whither shall I turn myself? How shall a creature endure all this, for it is not made of iron? Yet, who shall contend with Him? he cannot answer Him one of a thousand. He is God! who can stand against His will?" He had the LXXXVIII and CII Psalms read to him, in which two Psalms his condition was particularly described; and whenever anything was expressed that specially fit him, he would exclaim: "That is I!" His conflict was really not with the weakness of his flesh, but with the powers of the air; for, as I remarked above, he had sown too much seed in the fields of righteousness, whereby the spirits of righteousness obtained the right to cut off his approach to the kingdom of grace. Wherefore he often used to say, that he was fallen among murderers, and the hatred of the devil and the weight of hell were about his neck, and that he knew not whether he were humbled enough for God to protect him against these powers. He also had Tauler's "Last Hours" read to him, probably because this one's departure was like unto his.

These peculiar trials were not strange to the Superintendent, for he understood the good Brother's condition better than he himself did; but he was aware of still worse temptations impending, and feared lest even blasphemy against God might result therefrom. From this, however, God graciously preserved him. Meanwhile the Superintendent, in his priestly spirit, penetrated through all the powers of darkness, and reached with his prayers even unto the blood of the atonement, which he applied unto the salvation of this lost sinner. Wherefore the dying man at last spoke thus to him: "If thou hast nothing more for me, I am forever lost; I desire, according to the usage of the first Christians, to be anointed by thee."

Thereupon preparation was made to comply with his request. But they were amazed to notice how upon this the brother-balsam penetrated to him in his prison house, and the powers of darkness soon released their prisoner. His whole form and demeanor were changed, so that for joy he repeated the words of the prophet: "Now will I sing to my well-beloved a song of

foundations of a nursery for the boys. The Superintendent did not know what to say to these actions of the Prior; the welfare of those who were entrusted to his guidance, lay near to his heart; but to put a stop to this world-conformed life, was not in accordance with faith; for he had kept them for a long time under restraint, but now they had got the ascendency over him, and when they were brought to judgment on account of some worldly affair, they held out until it was over, and afterwards, nevertheless, did as they pleased.

my beloved touching his vineyard." Then he commenced to speak prophetically, and pronounced judgment against the spirits of evil who sought to close against him the entrance into the kingdom of God. Finally he said that he now saw his redemption; only God could take him up. Meanwhile, the 4th day of his sickness approaches, and with it his blessed end. He was overfilled with great joy, and at last broke forth in these words: "Oh how glorious a thing it is to endure unto the end ! Oh what peace does it bring, to persevere without yielding up to the last fight!" Thereupon he related how he had been delivered over to strange spirits, who had taken him to a narrow pass, and treated him harshly, so that he applied to himself the words of the 129th Psalm: "The plowers plowed upon my back, they made long their furrows." It appears as if it had been revealed to him that his end would come at the 9th hour of the day; therefore he looked keenly towards the hour-glass, whether the 8th hour was not soon to pass. As soon as it struck 9 he had himself set upright, and thus he expired, but when again let down, he once more revived and asked whether he had not yet died. After that he expired at the end of the 9th hour, aged 54 years, 4 months and 28 days, and afterwards was interred at the Settlement in a coffin neatly prepared for the occasion, May 21st. The following verses, taken from his funeral hymn, are notable:

> See all the anguish, trouble and pain
> I suffered before death in vain,
> Until the oil of grace so mild
> Refreshed my soul,
> Was poured upon my head.
> Oh comfort rich! which I enjoyed;
> The brother-balm, it entered me
> And made my heart at rest to be.

His epitaph is the following:
Here rests the godly wrestler, Agonius, died anno 1741, aged 54 years, 4 months, 28 days.

> Victory brings the crown,
> In the fight for faith, grace and renown.
> Thus blessings crown the warrior true
> Who bravely Sin and Belial slew.
> Peaceful he passed to his chamber of rest,
> Where now he is free of all pain and distress.

But it cannot be said that the Brotherhood in Zion had, at the time, fallen away from its holy calling, for their household was regulated in such a manner, that one could hardly live, so that whoever was not well accustomed to fasting, had to resort to stealing; and, perhaps, those good recluses in the Roman Catholic church experienced the same, notwithstanding the riches their convents possessed. The Superintendent, at least, saw herein the divine government when he thus writes to the Prior: "What else relates to the chief matters of the Brotherhood in Zion, I have, in consideration of how the matter rests with God, to overlook not a little in many things which have changed my opinion considerably; although only my opinion. As concerns the matter otherwise, as it lies straight before God, I have such a fullness and steadiness of faith, that I want nothing; neither do I, in this our Community, grant any good to either young or old, without its being connected with the suffering or the original good of the Brotherhood in Zion." (Vide Del. Ephr. Par. II, page 283.) And now let us leave the narrow boundaries of Mount Zion, and turn again to the great church.

CHAPTER XXIII.

CONTAINS THE DISPUTES WHICH OCCURRED BETWEEN THE SO-CALLED MORAVIAN BRETHREN AND THE CONGREGATION IN EPHRATA.

Hardly anybody would believe what difficulties this Community encountered on its arrival in Pennsylvania, in order to be received among the tribes as a Christian Community, did not many polemical writings plainly reveal it; for all different denominations declared against it, and although they were a complete Babel among themselves, they all were united in opposition against these newly arrived guests. It is remarkable that these good people came to this country to destroy the Babel therein, of which they might have heard in Germany; but, because they did not understand the language in which the Apostles had spoken on the day of Pentecost, so that they might have been able to speak with every one in his own tongue, the only result was, that the schism became wider, and there was one more faction in the land. The present account contains the subjects of dispute which occurred between them and the Solitary in the Settlement.

In the year 1739, two delegates of their denomination, namely, Spangenberg and Nitschmann, arrived in Pennsylvania, who met with great success, and might have proved of edification to many, had they had more experience, and not been novices themselves. After the Brethren had heard of them, three went down the country and visited them at Wuegner's, a venerable family, descendents of the Schwenkfelders; and because at that time the fire of first love was still burning, their spirits united into one, so that they returned with them. When telling of their institutions at Herrnhut, the Brethren became so perceptibly moved by it that little was wanting and some would have accompanied them thither. Having tarried a few days in the Settlement, and also been present at a love-feast, they were dismissed with the kiss of peace, in all tenderness, as became the messengers of such a renowned people; then they left there for St. Thomas. (See Chap. XVII.)

Some time after this, one by the name of Haberecht, who was decended from them, applied to the Superintendent for baptism, who complied with his request; in consequence he moved into the convent Zion; but brought upon himself many temptations thereby. Anna Nitschmann, however, when she visited the Settlement, drew him back to her communion; and then only it was understood why the Superintendent had baptized him into the faith of his own people. He again returned with them to Germany, and afterwards served their laborers in Algiers, from where he again journeyed to Pennsylvania and ended his life in their institution; may God give him a blessed resurrection. Meanwhile more important laborers of their communion arrived in the country —everyone of whom made the attempt to bring the people in the Settlement on the right road again; for they believed that he had no true faith in the blood of Christ, who was so much occupied with work. They must either have laid this plan in Germany, or many among them must have been possessed of a false spirit of priesthood. One of their most eminent single Sisters stayed for three days in the Sisters' House, during which time she enjoyed much love; this Sister afterwards spread the report in Germantown that most of the Sisters in the Settlement would like to throw off the yoke if they but knew of another retreat. When this became known to the friends of the Separation there they were much grieved, because they had much confidence in the House mentioned, and on that account wrote thither for information. Thereupon one of the Sisters answered that she had always been about the person mentioned, but she never heard any of the Sisters say the like of it to her. This letter can be found among the papers published against them in Frankfurth.

But, in order that the reader may receive a proper insight into this quarrel, let him know that it chiefly related to justification and the married state. The Superintendent complained a great deal that in the churches the blood of atonement was permitted to become a shield in the hands of the old

Adam, the consequence of which was a carnal security, and for that reason the blood of atonement was considered by us to be too holy to be talked about with levity, which they interpreted as not believing in Christ. But it must be known, that man committed a double fall; at first he fell off from God under the law of nature, after that he fell from the law into unrighteousness. Thus also there is a double conversion, the first through the drawing of the Father, where Moses holds the rule; here man tries to satisfy the demands of his conscience, and endeavors to do works of righteousness, whereby he gains a degree of blessedness, as is written: Do this, and you will live; but this is not yet the true blessedness. When man has fulfilled the righteousness of the law under Moses, he is sent by Moses to God. Now only the axe is laid at the root of the tree, and all his good works become sin, as Paul says : He has resolved all under sin, not the wickedness of man, for it already is sin, but his good works, for the great contention between God and man does not originate in the evil of man, but in his goodness, and here alone is the road to salvation where the primitive cause of all corruption is excited, and if here the blood of the covenant did not prevail, there would be no getting off, therefore says Christ: "Blessed is he who shall not be offended in me," namely, when his goodness is turned into sin for him. Whoever preaches the gospel to one who is still a debtor to the law, turns Christ into a servant of sin: for it is our schoolmaster who points to Christ; therefore also the good Master, when asked by that youth, what he should do in order to be saved, did not answer: Believe in me, but showed him the commandments. Such like speech he had with them at times, but it found no entrance. They said they could make a Christian in three days.

There were also difficulties respecting the married state; the Superintendent called it a house of correction for carnal minded persons, but they gave it a place in the sanctuary. Perhaps the spirit of virginity was given to them at their awakening, because there is no conversion without it, but it seems that the leaders of their awakening left their posts, whereby the married state became privileged again, for everything depends upon the government. However, the sealing of the elect number has been put back so far, since God cannot complete it, until the number of four hundred and forty thousand is made up. They gave great offence, in that they forthwith married a great number of young people by lot, who had visited them for the sake of edification, as happened to several daughters of a merchant, perhaps without his knowledge. One of their most prominent Brethren (as can be seen in his biography), when he intended to change his state, sought consent in the Scriptures; and came as far as Enoch, of whom it is written that he walked with God for 300 years, and begot sons and daughters. It would not have been necessary to go back so far; the example of the good Master would have been nearer, as also Paul's church ordinance, I COR. VII, for as far as Enoch is concerned, it is known that the fathers before the deluge represented but figures of the future, and that Enoch represents the fruitfulness of the Sabbatical church.

In the year 1742 the Ordinarius Fratrum arrived in Pennsylvania, and found soon after his arrival, a perfect Babel, as he himself acknowledged; he also saw that all parties were greatly alarmed by the works of God in Ephrata, and that it was necessary for him to declare for one or the other side. Meanwhile preparations were made for conferences, for the chief purpose of uniting all the different parties into one great church-body, which would have given joy to all the saints, had only the workmen themselves been separated from the Babel. He undertook a journey up the country, even before the conferences, but visited only the door-sill of the Ephrata House. The first conference was to be held at Germantown, and circulars were distributed through the land by Henry Antes; when they arrived in the Settlement, a church council was held, and resolved that one Brother in Zion, together with several Fathers, should attend; but the Prior whose dignity did not allow that another should be preferred to him, brought it about that he was appointed. Besides those of Ephrata, men of all kinds of opinions made their appearance, even apostates of the Settlement; for many hoped that a nearer road to the Kingdom of Heaven than known in this country, might be found, because the hand of God lay heavily upon men, and many were driven into such straits by his witnesses that they did not know what to believe. The Ordinarius received the Prior with all tenderness, and placed him at his side at the meeting. Then he reproved all the communions, because they had stricken the Ephrata Society off the roll of Christian fellowship. He spoke a good deal with the Prior about the economy of the Solitary in the Settlement, and foretold him that he would be the Superintendent's successor in office, which was an easy prophecy, for Tacitus says: "Cupido dominandi cunctis affectibus flagrantior est"—the lust to govern surpasses all passions. The prophecy, however, was not fulfilled, for the Prior departed this life perhaps twenty years before the Superintendent; but what he said behind the back of the Prior, happened, namely: That he was one of those who tried to deprive the Superintendent of his good. The Ordinarius showed his passionate temper at this conference, or at least pretended to, in order that others might find cause to dispute with him, and he succeeded well; for a delegate of the Baptist congregation, Joseph Müller by name, gave him a sharp reproof about his violent ways; whereupon he begged him on his knees to save him from this evil by laying on of hands, which the above-mentioned Müller did, by which act he was converted by him, whom he had endeavored to convert from his impetuosness, and became a proselyte. When the conference came to an end, the next was appointed to meet at Ephrata; and thus every one went his way.

When the Brethren in the Settlement heard that the next conference was to be held there, they complained greatly about the arbitrary conduct of their Prior, and said: "These people appeared to them like the foolish virgins, who tried to borrow the little oil left; they did not know what these conferences were for; people who were not sure of their road, might consult about it, they had no need of it, and no conference would render the road easier. This determined the Superintendent to write to Henry Antes, and to revoke the conference; among the rest he wrote thus: "With regard to the matter with which we have been mutually concerned through the Brethren delegated by our Community, I shall remain your kind patron and well-wisher; but in regard to the matter itself, I stand still, and will do nothing either against or for it, and try to maintain with my people, by the help of God, the peace in Christ Jesus, together with all who are children of the same peace." (See his 6th printed Epistle.) After the failure to hold the conference in Ephrata, the same was held in Falckner's Swamp, at Henry Antes', Jan. 29, 1842; but the particulars did not come to hand.

About the same time, the Ordinarius paid another visit to the Settlement accompanied by Brother Lischy, and they were hospitably lodged in the convent Zion, because his friendly manners were especially agreeable to the Brethren. The following morning he called on the Prior, and told of his intention to visit the Superintendent; and that he was going to use the lot about it. The Prior advised against the lot, and announced him to the Superintendent, who, after some reflection, answered: That * * * was no marvel to him, but if he were a marvel to him, he must come to him. This short answer made the Ordinarius doubt what to do, and he surely had cause, for here he had to deal not with a coat, surplice or vestment, but with the head of a united and organized Community which, moreover, was founded on the Testament of J. C. And had he had more faith, a beautiful crown might have been put on his head, for the sake of the great fidelity he showed in the work of God, for the Superintendent never bestowed his favor on any one whom he had not tested; but he made various pretences and departed without having seen the Superintendent; and thus two great lights of the Church came to each other's thresholds and neither saw the other in his life. But soon after he wrote a letter to the Superintendent, to the purport that he should descend from his spiritual height that others might sit along side of him without danger to their lives, of which the Superintendent remarked: "If I were as great as he supposes, he would not have been afraid of me." This letter was afterwards inserted into the Büdingen Collections, but joined with other remarks. About this time the Prior was attacked by a dangerous disease, and it was supposed that he had disclosed too much of himself to the Ordinarius, for just at that time a letter arrived for the Prior, wherein he mentioned many incidents of his life, which, however, was destroyed, because it was not thought advisable to burden the Prior with it during his sickness. Of this the Ordinarius complained, and commanded the return of his letter by an express messenger. Anno 1742 still another conference was held in Oley, at which four Brethren of the Ephrata congregation appeared; for the Solitary Brethren were so suspicious of the thing, that they did not want to have anything to do with it. They had composed a writing on the married state, namely, how much God had to do with it, and that it was but a praiseworthy order of nature; this they handed in, which occasioned a passionate dispute. The Ordinarius said that he was not in any way pleased with this writing, he had not commenced his married state in that way, and his married state occupied a higher position than the Solitary state in Ephrata. The delegates from Ephrata tried to smooth the thing over, and said: They were no enemies to the married state; there were families in the congregation who had a child every year. At that he lifted his hands in astonishment and said: He was amazed that people who pretended to bear such important testimony would lead such a carnal life. The Ordinarius became so violent after this, that he was deposed from his office in the conference, and a Scotchman was installed in his place; and thus the conference ended to the disgust of all present.

But their greediness for fishing drove them again and again to the Solitary in the Settlement, and often they quarrelled through half the night and called each other heretics, for the Solitary imprudently engaged themselves too much with them, and were enticed to leave their fortress; and when they did not do this, they engaged in spiritual whoring with each other. Therefore, when Spangenberg and a large following visited the Settlement at one time, amongst them Andreas Frey and several renegades from the Community, and as the Solitary seemed to make a covenant with them, the Superintendent was obliged to expose their frivolous behavior before the eyes of the visitors, wherefore Spangenberg accused him of being angry, and said afterwards to others that his scolding had opened all his pores, and that fire had shot out of them. The Superintendent, at last, found a way how to get rid of this man. He summoned a Brother, and commanded him to compose a writing, and to sharply rebuke these people because of their disorderly lives and carnal passion for making proselytes. The Brother soon had it finished and brought him a sketch, which he sanctioned; but observed that he might have been more severe, the Brother accordingly added more salt. The Brother Prior embraced this occasion to free himself again, because he had too freely communicated with them, and added a supplement not less biting. But that was not all, for a housekeeper by the name of Hildebrand brought still another supplement, in which he laboriously proved that the married state originated in the fall of man. The Superintendent gained his end by these polemical writings, since these people did not trouble him again in the future; there is nothing to be found to show that they defended themselves against these accusations, except what they did at the seventh and last conference in Philadelphia, where they attempted to declare by lot that the Solitary in the Settlement were a recognized masterpiece of Satan; but the lot not answering favorably, they changed this saying and called them a rabble of Baptists, who had stolen from them baptism and vocation, at which the Brethren of the Settlement were not offended, because they had already explained their opinion about the extreme unction, which the devil had poured out on the Christian Church. Soon after a printing press was set up in the Settlement, and there, by the Prior's orders, the same writing had also to be printed in the English language; but because he had done this arbitrarily, and soon after left the Order, all his acts were annulled, and also the English print condemned to the flames. These are the principal incidents which occurred between the two communions.

At the same time an Englishman, named Thomas Hardie, arrived and joined the Order. His biography will conclude this chapter. Of his descent he only revealed that his grandfather had been English ambassador in Spain, and that his father married a lady of Normandy and had lived in London. In his youth he studied the languages and law, but was early awakened by God, on account of which he left his father's house. When his father perceived that he had the intention to go on shipboard, he gave orders forbidding it at all sea-ports; but he assumed the dress of a sailor and safely escaped to Pennsylvania. On the voyage he threw his seal and everything by which his family might be recognized, into the sea; his other property, however, the sailors stole, so that he had to submit to the fate of being sold in Philadelphia; it was lucky for him that just then a German inhabitant from near Maxatawny, Siegfried by name, bought him for four years as an English teacher. His master realized great profits through him, for, because he was versed in law, he executed all necessary writings for the neighborhood, besides teaching school, which pleased his master so much that he made him the offer of his daughter and 100 acres of land; but there lived another spirit in him, so that he courageously declined the offer. After the termination of his bondage, he wandered about among the Germans, in order to find agreement to his holy calling. He came first to Bethlehem; but because he found hard opposition there, his wits were unsettled for the first time; of which failing he was never entirely free as long as he lived; thus God hides his treasures in such shells. But he never laid this to the charge of those good people, though he was of opinion that, if their head-master whom he greatly esteemed, had been present at the time, it might have turned out differently.

After his recovery, he undertook a journey to Ephrata, for these places, Bethlehem and Ephrata, were at that time, and still are, objects of interest for all foreigners who wish to get acquainted with the different sentiments in this country, because you find there everything *in compendio*. As soon as he got sight of the person of the Superintendent, the celestial Venus in him became so eager to embrace the heavenly Virgin, that he soon after entered into the *Actum* of betrothal in the water of baptism, since which time he entertained a child-like love for his spiritual Father, as is evident from the following letter which he wrote much later to the Superintendent in broken German: "'To Father Friedsam: I thank thee for all the acts of love done to me, for all thy innocent suffering on my account, for all thy faithfulness. My friend, my Brother, how beautiful thou art in priestly adornment when thou enterest the sanctuary with the golden censer, on the days of atonement, with many priests, when the bride Sophia, in a column of clouds, with many thousand saints, fills thy hand with incense. Praised be thy God, who elected thee. May he bless thee with everlasting comfort, from his loving heart, and be this the reward for all the affability thou didst show to the children of man. Now, my good heart, soul living in God, I wish thee inexpressibly much good, my dear prophet, thou servant of God, pray incessantly for me to thy and my God and the God of us all. Highpriest of God, in whom dwelleth his paternal love, to whom he delivered the kingdom in order that he might keep me from evil!

"Now, my dear one, receive from me, in spirit, a hearty, mutual, loving kiss, and enter the sanctuary in peace. Love the Lord in his holiness, praise the work of his hands, for his grace abideth for ever and ever. THEODORUS.

"P. S. Now I depart from thy presence with a weeping heart, the heart tells more than the pen. I shall greet thee above in the garden of him who has loved thee and me."

After he had entered the covenant of grace in the water of baptism, he entered the convent Zion, and was named by the Brethren, Theodorus. The office of translator from German into English was given him; but because he could not stand the confined way of living in the convent, he left it again after six months. And although he kept up in spirit the communion with the Brethren until he died, he did not from that time on live in the Settlement, but exercised the office of teacher in the back regions of the country under the protection of the Community. He could not bridle his spirit when making an address, and was frequently inspired in his preaching, so that often but little more would have been needed to upset the table. He led a very humble life, and loved poverty; but he often led so austere a life that it had to be forbidden him. Because his life is still in our remembrance, it will be needless to expose his foibles which originated in his national character, the altar of atonement must stand before them. His death[1] took place in 1784, and had something remarkable about it. When taking leave from his friends in Pittsburg, intending to visit his Brethren in the Settlement, one of his friends told me that he had seen

---

[1] The following was sung to his memory over his grave:

1. The call came loud from heaven's sphere
   To change my mind of sin,
   The Virgin's net caught me, and here
   A doctrine pure received my heart within.
   Others with me ran for the prize,
   Ready to die for it.
   That was a love-sick game, the choice
   Of many, to memory knit.

2. And hardly by the flood so pure
   Was I united with the warrior's throng,
   What love can do, I was made sure—
   Nor hate nor anger can outlive it long;
   Always I blew again upon
   The dying love-lit flame,
   For God Almighty's breath hath blown
   To guide our path unto his cross of shame.

3. Although I sometimes slipped as well
   As other warriors will, I ne'er did fly;
   Nor ever did I join to swell
   The crowd that spurned his might on high.
   I patiently did bear my shame,
   Like one who missed the proper road,
   Until again the day-time came,
   Brought comfort and relieved my load.

4. O, vigilance, thou pledge so dear,
   Thou open kept'st the broken gate in me;
   Not vainly did I strive, although with fear,
   To reach the goal, I and my brethren free.
   I always knew that I was bound
   In youth's spring-time, to Thee, High Priest;
   Thou are the bridegroom whom I found,
   And vowed to live for, unreleased.

5. Therefore did I not soil the garment white
   On my long journey, whilst on earth I staid,
   The virgin, she stood at my side
   Whene'er the fiend began his play, and said:

in a dream, that he would die there; he, therefore, delayed his journey for another week; but a hidden hand moved him to take up the project again, for it was decreed that his body should be again delivered to his Brethren as a pledge. As soon as he arrived in the Settlement, he was seized with sickness, and recollecting what had been prophesied of him, he prepared for his decease, and departed after a short illness. May God give him a blessed resurrection!

    Remember thy first ardent passion,
    When love of one did friendly aid afford.
    My favor will remain then, and not lessen,
    Be in the fight thy strength, until in port.

6. Now the fight is ended, all the pressure
    I once did feel is swept away;
    I woke, as my dear Lord's own treasure,
    I am clothed without shame's array.
    My mother dressed me in a new garment,
    And the change it suited well;
    Upon her lap receives he preferment
    Who gave to this vain world farewell.

7. So let us then conclude;
    I left the Brotherhood.
    Whene'er your journey, too, is ended,
    In unity we shall be blended.
    You from afar me oft remind:
    Remember those thou leav'st behind!
    Until, all spotless 'fore God's throne
    We meet again, through his dear Son.

CHAPTER XXIV.

A NEW CONVENT FOR THE SISTERS IS BUILT, CALLED SHARON; THE SINGING-SCHOOLS COME INTO VOGUE AT THE SETTLEMENT.

Above we mentioned that the Superintendent informed the congregation at a meeting, that it would be necessary now to build a chapel for them, in order that the domestic household need not be dependent on the Brotherhood in Zion, as this had been a cause of offence to several families, who left the Community. Hereby you can see again that the Superintendent stood under a high hand, since two chapels had already been built in the Settlement, and one might well have asked, who gave him the right thus to put a load upon a whole Community, and had God not secretly urged him on to this work, the people would certainly soon have been done with him. But he had learnt so much by experience, that nearly all the awakened, having expressed displeasure for a time, will soon again prepare for themselves a resting place in the ease of their natural life, and he, therefore, always took care not to relapse again into comfort after so tedious a journey. He consequently frequently used to say that he had renounced himself to such a degree that not even a melting-pan was left him.

The building of this new church was commenced in spite of all opposition, and finished in September, Anno 1741, after the Community, together with the Brotherhood, had worked at it for ten months. In December following, the house was consecrated by a meeting and love-feast, and called Peniel. A brother, Elimelech by name, who has been made mention of before, was put over the house as Superintendent, and divine service was held therein for the Community until 1746; but how it happened that Peniel with all its belongings got into the hands of the Sisterhood, will be mentioned in its proper place.

Soon after these events, the house-fathers and mothers were induced to attempt to bring their state to a higher condition, for they were convinced that it was founded on sin, and they knew that Rudolph Nägele and Sigmund Landert, who still lived at that time, had succeeded. The Superintendent gave his moral support to the matter, although it was conjectured that the affair was instigated by the Eckerlins, for it was known that they intended to turn the farms of the household into convent-land. Meanwhile the households courageously furthered the work. They built a great convent adjoining their chapel. The same was divided into two parts, of which one was arranged for the fathers, the other for the mothers. Besides this the house was provided with rooms, chambers and a hall for love-feasts, just as it had been done in that of the Solitary. And in order that the house might be thoroughly incorporated into the Community of the Solitary, some Brethren of Zion moved into it, and administered their divine service, because at the time a particular harmony existed between the two Orders, since both held the unmarried state high. After the household was thus arranged, a venerable house-father, John Senseman by name, was installed as steward, who had the management of the household. But, when the house was to be inhabited, the house-mothers objected, and said: They had first again to be on a free footing, and this must be done by divorce; for, although they had thus far lived a life of continence, they still stood under the will of their husbands, and lived at their mercy. The Superintendent granted their request, to which the care for their eternal salvation had actuated them. Consequently one of the Brethren had to write the letters of separation, which afterwards, being sealed, one part handed to the other.

This new institution was for some time richly blessed by God, for these good people were not only very simple minded, but bore a great love towards God; they also were very benevolent and harbored many poor widows whom they maintained out of their own means, so that their household resembled a hospital more than a convent. But the tempter pressed so hard upon this work, that it was sifted to the utmost, and at last broke up. The beginning was made by the house-mothers, every one of whom, being excluded from creature-comfort, took hold again of her husband; and this was not to be wondered at, for their children, who they had vainly hoped would follow them, remained on the farms in a neglected state, and drew the hearts of the mothers towards them. Another cause was added, for about this time the Eckerlins, who had been a great defence against the natural life, left the Settlement. When the Superintendent observed that the means of the household were not sufficient to continue in these limits, he again gave these dear people their liberty, and advised every house-father to again receive his helpmate, which they did, and then all letters of separation were burnt on one pile. And thus, according to human insight, we often work in vain when we think to have done our best; as happened to these dear people, all of whom have by this time entered eternity, where they perhaps received through grace what they strove after with great labor here below. For although God cannot allow man to believe that success rests with himself, (how else could he be humbled?) yet he will not allow anyone to be deceived in him. Oh, that such a zeal might awake again within the household! Then salvation would obtain in all the boundaries of Israel. The people of the household, therefore, moved upon the farms again, and left the widows and all the rest of the poor to the Settlement, who were maintained in Zion by the diligent labor of some of the Brethren, until at last they died. The expenses which the household had incurred were partly refunded, as much as possible. For instance, one house-father was paid with 100 acres of land; besides, the Zion's Church was handed over to them. In return, they renounced all claim on the newly erected house, which later on was given to the Sisters as their convent, and called Sharon; they have possession of it at the present day. Thus God secretly carried out his counsel, and helped them to a house, and the households unknowingly had to assist him in it, which God at the day of judgment may remember to their benefit. Although the Superintendent has been falsely accused of having outwitted the households, this is only another proof that Ephrata was not built after a previously conceived plan.

Now we will again return to the Solitary. Thus far they had sought self-sacrifice in hard labor; but now the Superintendent was urged by his Guide to establish higher schools, of which the singing-school was the beginning. This science belongs more to the angelic world than to ours. The principles of it are not only the same all over the world, but the angels themselves, when they sang at the birth of Christ, had to make use of our rules. The whole art consists of seven notes, which form two thirds and one octave, which are always sung in such a way that you do not hear the tone which stands between two notes, thus occasioning a sweet dissonance, which renders the art a great wonder. It is also remarkable, that, although so great confusion of languages arose, the singing remained untouched. But as everything necessary in the Settlement had to be stolen from the world-spirit, so also in respect to singing. The Superintendent did not know anything about it, except some notes which he had learned on the violin. But a certain house-father, by the name of Ludwig Blum, was a master-singer, and was also versed in composition; he once brought some artistic pieces to the Superintendent, which induced him to make use of the Brother in his church building.

Now those of the Solitary, of whom about seventy of both sexes were in the Settlement, were selected who had talent for singing, and the above mentioned Ludwig Blum, together with the Superintendent, arranged a singing-school in the Settlement, and everything prospered for a time. But the Sisters at last complained to the Superintendent that they were sold to one man, and petitioned him to manage the school himself, saying that they would steal the whole secret of the schoolmaster and hand it over to him. The Superintendent soon perceived that this advice came from God, for as the event proved, quite different things were hidden under it, for which the good school-master's hands were not made. And now the Sisters told the Superintendent everything they had learnt in the school, and as soon as they saw that he had mastered the art, they dismissed their school-master, at which he took such offence, that he left the Settlement, and did not walk with them any more, and when asked, why he had left the Settlement he said: The singing broke my neck. Before he left he made the following declaration to the Superintendent: "A king's daughter took a poor peasant's daughter into her company, because she was gifted with various arts and abilities; however, after she had learnt all her arts, she thrust her off and banished her into misery. I, therefore, ask the Superintendent, whether the king's daughter treated the peasant's daughter justly?" The Superintendent thereat showed him all kindness, and promised him, since there was not anything more for him to do in the Community, he would go with him in spirit, and remember him in his prayers before God. He afterwards showed him much favor, and thus the Superintendent was against his will inveigled into this important school.

Before the commencement was made, he entered upon a strict examination of those things which are either injurious or beneficial to the human voice, in consequence of which he declared all fruit, milk, meat, to be viands injurious to the voice. One might have thought that he borrowed this from the teaching of Pythagoras, in order to break his scholars of the animal habit of eating meat, of which habit he was never in favor. When bringing all this before the Brethren for examination, they observed that he crossed some words with his pen, by which he had declared the love of women as also injurious to the voice. When asked why he did this, he answered that some might take offence at it. But the sentence was retained with full consent of the Brethren, and the writing was added as preface to the hymn-book. This was but fair, for who does not know that carnal intercourse stains not only the soul, but also weakens the body, and renders the voice coarse and rough; so that the senses of him must be very blunt who cannot distinguish a virgin from a married woman by her voice. Much concerning the fall of man can be explained from the voice. It is a well-known fact that the voices of nearly all people are too low, and this occasions the sinking of the voice in church-songs. On the contrary, it cannot be explained how the voices of friars who keep their vows change for the better; he who in his youth was a skillful bass singer, may become an excellent tenor singer in his old age.

But he also added to the things necessary to be observed in united song, that godly virtue must be at the source of our whole walk, because by it you obtain favor with the spirit of singing, which is the Holy Spirit. It has been observed that the least dissension of spirit in a choir of singers has brought confusion into the whole concert. The singing-schools began with the Sisters, lasted four hours, and ended at midnight. Both master and scholars appeared in white habits, which made a singular procession, on which account people of quality frequently visited the school. The Superintendent, animated by the spirit of eternity, kept the school in great strictness and every fault was sharply censured. The whole neighborhood, however, was touched by the sound of this heavenly music, a prelude of a new world and a wonder to the neighbors. But it soon appeared what God intended with this school. Afflictions were aimed at, and these were plentifully imposed upon both sexes, in so far that a lesson seldom ended without tears; although within the Brethren the essence of wrath was stirred. And though strange scenes occurred, no one ventured to check the Superintendent, for so far everyone believed that he acted as God's commissioner, until at last Samuel Eckerlin, one of his principal adherents, when required to submit to the rules, left the school, whereby he fell under the hatred of the Brethren, and his spiritual growth faded in consequence of it.

The Superintendent conducted the school with great sternness, so that whoever did not know him, might have thought him to be a man of unchecked passions. At times he scolded for one or two hours in succession, especially when he saw that they were under a ban, and at such times he looked really majestic, so that even his countenance glistened. When the Sisters saw that a continual quarreling was going on in their school, they took counsel among themselves to find out the cause of this quarreling, and came at last to the conclusion that it must be in the difference of sex, and, therefore, determined to give up the school. But they were greatly mistaken in the cause. It was the very opposite. For God assigned to him a dangerous post, where many a saint had already lost his crown; besides some had even tried to cut off his locks, and who knows whether some such people were not among his choir. Meanwhile they sent a Sister, Tabea by name, who was bold enough for such a mission, to inform the Superintendent that they would break off all connection with the school entirely. Thereupon the Superintendent asked them, whether they would free him of all responsibility before God, to which they answered "Yes." Thus was the spiritual union between the Superintendent and the Sisters sundered by this imprudent counsel, and he entirely withdrew his favor from their house.

About this time a young man, named Daniel Scheibly, was bought from a ship by the Brethren, and because he was of good manners, they extended to him the right hand of Brotherhood. Because the above mentioned Sister Tabea had thrown off the yoke of Christ and was become a freedwoman, she incautiously engaged in a secret correspondence with this young man, and at last promised to marry him. Such an uncommon thing in the Settlement soon became rumored abroad. A conference was held about it, and she was asked by the Brethren why she had seduced their servant, and they demanded back the money they had expended for him; but at last they came to an amicable settlement for conscience sake, and relieved her of the debt. Finally the time of their marriage arrived. One of the house-fathers was to officiate; then, while she stood before him in the dress of a matron, having laid aside the habit of the Order, and the moment had arrived for them to be united, the Superintendent called her apart, and took her again under his protection; whereupon she dismissed her bridegroom and again entered the Sisters' House. To atone for the scandal she had caused she shed many tears of fervent repentance, by which she washed off the stain from her habit, wherefore also her name Tabea was changed to Anastasia,[1] which means "One

---

[1] It seems fit briefly to mention some incidents in the life of this Sister. She was the youngest child of a respectable family in the Canton of Basel,

risen from the dead." Her bridegroom, however, left the Order, and fell back into the world.

The example of this Sister influenced the others again to submit to the guardianship of the Superintendent, so that the school was re-commenced. Soon after a choir of Sisters appeared in the meeting, and sang the hymn, "God, we come to meet Thee," with five voices, which was so well received in the Settlement, that everyone had his name entered for the choir, so that one did not know who should perform the outside work. But this heavenly art also soon found its enviers, for one of the house-fathers publicly testified and wrote against it, but the Brethren reprimanded him and said: The wisdom of God had ordered this school to their sanctifi-

---

Thomen by name, and she was the first in the family who was among the elect, and entered the Sisters' convent in the bloom of youth. Her brother and sister soon followed her, joined the Order, and ended their course in the Settlement, and last the parents followed. That is what a pious minister in Switzerland, Lucius by name, had told them when taking leave, namely, that there were many sects in the country they were going to, therefore they should join the most despised. She was accomplished and well formed, endowed with fine natural gifts, and was an excellent singer, on which account she was of much value to the Order. She was fortunate also in enjoying the confidence of the Superintendent, and was his right hand in the important work of the singing-school, spending many a sleepless night over it. At one time he gave her many tunes of his composition to copy, which so fatigued her that she at last fell asleep, and cut his tunes into pieces.

Her subsequent fall was the consequence of her excessive human nature. The Superintendent had at that time often warned the Solitary against the outward church, because it usually produced husbands and wives. She, nevertheless, was always prominent in church visitations, and her friendly disposition drew everyone toward her, so that her fellow-combatants were little noticed aside of her. This stirred up envy within them, and they mockingly called her Court Cavalier. To this was added, finally, the death of her faithful guide, the Superintendent; in consequence of which she confided in others who could not help her in her Solitary life. Meanwhile by her travels she lost her fellowship with her Sisters, and thus also her home in the convent, which obliged her in her old age to marry a rich merchant, after having been a nun 30 years. For all this she was indebted to her unsanctified natural gifts. This, however, was a great loss to her, because she had taken the vow of perpetual virginity, and had on that occasion allowed her head to be shaved. After a short period of wedlock she was transferred into eternity. May God give her a blessed resurrection, and not repent him of His gifts and calling.

cation, they had sweated in it and endured school discipline, therefore they would not permit a stranger to interfere. After the Superintendent had with much trouble broken the ice, and taught the first principles of singing to the scholars, he divided them into five choirs with five persons to each choir, namely, one air, one tenor, one alto, and two bass singers. The Sisters were divided into three choirs, the upper, middle and lower; and in the choruses a sign was made for each choir, when to be silent and when to join in the singing. These three choirs had their separate seats at the table of the Sisters during love-feasts, the upper choir at the upper end, the middle at the middle, and the lower at the lower end; in singing antiphonally, therefore, the singing went alternately up and down the table. Not only had each choir to observe its time when to join in, but, because there were solos in each chorale, every voice knew when to keep silent, all of which was most attentively observed. And now the reason appeared which induced him to establish such choirs of virgins. It was with him as with Solomon, he was zealous to make manifest the wonderful harmony of eternity, in a country which but lately wild savages had inhabited; for God owed this to North America as an initiation into the Christian church, therefore these choirs belong to the firstlings of America. The contents of these songs were entirely prophetic, and treated of the restoration of the image of Adam before his division, of the heavenly virginity, the priesthood of Melchizedek, etc. The gift of prophecy overflowed the Settlement like a river at that time; and close observation showed that the beautiful sun of Paradise had then already reached its meridian, but afterwards inclined towards its setting, and was at last followed by a sorrowful night, as will be shown in its place. This wonderful harmony resounded over the country; whoever heard of it, wished to see it, and whoever saw it, acknowledged that God truly lived among these people.

And now let us tell for the information of those who are versed in this art, how he explained the first principles of singing so simply that even a child could understand them; therefore he did not care for the artificial terms of the masters, which rather obscure than enlighten the art. Accordingly, whenever he took a hymn in hand, in order to compose a tune to it, he was careful to represent the spirit of the hymn by the tune; then after he had composed a choral-song, he fixed the metre, not according to custom, but as the nature of the thing required it. He, however, soon found out that some of the melodies were very strained, and that notes occurred which did not belong there. Thus he discovered the key, for every key has its own peculiarity, and adopts only such notes as are natural to it, and this is the reason why the melodies of Lobwasser have a strained sound, because the key to them was not understood, and notes were thus used which were not suitable. In order that he might not make mistakes in composing, he had for each key certain dominant notes, commonly four to the octave, which he called rulers, but the three other notes, servants. Thus in the f tunes, f, a, c, f, are the rulers, but g, b, d the servants, and although it sounds ill if a servant is made ruler, the composer, nevertheless, must know when it is proper to swerve into another key. This gives a very charming variation to the song, provided it resolves itself again into the original key before the end. The Superintendent was a master in this, but his scholars suspected that he had done it in order to find a cause for fault-finding with them; for as soon as they changed to another key their voices fell into disorder.

When he attempted to compose the bass and middle-voices he encountered new difficulties, for you must know that vocal music, as well as *mathesis*, have their unalterable first principles, which angels even observe in their song. These he did not know, neither was he able, like masters in music, to find the concordance by means of instruments; at last he invented certain schedules, a special one for each key, in which he laid down the proportion between the soprano and the other voices, whereby composition was greatly facilitated. For instance, in the key of f, the f in the soprano corresponds to a in the tenor, and c in the alto; the bass, however, has the octave of the middle voices. All his tunes have two basses; but he also composed some for six voices, and even for seven, namely, two soprano, one alto, two tenor, and two bass; for that purpose, however, he after all had to use two octaves. His last work, by many masters declared the most important, were the choral-songs. They were brought to light, partly printed, partly written, Anno 1754, under the title: "Paradisiacal Wonder Music,[2] which in these latter times and days became prominent in the occidental parts of the world as a prevision of the New World, consisting of an entirely new and uncommon manner of singing, arranged in accord with the angelic and heavenly choirs. Herein the song of Moses and the Lamb, also the Song of Solomon, and other witnesses out of the Bible and from other saints, are brought into sweet harmony. Everything arranged with much labor and great trouble, after the manner of singing of the angelic choirs, by a Peaceful one,[3] who desires no other name or title in this world."

It is reported that the angels singing antiphonally appeared in a vision to St. Ignatius, and thus their methods found their way into the church. It is possible that in former ages they were more in use in the convents; now but little is known of them. Yet one of these tune-books came over the ocean, and we are informed that, being engraved on copper, it was printed at Augsburg; but we cannot answer for it. When already half the Settlement was burdened with this work, the house-fathers, too, came to engage in the wonderful music, for the powers of eternity, which were embodied in it, had such an effect that whoever heard the song was forcibly attracted by the goodness of God. Some time during the night was fixed for the school-hour, and two Brethren were appointed teachers; but they showed such diligence in the school during winter that they neglected their domestic duties, which rendered it necessary to close the school. But the Superintendent, in consideration of the fact that such gray heads had paid so much honor to the work of God, in so far that they suffered themselves to be children again, had a music book for four voices written for them, which he presented to their Community. Their veneration for this music was so great that everyone wished to possess the book, and who-

[2] [Paradiesisches Wunderspiel].
[3] [Einem Friedsamen, the Superintendent's "church-name" was Friedsam].

ever had it accordingly fell under judgment, as happened yonder with the ark of the covenant. The book thus wandered from house to house, till at last nobody wished to have anything to do with it.

After the Superintendent had accomplished such an important work for the benefit of the spiritual Order in Ephrata, it was resolved, at a general council, that both convents present him with a worthy reward as a testimonial of filial esteem. This was to consist of two complete music books, furnished for all voices, one of which was to be made by the society of the Brethren, the other by that of the Sisters. Both parties put their most skillful members to the task. On the part of the Brethren three of them worked at it for three-quarters of a year. It contained about 500 tunes for five voices; everything was artistically ornamented with the pen, and every leaf had its own head-piece. The Superintendent's name stood in front, skillfully designed in Gothic text; around it was a text of blessing added by each Brother. The work of the Sisters was not less remarkable. It was artless and simple, but something wonderful shone forth from it, for which no name can be found.

These two books were reverently presented to him, and the Brother deputed thereto thanked him in the name of the whole Brotherhood for his faithfulness and care. He accepted their present graciously, and promised to remember them in his prayers. There were some instances when the Superintendent showed himself to be a great man, and this was one of them. Many might object that he was ambitious, but those who knew him more intimately, know how far he was from it. But the fact is, he was to make manifest the manners of the New World among his followers, and how everyone must esteem his neighbor higher than himself; and herein did his disciples faithfully follow him, according to the simplicity of those times.

Before we conclude this chapter, let us mention the writing-school, where the writing in ornamental Gothic text was done, and which was chiefly instituted for the benefit of those who had no musical talents. The outlines of the letters he himself designed, but the shading of them was left to the scholar, in order to exercise himself in it. But none was permitted to borrow a design anywhere, for he said: "We dare not borrow from each other, because the power to produce rests within everybody." Many Solitary spent days and years in these schools, which also served them as a means of sanctification to crucify their flesh. The writings were hung up in the chapels as ornaments, or distributed to admirers.

CHAPTER XXV.

Concerning the Domestic Contentions in the Settlement, Up to the Time When the Eckerlins Moved Into the Desert.

The course of events brings us to the strange division which took place in the Brotherhood of Zion, which had its origin in the dissensions which arose between the Superintendent and his first-born spiritual son, Onesimus, the Prior of the Brethren, whereby such a winnowing was brought about in the Settlement that it almost ended in a complete disruption of the same. It has already been mentioned that the Prior frequently became too powerful for the Superintendent, and that the Superintendent had much trouble to bring him to order again with the assistance of the Brethren; but what prompted the Prior to act as he did, was at that time still hidden from him. It was the secret of apostasy which was to be revealed through him, and which the Superintendent's spirit still hindered at that time. Because these events have a great resemblance to the fall of the angel of envy and of the first man, let us go back to the source from which this evil flowed. Whoever is acquainted with the affairs of the Superintendent knows that much was entrusted to him by God at his awakening, namely, it was that good through which the grand-duke Lucifer was turned into the devil, and which also occasioned the fall of the first-created man, because both of them tried to bring this same good into they own possession. For the Superintendent, a man of great simplicity before he was taught wisdom by experience, it was impossible to imagine that any of his disciples would dare to rob him of this good, especially since he himself had nothing in his own hand, but had to do as God had imparted to him. Being thus minded he entrusted many things to the Prior, hoping that he would not betray his trust. And during the first years of his official employment the Prior was so faithful to his spiritual Father that he did not enter into intimacy with any of the other Brethren, not even with his own brothers. This intimacy between the Prior and the Superintendent was often the talk of the whole Settlement. The Prior, therefore, was often in the balance against the whole Brotherhood, and yet they could not outweigh him, so strong was the confidence of the Superintendent. But it was no small matter to continue this intimacy with the Superintendent, for his intercourse was like unto fuller's soap or a refiner's fire. Therefore, as soon as the Prior perceived that in this narrow life the Superintendent never would put any advantage into his hands, but that he would always be obliged to live by his grace, he gradually withdrew from him and joined his own brothers, and thus betrayed the trust which the Superintendent had put in him. The Brethren also objected to being any longer used for the latter's humiliation by the Prior, saying: "It is only a war for the cap."

Thus was the household in Zion conducted amid incessant changes, because the Prior did not possess sufficient righteousness to humble himself before his spiritual Father, nor sufficient boldness to withdraw from his subordination. Yet was his fall meanwhile a foregone conclusion, for the Superintendent, possessed of a keen perception, knew very well that the Prior had betrayed his intimacy with him to his natural brothers, to such an extent that they became masters of him and of his goods, and he was in the same situation towards them as David to Zeruiah's children. They, meanwhile, usurped the government, and commenced great things, which they were also able to carry out, because they had the whole Brotherhood on their side. For it was their intention to add yet another wing to the convent, to purchase more bells, a clock, doors and other unnecesssry things, wherefore they kept four wagons, two for the purpose of maintaining the trade with the forges and with Philadelphia, and the other two to bring together an indescribably large quantity of lumber. All this the Superintendent did not hinder. He did not consider it advisable to check it with his own will, because the whole of Ephrata was built on the foundation of his self-denial and the sacrifice of his will to the will of God; and therefore the poor Brethren of Zion also had to deny themselves well.

About this time adverse circumstances brought it about, that the Superintendent fell sick, and everybody thought he would depart this life, which, at the time, would have been welcome to many, since he was a great burden to some as a witness before God. The Prior, at least, entertained this hope; for although the Superintendent outlived him by fully twenty years, the Prior used to say of him: The Superintendent, to be sure, had received of God the gift to awaken men, but not to be their spiritual guide, and therefore, as soon as the Father had transferred his witnessing power to the children, he had to give way, and leave the work to the children; the Superintendent has finished his day's work. Besides, the tomb-stone of the Superintendent was already made and laid by for use. So every one could perceive what their opinions of the Superintendent were. During this illness, the Prior visited his spiritual Father, and since the Fathers of the old covenant when departing this life blessed their children, he asked that he also should please, before he departed from the Community, honor the Brotherhood with his blessing. The Superintendent consented; and these blessings were afterwards entered upon the minutes of the Brethren.

But the Superintendent recovered, and, although very weak, appeared again publicly at the meetings, at which many rejoiced. But the Prior did not know how to conduct himself, for he had already instilled too much of his own will into the work, and did not know how again to disentangle himself. Only two ways were open for him, either to lay down his office voluntarily, or to try to bring the Superintendent under his feet; the first would surely have been the safest, provided he could have endured all the judgment and shame connected with it without running away from school; then he would again have been an ordinary Brother, as others who had fallen under the same tribulations, tried after him with good success. But he was too great a man for this, therefore he followed the second way as the nearest, and thereby brought about his fall. The Superintendent foresaw all this, for everybody could see that the Brethren's household in Zion was not founded on the rock Jesus Christ, since you heard there no other talk but about buying, selling, taking in or lending out money, dissolving marriages, acquiring land, keeping servants, wagons, horses, oxen, cows, etc. The Governors even were induced to notice this new institution, and yet all this was put to God's account. Therefore he prophesied several times that the Brotherhood in Zion would yet have a great fall. And of the Prior in particular, he said, he resembled one, who climbed too high, and the ladder was taken away from under him. This the poor Brethren did not believe, because they were already so heavily laden that nothing heavier could befall them except martyrdom. But it was as little his part to advise, as it had been God's part to prevent the fall of the angel of envy. For if the Superintendent had held back anything from him, he might have been accused of not having dealt honestly with him. On the contrary, he afterwards accused the Superintendent of being the cause of his fall, because he had loaded him with more good than he was able to carry, which even now is the accusation of the fallen angels against God. Thus you see that everything has to be brought to an end by the goodness of God. The Prior himself was not without experience in these dangerous ways. He was several times heard to say: "If a vessel on a potter's wheel turns out badly, he can work it over again and make something else out of it, but when it cracks in the fire it cannot anymore be made use of;" by which he meant himself. Again he said at times: "God be gracious to me, that I may not run away from school, for if I once run off I shall not return as long as I live." And he was his own prophet.

All these things were hidden for a while in the breasts of the Superintendent and Prior, without the public noticing anything of it, for the Superintendent treated him at the time with all the honor due to his office. An especial dress was made for him, which he put on when officiating at a baptism, which no one wore either before or after him. The Sisters had to stitch a clever breast-plate on it, which he, like the high priest of the old covenant, wore on the breast, as a sign that he had to bear the sins of his people on his breast, to which fancy, it is reported, he clung to his death. He also bestowed upon him a title of honor, so that the whole Settlement had to call him par excellence "The Brother," and he consigned his own house to him as residence. But because the same stood too near the Sisters' convent, he hindered them; for they soon perceived that his intention was to bring their house under his man-power. Although their Mother visited him at least once a week in her virginal pomp, as already mentioned, their intercourse contributed much to his misfortune. Whilst the Brethren's Prior and the Sisters' Abbess made such an ecclesiastical show together, the Superintendent sat in his house forsaken by God, men and angels, wherefore no judgment could be passed against him, since he did not lay claim to any good for himself, while on the contrary the Prior and the Mother had to pay dearly for this ecclesiastical show. The greatest wonder of the whole play was that the Prior always imagined himself obedient to the Superintendent, though after the case was carefully inquired into, it was found that the Superintendent in everything he did stood under the Prior's influence. I will not deny that this was the severest school through which the Superintendent went in all his life, and that he was greatly humbled during the domestic administration of the Eckerlins. As for the Community, most of the members were ignorant of these things, and therefore pleased when the Superintendent charged the Prior with keeping the meetings in the Community. Thus he conducted the divine service for nine months in Peniel, the chapel of the Community, during which time the Superintendent remained quietly in his retirement, and thus proved that he had learned, if necessary, to dispossess himself of everything. The meetings lasted mostly four hours, and were a medley of useless repetitions without any connection or order; they aimed at sternly trying the patience of the listeners. It was a wonder that so many gray heads were able to bear all this in patience, but respect for the office and esteem of the Superintendent's person restrained them, though some publicly called him a babbler, for which, however, they were very sorry. The Superintendent, besides all this, surrendered also the love-feasts to his charge, and allowed him to break the bread for him, as for an ordinary Brother; so that everything was now in his hands, and nothing in those of the Superintendent. But all this did not satisfy him, for he was still in his exaltation and not yet humbled; he wanted to have all this absolutely in his possession, but that could not be. His domineering was so easily detected, that once he and another Solitary Brother, G. A. Martin, had a violent altercation on their journey, and the Prior told him: "You will have a wife within three years;" he was answered, "And you will not be in Ephrata after three years," which was easy for him to prophecy, knowing the Prior's affairs, and this was exactly fulfilled to both of them. All this is not mentioned in order to derogate from the Prior's personality, for there are thousands who have been converted and do not get into such a dangerous position as he occupied at the time; even the Superintendent acknowledged that God stood in debt to the Prior, for he was dragged as by the hair to his office.

All these things were very sad to the Prior, and had to be bewailed, especially when he considered how tenderly he had loved his spiritual Father when still an ordinary Brother, so that he would have given his life for him at any time, and how happy he had been while he was still a hermit and sought to win the grace of God by watching, fasting and prayer. But now it had turned out through the guile of the tempter that the Superintendent and he had mutually come into each other's way. He, therefore, determined to go out of the way for some time, hoping that meanwhile his place might be filled by another Brother. This he made known to the Superintendent, who gave his consent to it, and gave him as travelling companions his most faithful Brethren, Jephune (he was his oldest brother after the flesh), Timotheus and Jabez. The Superintendent meanwhile himself attended to the meetings which the Prior had conducted for nine months, and also installed another Brother as steward of the domestic household in Zion.

Now it will be necessary to drop the main subject for some

time, and to give a circumstantial account of this visit. These four brethren commenced their journey September 22d, 1744, and having in Jersey visited the Baptists at Amwell, they turned towards East Jersey to a place named Barnegat, situated by the sea. There some Baptists lived, who had come from New England, and had paid several visits to the Settlement; the name of this family was Colvert. The founder of these people was John Rogers, on which account they were called Rogerians. He was the proprietor of a large tract of land in the Connecticut province, but because he differed in his religious belief from that of the country, he had been persecuted, (some say condemned to death, but pardoned under the gallows). His followers still are very troublesome to the government on account of their untimely zeal; and thus far no way could be found to satisfy them. These dear people of Barnegat received their German Brethren with special love, arranged several meetings in their honor, to which they brought their sick, in hopes that they might be cured. They also spoke a great deal to their visitors of their Brethren in New England, and said at last it might prove edifying if the Brethren would pay a visit there. This was a desirable opportunity for the Prior to execute his plan, and therefore they undertook the journey to New England. Having taken leave of these good people, they journeyed through Crosswick, where they visited an old Pythagorean, John Lovell by name, to Brunswick, where they took passage on a ship which was just ready to sail to Rhode Island, where they landed seven miles from New London, at a place called Black Point. Now they were in a strange country, 300 miles from their Settlement, without friends, and so despised on account of their dress, that whoever saw them, ran off. They at last gained their object, and came to a respectable family, Boles by name, who were members of the Rogerian congregation. These received them very affectionately, after the Brethren had delivered the greetings of their Brethren at Barnegat. Meanwhile the rumor about these strange people reached New London, and because England was at the time involved in a war with Spain, it was suspected that they might be Jesuits of New Spain; therefore they sent messengers to them and inquired into their circumstances, and hearing that they were Protestants by birth, they permitted them to pass. Now they had the opportunity to visit the above mentioned Rogerians, who were distinguished from other people by their quiet life; among whom the Brethren found so much favor that wherever they went they had a train of more than fifty persons, white and black, about them. In this very region the pernicious custom of disputation was at that time carried to its highest point; whenever they came together they placed two chairs in the middle of the space, on which the disputants sat, the listeners sitting around them in a circle, when they often gave vent to violent passion. At that time they mostly disputed "about the Perseverance of the Saints."

After their country visit came to a happy end, they were brought into the town of New London, and lodgings were prepared for them with a merchant, Ebenezer Boles, who was a member of their Community and a blessed, virtuous man. He, at that time, lived single; but married afterwards. His death was brought about by poisonous wood, against which the principles of the Rogerians did not allow him the use of medicine. May God give him a blessed resurrection!

The town of New London resembled at the time a fruitful garden of God, and everybody was anxious to prove his good will to the newly arrived strangers, for there were many converted souls among them who were commonly called "Newlights." May God remember them graciously on the day of judgment! When the time for their departure approached, their friends hunted up a ship for them, paid for their passage, and gave them so much for on the way, that they returned home richer than when they left. When they went on board, the town accompanied them to the harbor with many blessings.

They would have been imprisoned in New York, under suspicion of being Jesuits from New Spain, had not a justice of the peace, who was acquainted with their circumstances, gone bail for them. After having arrived at the Settlement, they handed in a journal of their doings, and everyone returned to his work. But the Prior was greatly deceived in his calculations, for his office called him again, and his former burdens rested once more on his shoulders. Since he saw that he could not get rid of his office, and far less could master the same, because the Superintendent stood in his way, he at last came to the determination to act as the tempter had insinuated, and make himself independent of the Superintendent. This he disclosed to one of his most confidential Brethren, adding that he had determined to leave it in the hands of God. The Brother counselled against it, and represented to him that he had to do with an old warrior, who had learnt many a stratagem; he might easily lose. But he insisted upon it, and to prove it he tore up, before the eyes of the Brother, a letter which the Superintendent had written to him; and thus the dark *magia* took hold of him, finally breaking out into a mighty storm, by which the household of the Brotherhood in Zion at last found its end.

The Superintendent, who felt all this very keenly, knew that henceforth he would have to battle again with the Prince of Wrath. But he found consolation in this, that he had been compelled by God to build up the Community, and was not conscious of any transgression, except that he had given into the hands of the Prior, while yet a novice, too intimate a fellowship, by the power of which the Prior was enabled to put his foot upon him, of which the Superintendent had deeply to repent. The Superintendent, soon after the return of the Prior, assembled the Fathers, and they deliberated who should be appointed over the new domestic household of the Fathers, when some of the household and some Solitary were proposed. The Prior, perceiving this, said: That he was greatly surprised, that in regard to such an important position the rule of the covenant was not taken; which in plain German meant that they should appoint him. This induced the Superintendent, in the Prior's presence, to entreat the Fathers in the name of God to relieve him of his office, else death would overtake him; which they did, and thus it came about that the Prior was his successor in office, of which he jocundly remarked: That the Superintendent had made him dance with an old woman.

All these happenings occasioned great disorder in the Community, which is always the consequence of a change in the priesthood. For now it became evident that a spiritual separation had taken place between the Superintendent and the Prior; many were anxious to see the end of it, knowing that the Superintendent stood under a high Guide, and God had always been his God in all his troubles. Some of the Community held back and did not want to desert the man who, for their sake, had poured out his soul, and to follow a novice instead. Some said: The thing could not last, for nobody ever heard that an Apostle had revolted against Christ, or a disciple of the Apostles against the Apostles. Many, however, of the Community accepted him as their priest, and permitted him to break bread in their houses; but I suppose there was little blessing connected with it, because these were thievish burnt-offerings, which cannot be pleasing to God. All the Brethren stood at the time, at least to outward appearance, obedient to the Prior, and bore their yoke willingly, because they had no hope of regaining their liberty again. But in the Sisterhood there lay a heavy stone for the Prior to lift, and although he strenuously tried to force himself upon them, they opposed him so vigorously that he at last had to give it up.

But there was still another task which gave the Prior much trouble; for the Superintendent still stood in his way, and he could not think of any means by which he might render him submissive. He at last seized his person, and obliged him to change his dwelling five times within one half year;[1] and if he should not effectually gain his object

---

[1] Of this fight he wrote the following to Euphrosina, a Sister in Sharon: Regarding my journey and wanderings, in the midst of which I am still engaged, it will, without doubt, be known that it happened during very cold days of winter, when an agreeable and fine day was hardly to be expected, which proved to be the case. The rough and severe weather continued almost to the present time; for surely, should I tell by letter all that happened from the beginning, when I was obliged to wander forth out of my little house, and endure hard procedures, I would hardly be able to do so. For there was nothing but a continuous martyrdom, during day and night, and this from within and without, so that nothing else was left to me but incessant prayers and supplications, by day and by night, that God might not let me be quite ruined, and fall a prey to my enemies. And

so, he had determined to make him live in one of the rooms of the Brethren, and thus to degrade him to the state of an ordinary Brother. But before he put this in practice he was himself overthrown. To give a correct report of this, it happened that as the Prior, with his most faithful Brother, Jabez by name, worked at the composing cases, God suddenly revealed to that Brother that the founder of that Community was being persecuted; wherefore he said to the Prior: "Why did you cashier the Superintendent?" The Prior answered, "That is none of your business; you attend to your work." Hardly was this said, when the Superintendent knocked at the door of the printing office (for the reader must know that at that time the language of the spirit, which requires no words, was still spoken in the Settlement, and therefore the Superintendent was able to understand the matter at once). He called the Brother out, and spoke with him about different matters, and then went his way. But when the same Brother entered the room again, he found the Prior sad and dejected. The Superintendent, after he saw that God himself had sown the seed of discord between these two Brethren, took advantage of the occasion. He consulted with the Prior's youngest brother after the flesh, called Jotham, how this Brother, who formerly had occupied a high office in the great church, had come to this Community by divine will, and had without cause become entangled in the quarrels of the Brethren; that he wished to tell him this as a word of truth from the Lord, that, if he should miscarry in this institution, it would never gain any prosperity. He at last persuaded him in conjunction with this Brother to take up the work of God, which was at its last extremity. After having obtained his consent, he commanded the house-fathers to be called together, and having spoken a great deal with them about how the testimony of God had fared thus far, he said: "Two Brethren of Zion have ventured their lives for the general good, whom I hereby recommend to your prayers." For he said it might

---

although I remained well preserved, still I could not be relieved of the bitter draught; for the bloody wine press had to be trodden, and I shall remember such wretchedness all my life long, etc.

likely cost them their temporal lives. And he was not mistaken in this; for dark powers had taken possession of the Prior, which tried to destroy the work, and therefore the task of these two Brethren was considered highly dangerous. Afterwards he put a warrant[2] into the hands of these two Brethren, by virtue of which they should fearlessly undertake the work of God. They, therefore, went to their Prior, and declared to him that their consciences did not permit them to be any longer subject to him, because he had rebelled against his spiritual Father, and, therefore, they renounced all obedience to him. There were at the time two Brethren with him who considered these proceedings very bold; but the Prior himself frustrated their doings, and tried to get over it all as well as he could. It is remarkable that whenever the power of God has manifested itself in a people, the powers of darkness also stood forth to obstruct the good, as happened to Moses through Jannes and Jambres, and to the Apostle through Simon the sorcerer. And the same happened here; but it is a pity that the Prior permitted such dark powers to take possession of him. He knew well how to bring God's wrath into the soul of others, as if by magic, and on this he relied. But he knew little of that magic of the light by which the fiery darts of the wicked are quenched, through holy humility.

This conflict continued for three weeks, without anybody knowing what would be the outcome of it, during which time the Prior, whenever he found a door open for his dark magic, went there, and like a prophet pronounced judgment in the name of God, which, however, had no other effect on them than to make trouble; for they knew that he had trampled under foot a man to whom God stood as debtor, because he had hazarded his own dearly gained life for the salvation of others. But the Superintendent had no intercourse with these two Brethren during this time, for he had

---

[2] The warrant was in these words: "To Brother Jabez and Brother Jotham: Be valiant, and do what you have to do, and leave nothing undone which might prove a hindrance to bringing the matter to its proper end. I, for my part, am strongly engaged in my mind before God, that this is the right way. May God give to all of us life, and the enjoyment of him in the world to come.   FRIEDSAM, a Nonentity."

to await the result from God. The Prior at this time worked at the saw-mill, for all the Brethren had their hands full with the convent, which was about to be built. But he had been mortified to such a degree, that he outdid all the Brethren, and by these means often saved himself from severe judgment, wherefore he hoped, although in vain, that he would now also succeed. The Superintendent once visited the supper-table of the Brethren, and when he saw him staggering towards the table as if he were going to fall, he said to him: "Do not mar it, there is something good in it." For he well knew that the Prior intended to get rid of his life in an honest way. How he must have felt to see his darling child, whom he had so tenderly loved, in such a sorrowful state, can easily be conceived.

Meanwhile the Brethren began to awaken and to comprehend that the day of their liberation was at hand. They entered into fellowship with those two Brethren; all of which came from God, for in a short time they had the whole Brotherhood on their side. When it was rumored that the Prior had rebelled against the Superintendent, the Brethren began to revile everything he had done when in office. It has already been mentioned that a writing had been published in the English language in the Settlement; this was burnt, because it had been printed by his order without general consent. There were also condemned to the flames a title and preface which he had written for the Superintendent's printed Theosophic Epistles; for both were offensive, because he had extolled the Superintendent without measure in the title, and had rashly said in the preface that most mystical books were not worth more than to be burnt afterwards; however, another title and preface were substituted. The Sisters followed this example and burnt all hymns and writings they had which were composed by him, among which two writings especially are to be named, one, "The Life of a Solitary," and the other, "Rules and Precepts of a Soldier of Jesus Christ." The Brethren likewise collected everything that originated with him, and delivered it to a Brother to have it burnt.

This was a heart-thrust to the Prior, and now it became

evident that he had his greatness only through the fellowship of the Brethren, so that when he lost this, he felt so forsaken that he was seized with sickness. It is strange that at that time he was kept prisoner in the same place where the Superintendent shortly before had undergone the the greatest temptations he had met with in his life; though he never was really in prison, it was only a common saying. But when it was noticed that some Brethren wanted to carry water on both shoulders, and always betrayed to him the secrets of the Brethren, it was ordered that whoever should visit the Prior without company, such a one should not be considered a Brother any longer. Some did not mind this, and these afterwards escaped with him into the desert. Thereafter two Brethren were ordered to attend him in his sickness, and then the whole Brotherhood clung again to the Superintendent as the man who under God was the cause of their conversion. They also arranged a night-school in their hall, at which they always had him with them, which the Prior in his spiritual prison could hear to his great grief. At last, when the Prior became aware that the loss of his office and his priestly dignity was in store for him, deep repentance took hold of him and he wept Esau's tears for a thing which he had once possessed in his own person, and which to all eternity could not be his again. Nevertheless, he took forty pounds out of the Brethren's treasury, and with it tried to bribe the Mother of the Sisters to intercede for him with the Superintendent. But the Sisters did not agree about this money. The most of them declared it would bring some misfortune, and should not be accepted. But the Mother took it. Her intercession, however, was of no avail. A Brother of Zion did the same; but everything was in vain. The good Prior would have done better had he laid down his office forever, because he only administered it in selfishness; it could only aggravate his fate. When he saw that the Superintendent was firm against entreaties, he made an attempt with the Brethren. He appeared before them, reduced by deep grief to be more like an incorporeal spirit than a human being. They were just assembled in writing-school. He said: "I beg of you for God's sake, Brethren, receive me again, for I cannot be separated from you in time and eternity." But no one had an answer for him, for everyone understood that he wished to regain his office. But in order to satisfy his entreaties, they held a council in the presence of the Superintendent, in which it was agreed that he should leave the Settlement for a time, and manage the business in the fulling-mill. The Brotherhood should meanwhile be reformed and as soon as everything stood on a proper footing again he should have the choice, either to again live with them, though only as a common Brother, or if this did not please him, that a small house should be built for him in the Settlement and he be cared for there as long as he lived. When this resolution was communicated to him, he by no means objected, but promised to move next day into the fulling-mill, and was greatly rejoiced, because he perceived that the severe judgment, which was the result of his administration, would soon reach its end. But, good God! it was a short joy, for when his oldest brother, to whose advice he had always paid more obedience than to that of his faithful spiritual Father, came home and heard the resolve of his brother, he said to him: "It is time again to turn to a hermit's life;" that he should escape with him into the desert, and leave misfortune to the Brethren; they would not carry on matters for any length of time, for they had not intelligence enough to conduct a household. This proposition pleased the Prior, therefore he left the Settlement on the following day, September 4th, 1745, with his above-mentioned brother Jephune, and another, Timotheus by name, and moved towards the wilderness, after having administered the office of Prior among the Brethren for not much longer than four years. They fled about 400 English miles, towards the setting of the sun, as if some one were chasing them, for justice pursued them on account of the spiritual debts which they had contracted in the Settlement, until, beyond all Christian governments, they had reached a stream which runs towards the Mississippi, New River by name. Here they settled, in the midst of a pack of nothing but raggamuffins, the dregs of human society, who spent their time in murdering wild beasts. These they had to take into their companionship instead of the Brethren they had left behind. But how incomprehensible, O Lord, our God! are Thy counsels, for those who dishonored Thee to stumble and fall, because they followed their own understanding more than the guidance of Thy cross; therefore they were despised; but Thou who scatteredst Israel wilt gather it again, for Thou canst not repent of Thy gifts and calling; Thou wast our God in our great misery, therefore build us up again and mend our faults for we are Thy people and the flock of Thy pasture.

It was necessary to give a clear record of these matters, because nearly everyone had the suspicion that the Superintendent had persecuted the Prior and his brothers; and no one can be blamed for it, because many in the Community were not cognizant of the condition of the household in the Settlement. The rock of offence[3] and the stone of stumbling were erected in the Settlement, and this was the cause why hypocrisy did not thrive, for everyone's secret was brought to light.

The first who stumbled over this rock was the Superintendent himself. But his trial was between God and him-

---

[3] Of this he sings in the large hymn book, page 227, thus:

> This hardest priest's condition
> Scarce hath aught to deplore,
> Since he's God's near relation
> Such things he must endure:
> In the end
> Peace is sent
> E'en to those despising
> Things of God's devising.
>
> Such task to me is hardest,
> Too hard for words to tell,
> Which Thou, O God, demandest
> Of me to learn full well;
> That e'en they
> Who to-day
> Treat God with derision,
> May have his salvation.

self, and therefore all the more weighty, as he sings in a hymn:

> "Now all vexation it is still,
> God, he himself avenged it;
> That rock, so hard, has crushed my will
> And all to pieces broke it;
> Because I took offense thereat
> Which no one else escaped had."

To his successors, however, he was a source of offence. At least it appears from the Superintendent's testimony that he bore this condition for them, and most likely carried it with him to eternity, where only such hard states are resolved.

Since the time of the Superintendent's flight into the wilderness where Ephrata now stands, which happened in October, 1732, to the flight of the Prior into the wilderness, which happened September 4th, 1745, a period of thirteen years intervenes. Let this be the end of this chapter.

CHAPTER XXVI.

THE BROTHERHOOD RECOVERS AGAIN FROM THE VARIOUS TRIBULATIONS CAUSED BY THIS SEPARATION. NEW CHURCH-WORK TAKES PLACE IN PHILADELPHIA, BESIDES AN AWAKENING AMONG THE ENGLISH PEOPLE.

While the vengeance kindled in the Brotherhood of Zion ferociously raged, it looked as if each Brother were about to turn out the others, and as if no deliverer were at hand who could control the conflagration. For when judgment had driven one Brother out of the Settlement it soon took hold of another, so that even the oldest Brethren were in danger of becoming victims of vengeance. As soon as the office of Prior had become vacant by the departure of the Prior, his youngest brother Jotham successfully worked himself into the position, for the Eckerlins had the delusion that the office was hereditary in their family, so that the Prior was once heard to say: "The Community is mine," to which his brother Jotham answered: "Then the Brotherhood belongs to me," which the third, Elimelech, heard and replied: "By God, brothers, both of you are mistaken," for in his opinion both belonged to him! It is strange that men who were already divorced from the wife of the world were still thus extraordinarily tempted by the false priest-spirit; and it seems that this was harder to overcome than the attractions of a mortal wife. Even Aaron's priesthood availed no more than for the reconciliation of Aaron's murderous church, wherefore it was overthrown when the true Priest appeared from heaven. Soon after Brother Jotham assumed the office the spirits of judgment, which had overthrown his Brother, took possession of him also, for he began arbitrary reforms. There were several Brethren of the household whom he would have mustered out of the Settlement if the Superintendent had not opposed it. He also had various plans of his own, and did not know that this had been the cause of his brother's downfall. The Brethren, however, did not allow him to get warm in his seat before they declared against him; they did not want again to have an Eckerlin as their Prior; they wanted him to move into the house which the Eckerlins had in the Settlement, and to let them reform the Brotherhood; after that he might again dwell with the Brethren. He, however, did not wait that long, for in the winter following his brother Jephune came for him and took him to the New River. Thus all the Eckerlins lost their right in the inheritance of the Lord, for which they had to thank their carnal connection alone, which had helped them to bring everything, even the Superintendent, under their sway. But the scandal of this schism spread through the whole country, and just as formerly this small Community had by its harmony brought everything close together so did this disunion now dissolve everything. The merchants of Philadelphia, who had traded with them, were displeased at this loss. They had expected to find indulgence for their worldly life from these supposed saints, and if the government had been able to interfere the affair would have been brought before the courts; but the sins were not against the government, but against God. Everybody wished them well, for it was hoped they would discover a nearer road to the kingdom of God than the one the Solitary in the Settlement thus far had walked in. The pious of the country were the most beguiled by this deception towards God; the friends of the Separation in Germantown were all ready to follow them, but were prevented by the subsequent Indian war; for nothing is sweeter in the world than to again desert God after having lived for some time nearer to Him. It is this that does more harm to the kingdom of heaven than ten Neros. A man of note wrote from Frankford: "The flight of the Eckerlins into the wilderness is a great marvel, let me know the result of it." And now a pilgrimage was undertaken to those regions, for whoever became troubled about his salvation took refuge with them, and they understood how to cure him. Others hoped to find out some of the sins and infamies which, as was supposed, were carried on in the Settlement. A famous doctor was most likely induced thereby to undertake his long journey to them. A young Brother in the Settlement, Henry Zinn by name, also longed at last for such a life of license; he begged the Brethren to accompany him thither, and promised in return to love them all his life long. He and the whole family of Bingeman were there killed by the Indians.

When judgment blazed so fiercely to sift the Brotherhood in Zion, the Superintendent gave his assistance to the same, as a test, whether their work were of God or not; therefore he said he would not desist from tearing down, so long as one stone was yet resting on the other in the household of Zion. And because he knew that several Brethren were but outwardly captured by the power of God's testimony, and that they did not internally live a life of mortifying their carnal senses, he made known by one of the Brethren, that whatever Brother were inclined to leave the Settlement, should at once make use of his liberty. The fence was thus completely torn down; some left in the day time, others secretly at night; some asked for their wages, others demanded again what they had contributed. About this time the printer in Germantown, urged by a hidden authority, proclaimed in the paper, that any who had contributed anything to Ephrata, should make application for it at that place, and it would be restored. Some in the Sisters' House also took their leave, and followed this licentious life, which gave rise to marriages and other forbidden deeds. It was observed that very few of them met with success. This disorderly crowd of people turned towards the New River. Several of the Community also followed them, for there they found an altar erected for flesh and blood, and the number of disorderly persons increased so fast among these Solitary that they sent a request to the Settlement not to send any more people to them. Although they tried to establish divine service, they could not accomplish anything with people who had stepped beyond God and trodden his testimony under their feet. At last they were dispersed through all countries. The last who left the Settlement was Beno, and therewith the judgment against the Brethren ended. When about 100 miles distant from the Settlement, the Spirit told him to stop, and he turned back, and was again received in the Settlement after much supplication. He ended his life there.

Thus the household of the Brotherhood in Zion, after a short but lamentable period of time came to a sorrowful end; all of which the Superintendent had predicted. It is remarkable that by this schism the whole was divided into three parts, according to the three principles, for some fell into possession of the empire of the outer world, and again become through marriage, citizens of it. The Eckerlins and others permitted themselves to be captured by the dark magic, and consumed their time in judging and calumniating their innocent Brethren, from whom they had wickedly separated. The remnant was a small, poor and despised crowd. The Superintendent remembered this business at times with sadness, and said: He was the cause of this misfortune, because he had put too much into the hands of inexperienced men, and if he had not been too weak he might have prevented it all, but thus he had exposed himself to the danger of falling. The Eckerlins did not possess the least degree of learning before their conversion, but because they were the first of the civil world who joined the Community, they revived secular life therein, tore the Superintendent away from the supposed holy simplicity of the Mennonites, and invested him again in his former secular way of living. And as they endeavored to gain his favor by various acts of goodness, they at last brought him under their influence, and thereby they became important men. However, after they had left the Settlement, and the Superintendent had suffered enough for the good he had accepted of them as long as he stood under their sway, he commenced an important work, namely, to deprive them again of the benefits which they had secured through church-robbery, and again to withdraw his fellowship from them, for he was one of the magi of light to a high degree. At this time he was always to be seen on his feet, and after he was done with his work in the spirit, his good which they had taken from him, returned to him, and there was nothing left them but their own good; and because they had possessed this in selfishness, they became a laughing-stock to the tempter in their hermitage; for God is not opposed to himself. Therefore they could not remain there any length of time, but returned again in order to commit a new church-robbery, which will be mentioned at the proper place. Besides all this, it must be said to their credit, that they did a great deal of good to the Brethren by the strictness of their rule in Zion, and that those who bore their yoke in patience had a great advantage over others in subsequent times.

Of the reform undertaken in the Settlement and of its success, the following is in a few words to be mentioned. A Brother of Zion visited the Superintendent and disclosed to him his wish, namely: That it was his intention to renew his covenant with God by a repetition of his baptism. The Superintendent agreed to his request, but asked him to wait yet awhile, as he expected some more work of the same kind. And he was not deceived, for on the following day two other Brethren came to the Superintendent for the same cause; in consequence of which the 27th day of September, 1745, was chosen for this festival, on which day ten Brethren renewed their covenant with God by baptism, as a tribute of gratitude, because his mercy had sustained them in their adversities. These were at another time succeeded by fourteen other Brethren; the others stood back. The Superintendent himself performed the act, and gave his sorely wounded heart to the Brethren who had been spared by the sword. After baptism the customary hair-cutting was performed, to which the Superintendent also submitted; the tonsure, however, was omitted, in order to avoid offence. The following day a breaking of bread was held in Zion, at which the venerable Sisters were also present. That was a day of great joy, since not only those expelled from Israel were again assembled together, but also because the Superintendent was again installed in his office, after having been a fugitive for one year, six months, and one day, on account of his wicked son Absalom, during which time he had to flee out of one house into another in the Settlement. O, how blessed he, who in dark days, does not depart from the guidance of his God, and does not take offence when the cup of affliction is filled for him! Oh, how richly does God reward all those who have been steadfast in the faith even unto the sweating of blood! This edifying act of the Brethren moved the Sisters so that all of them were re-baptized by the Superintendent in two days, namely, October 3d and 15th, 1745. Afterwards it was proposed, that in memory of this time, this day should be celebrated every year, and that all members of the Order should submit to re-baptism; but the necessary harmony was wanting. The reader can see from this, that re-baptism was rather a church-rite in the Settlement, than that it originated in hatred towards other Communities. When the last of the Brethren were baptized, as above mentioned, another breaking of bread was held in Zion, which also was the last held there; it lasted till two o'clock after midnight. The cause of its long duration was because there still lay a ban upon the Brethren which the Superintendent felt in his spirit, and which impelled him to speak so long and ardently, until three Brethren went off, thereupon the bread-breaking was considered as blessed.

Soon another just as important work presented itself. The Brethren represented to the Superintendent that this convent was built under the direction of the Eckerlins, and therefore, these would have a right over them, as long as they lived in it. Therefore they had a mind to leave the hill and build a new convent near him in the plain, to which plan he gave his consent. This undertaking produced many changes in the Settlement, for the widowers and widows who at that time inhabited the convent Kedar, which belonged to the Sisters, made room there for the Brethren and moved into Zion, which the Brethren had left empty. The 22d of October, 1745, was the memorable day on which the Brethren moved down the hill out of their convent Zion, and handed this over to the Congregation for its poor. The first Brethren moved into Zion in October, Anno 1738, thirteen in number, and from that time on for seven years the Brethren had lived in Zion. The rest of the Brethren followed them August 13th, 1740, as has already been mentioned. September 21st, 1740, they held there the first Night Watches, and the last on August 4th, 1745. Since the death of Brother Agonius, when the government came completely into the hands of the Prior, the latter had ruled four years, two months and nineteen days. The number of Brethren who left Zion at that time was thirty-four. On December 27th, 1745, the Brethren commenced to abolish their Babylonian bell-trash; they sold their clocks and bells to the Reformed and Lutheran congregations in Lancaster, but tore down the spire in great zeal. And because it became known that young people used the common wash-house at night for courting purposes, the same was burnt down. At this time a pretty large bell arrived in Philadelphia from England, which the Eckerlins were said to have ordered. The following was inscribed around it: *Sub Auspicio Viri Venerandi Onesimi Societatis Ephratensis Praepositi.* Having received intelligence of this a council was held in presence of the Superintendent, which resulted very unfavorably to the bell, namely, that it should be knocked to pieces and buried in the ground. But how to pay for it nobody could tell, for its cost was £80. The next morning the Superintendent appeared again in the council and said he had considered about it. Because the Brethren were poor, the bell should be pardoned, and that is how it became the property of the Lutheran church in Lancaster, as mentioned above. But the following incident sounds still stranger. The Eckerlins had laid out an orchard of 1,000 trees near their convent. The Superintendent once passed by it with several Brethren, and the question being asked, what to do with so much fruit, one Brother said: "Cut them down." The Superintendent agreed to it, for he had received the charge from God to lay open the inner man. This orchard, therefore, was rooted up during the night, to the great chagrin of the whole country; and when the originators announced it to the Superintendent, he asked them whether they had done right? But they could not answer him. These were cases of judgment such as are common over the whole world, namely, that one nation sweeps away the other.

After the building of a new convent for the Brethren was agreed upon in the council, the choice of the place became the common consideration, and this fell upon a fine orchard, which was speedily rooted out. But after a considerable time objections were raised against this spot by the Superintendent, and they looked in common for another. The Superintendent always tried to have it near the Sisters' convent, but the Brethren checked him, for they would have preferred to have a high mountain separate these two convents. At last the site for this new building was placed so near the Sisters' House, that conversation could be carried on from one to the other. The Brethren, in retaliation, afterwards played the Superintendent a trick; for when a new dwelling house was to be built for him, they selected the space between the Brethren's and the Sisters' convents, at which some of the Sisters were not well pleased, and said it had exactly the appearance as if the Sisters could not live without the Superintendent. About the same time the Mother, accompanied by some of the oldest Sisters, most likely in company with the Superintendent, paid a visit to the Brethren. It was a very edifying and blessed one. May God recompense them on the day of judgment; for they needed consolation, especially since their church-body was still bleeding from those many wounds which they had received in their strife with the Prince of Wrath. After the Night Watches had been omitted for three months and twenty days, dating from the Prior's flight, they were again commenced December 24th, 1745, by the Brethren in Kedar, where they lived for the time being, and December 25th following, a morning and evening service was added.

On March 23d the office which Brother Jethro held since the time when the Eckerlins left, was again taken from him and given to another Brother, called Jabez, after the former had been in charge of it for four months. There were always candidates enough whenever the Prior's place was empty, but as soon as it was again filled the Brethren either submitted in blind obedience, as they had done to the Eckerlins, or they abstained from all fellowship with him. Therefore the post of Prior was always a dangerous one; but the Superintendent had learnt to sail with all kinds of wind, and was careful not to infuse his own will into any act. During the administration of this Prior the building of the convent was commenced, March 31st, 1746. This house met with strange changes. At first it was intended as a wing to the Zion convent, large enough to accommodate about 100 Solitary. The foundation had already been laid for this purpose, and a surprising mass of lumber procured for it by the Eckerlins, all of which the Brethren made use of. And because heaven was again open for the poor Brethren their work progressed in a blessed and quick manner, especially since one of their Brethren, Sealthiel, was an experienced carpenter. The house was so durably joined together by posts, beams and joists that you will hardly find its equal in North America. All this carpenter work was finished in thirty-five days. On May 11th it was raised, which took three days, at which dangerous task Providence took care of the work, so that nobody was hurt. Then they resolved to build a chapel, for which the remaining timber was used. They raised it in November, 1746, after having worked at it for five weeks. This was a stately building, contained a meeting-hall for the Community, specially ornamented with Gothic letters, besides galleries and halls for the love-feasts. After these extensive buildings had been so well completed under the blessing of God, the Brethren moved into their new convent, called Bethany, where their different domiciles were distributed to them by lot.

September 5th, 1746, Brother Jabez again lost his office, and Brother Jethro was installed the second time; and this was the way it happened. It was the custom of the other Priors to try to establish themselves firmly in their office by gaining the favor of the Brethren; he on the contrary never cultivated any fellowship with any of the Brethren, which indeed was one cause of his early fall. With this he also came into too close intimacy with the Superintendent, whereby he was more heavily burdened with the weight of his spirit than his human nature could bear. For some time it appeared as if he might lose his senses; wherefore some of the Sisters entreated the Superintendent to set him free, lest he might break down under his hands. But the Superintendent had no intention to do so, and said nobody need think that the Prior had lost his senses, there were other causes. Yea, verily, other causes; for it was a most melancholy wedlock; the Superintendent was too great and too small for the Prior, so that he could neither put him down, nor gain ascendancy over him. Being brought into such a wine press, and deprived of all hope of living, he proposed to lay down the office. But the Superintendent soon had a spiritual intimation of this, and warned him to take care, that there was danger of life connected with it. He, nevertheless, at last was brought to the determination by these temptations, to pack up everything belonging to the vesture of a Prior, which had been handed over to him, and with it to pay a visit to the Superintendent. He then represented to him in a proper manner, how strange a life he had led thus far, though it had been more like dying than living; that after close inquiry he had found that all his misfortune was contained in this dress, therefore he desired to return it to him; then he went his way. After this the Superintendent took counsel with three Brethren, and these, in company with the Superintendent, communicated their decision to the Prior, namely, that he should be freed and be again an ordinary Brother; to which he replied that he thanked God for their decision, if he were but permitted to remain in the Settlement, for he did not know whether any guilt was resting on him, because he had had a hand in the overthrow of the Eckerlins. After these events the Superintendent was attacked by severe sickness, which almost sent him to eternity, and which was commonly supposed to be the consequence of the dissension which had occurred between him and the Prior. When able to go out again he summoned him into the new Prior's dwelling, and after he had talked with him about this and that concerning his release, he commended him to God, and then turned his attention to the new Prior. Thus it happened that this Brother, after having enjoyed this dignity for six months, became an ordinary Brother. This was the divine comedy, which had to be learned with such pains in the Settlement, namely, that you must learn to be both high and low, rich and poor, etc., without a change of mind. But the hardest for him was, that access to the Superintendent's person was prohibited him except by permission of the new Prior; and because the new Prior stood so much above him by virtue of his office, he endeavored again to gain the fellowship of the Superintendent. For that purpose he composed a hymn about the virtues of his spiritual guide, (to be found among the Brethren's hymns, and commencing: "Come, come soon my friend," etc.,) which, after having enclosed it in a letter, he sent to the Superintendent through the above mentioned Prior. It produced its desired effect, for when the Superintendent read it to the latter, and the flattery it contained, his countenance paled, and he began to doubt whether he would ever master his office. Some time after this the Superintendent came into the Brethren's writing-school, nodded to this Brother, led him aside, addressed him in a very friendly way, said that he had received his holy remembrance in the song, and that he would stand up for him. Thus was the union of spirit again established between him and the Superintendent and he advanced to a higher school, in so much that he was afterwards freed of all subjection to the Prior, and entrusted with more important work. It is yet to be mentioned, that no Prior of the Brethren (with exception of the first) was ever clothed with the honors of priesthood; the Superintendent himself administered the mystery of the altar and holy baptism, and only permitted a Brother to have a hand in it in extraordinary cases.

After the departure of the Eckerlins, an awakening took place among the English nation in the region of French Creek and Brandywine, in Chester county, to which the Settlement in Ephrata extended its hand. Anno 1746, the following households joined the Community, namely, Jeremiah Pearcol, John Derborough, Job Stretch, etc., likewise some single persons, as: Abel Griffyth, Thomas Peascify, David Roger, Israel Seymour, his sister Hannah Hackly, and several others. Israel Seymour, his sister, and Abel Griffyth lived in the Settlement for some time, but because, according to their allegations, they could not stand the confined way of living, they left it again. Of these Israel Seymour was a man of special natural gifts; the Superintendent, therefore, baptized him again after he had entered the Settlement, and ordained him to service among his nation. His nation afterwards accepted him as teacher, and as such, in companionship with the Brethren, he held a meeting every three weeks at Bethany, in West Nantmill. But there was reason to believe that this work might deliver him into the hands of the tempter, because he was still a novice and rising, as the end proved. He soon took offence at many things in the Settlement, especially at the person of the Superintendent. The Brethren, therefore, erected a hermitage for him at the above mentioned West Nantmill, for his way of life was greatly admired by his people and he was daily overrun with various visitors. A young girl among the Sisters, who most likely had found little pleasure in her convent, moved to the above mentioned Seymour, in his hermitage, under pretence of learning the English language from him; but her actual desire was to cut off the locks of this saint. Another visit was made after this by some from the Settlement, to see these people, because there was bitter complaint against their teacher in all the houses, that he could not preach so forcibly since the Sister lived with him. Then he was notified by authority of the Community, that if he wished to get rid of the Sister, he should come to them, they were ready to extend their hands to him; but if he desired to marry her, they had nothing to say against it. The Sabbath following he came to the Settlement with a long letter of divorce, which he had read to her in both languages in presence of all the Solitary; she then gave her assent to everything, and promised to renounce her right to him forever. . Knowing people said: "Now they have published their engagement." And so it was, for the next week their wedding was celebrated.

A married life thus commenced in fraud and hypocrisy. could not bear good fruit, for he had not learnt to descend from his spiritual height and priestly dignity, and to take upon himself the burden of a household. And she, as a spiritual virgin, was not accustomed to submit to a man. After this he left the service of the Congregation and his hermitage, where the tempter had mocked him with false sanctity, and the Brethren erected for him another dwelling house. But the tempter did not rest. He breathed into him very suspicious thoughts towards the Superintendent, namely, that the same had envied him his gifts, and that this female, therefore, had been made use of to bring about his fall. All this caused him to lose his senses, and he was for some time a victim of madness. For all this he had to thank his having with unwashed hands engaged in so important official duties. After he had regained his reason he engaged in such cunning frauds that neither magistrate nor jurist could get behind his artifices, whereupon he left the country and fled to South Carolina. From that time on nothing was heard of him for fifteen years, until at last a letter from him was received in the Settlement, in which he gave the following suspicious account of his affairs. He had not expected to hear anything of the Community in Ephrata before the day when he would have to appear before the judgment and be condemned by them. After he had committed all kinds of wickedness he had added the folly of taking part in the Iroquois war. But when in battle he had seen men and horses fall down, and his own horse had been shot, he earnestly prayed to God, and made a vow that if God would save him out of this danger he would mend his life; then, after victory was won, he had retired from service, intending to return to his Community in Pennsylvania, but weakness had prevented him from getting further than to Little River, where he had since lived as a settler. This letter was followed by another, Anno 1783, signed by him and more than forty members of the Congregation, which shows that God afterwards made use of him to build up an English Congregation according to the plan he had projected when still living a Solitary in the Settlement. And since he put his hand to the plough again, according to his vow, and returned to his former faith, the preceding narrative will not be prejudicial to him, for the ways of God are incomprehensible, and all of us will fall, although it were better we fell into the hands of God than into the judgment of the world.

At the same time there lived in Philadelphia a Pietist, W. Y.[1] by name, who was accustomed to ingratiate himself with the pious and to raise money by all kinds of frauds. He is said to have done the same in Germany, and in Germantown

---

[1] [William Young].

he practiced the same with the Separatists. This man wrote a letter to the Superintendent, September 26th, 1746, and requested of him to read it to the whole Community. The contents of the letter were, that he had bought a house for £300, but that he still needed £40 or £50, which he requested the Community to lend him. Besides this he also related much of his career, which had already commenced in Germany, and that there already he had determined to become a Capuchin, but that he was prevented from carrying out this holy design. He thought now he might attain his end in a different way, for after having paid for the house he had bought, he intended to set up therein a shop for his wife, and then to set out for Ephrata with his three children, and by these means to escape from his captivity. Two Brethren were sent to him, in consequence of this request, who in the name of the Community, made the following known to him, namely: As regards the money, they could not assist him this time, but in regard to the separation from his wife, they advised him to desist from it, because experience had taught that it would not be accomplished. For there had happened in Ephrata not a few matrimonial separations in times past, and on that account letters of divorce had been executed; but when the Eckerlins had lost the management of affairs, and the Superintendent had again assumed it, he stopped these disorders, ordered the letters of divorce to be burnt, and obliged the married couples to live together again. This unexpected answer greatly disturbed him. But nevertheless he sent another letter to the Superintendent by those two Brethren, in which he renewed his request for £40 or £50. The Superintendent, who, according to the doctrine of Jesus Christ, "Give unto him that asketh of you," could not easily refuse anyone who applied to him, at last, after two months, procured the money for him as a loan. The Superintendent hereby found an open door in the spirit to get further acquainted with the man by letter, and several long and important letters were sent to him at the time, which had such a powerful effect that he submitted to baptism in Ephrata, February 28th, 1747. While still standing in the water he delivered an address, in which he called the water, trees, etc., to witness that he had betrothed himself to Jesus Christ. And because at a future time he wickedly broke the covenant entered into by water, it is to be believed that this innocent element will bear witness against him on that day.

But the baptism did not bring him to himself, for soon after the same he commenced an unnecessary war with the friends of the Separatists in Germantown, and drove them into sore straits by means of the Community; he always took care first to send the letters which he wrote to them to Ephrata for sanction. But after he had discovered the good nature of the Community, it was clearly to be seen that the sole motive of his conversion was to obtain money. Many people pitied the Brethren at the time, that they had been deceived by so great an impostor; but they did not understand the guidance of God, which had for its object to make manifest the innermost depths of the human heart. The next year he again demanded £30 to pay on his house. This greatly enraged the Brethren. It was strongly conjectured that the Superintendent used this opportunity to reduce the Brethren to their blissful state of poverty, for it is sure, that from that time on many refused to put their money into the treasury, under the pretence that they could themselves expend it more profitably on the poor. However, respect for the guidance of God was still so great at the time that some Brethren in the paper mill made up the money in a short time, and satisfied him. But in the autumn following he bought two shoemakers with that money, the trade which he followed, and permitted the Community in Ephrata to take care of the debt on his house. Soon another letter of his arrived in the Settlement, in which he again wanted to borrow the above mentioned £30. Everybody now saw quite plainly that the man was a cheat; the Superintendent alone did not allow any suspicion against him to enter his mind, for he stood under an extraordinary guidance, totally in opposition to the general doings of man; and he, therefore, did not yield until the wishes of the man were in this case also complied with.

This man, being thus thrown into the lap of the whole

Community, became so intoxicated with spiritual affairs that powers of inspiration appeared; for once in a letter to the Community he prophesied of the awakening in Virginia, Maryland, etc. He was, besides, possessed of such an acute feeling that he could tell to the minute when Brethren arrived in Philadelphia, and usually reprimanded them if they did not at once report to him. When the Superintendent became aware that the man was pregnant with priestly buffoonery, he felt impelled to grant him full fellowship, most likely in order to bring to light the mystery hidden in the man. And now he commenced to win recruits for the Community, and to proclaim himself their representative. For this purpose he demanded for himself a complete suit of a Solitary in Ephrata, as also for his daughter the garb of a spiritual virgin, and all of the finest cotton, which was also granted to him.

In general, whenever he sent such new recruits to the Settlement, he did not forget to mention that their needs would have to be supplied, and thus he at once transmitted his impudence to them also. The first one recommended by him who arrived in the Settlement was the wife of a shoemaker, John Mayer. She was baptized October 16th, 1747. In the year 1748 he again sent two single Brethren, Henry Sangmeister and Anthony Höllenthal by name, who were baptized on the very same day, and the first received the name Ezekiel. John Mayer and Peter Schmidt were baptized on April 9th, 1748. Soon after he also brought his sister to the Sisters' convent, where she was called Seraphia.

Here I have to introduce several things, on account of the order of time, although they have no connection with the subject itself. There lived a fallen woman in the Settlement, Blandina by name, for whose conversion they had good hopes for some time, but when she was accused before the Superintendent of attempting to seduce young Brethren, of which he had already a spiritual monition, the spirit flamed up in him so violently that she had to quit the Settlement at once, although the house-fathers offered to go bail for her conduct. Because the house which formerly had been the residence of the Eckerlins was under suspicion of similar disorders, it was,

by common counsel, torn down and cut up for fire-wood.
Meanwhile a love-feast and breaking of bread was announced
to be held in Philadelphia at the house of the before mentioned W. Y., to which the Superintendent went with twelve
Solitary Brethren and Sisters, June 2d, 1747. This love-feast
was kept at the expense of the Community, and cost them
a great deal, for not only flour, butter, and whatever else
belongs to it had to be sent from the Settlement, but all the
necessary tinware, window-curtains, tables, etc., were also
bought on account of the Community, which amounted to
a large sum of money, since the tables alone cost £10. I
observed that during this whole journey the Superintendent
stood entirely under the influence of this man. Thus he would
not permit the poor Sisters to drink water on the way, merely
because the same had written to him he should take care that
the Sisters did not suffer any injury from drinking too much
water on the journey. And when after the festival was over
everyone prepared for the journey home, he requested the Superintendent to stay yet another day, which had to be done,
notwithstanding it was hard for the company to be confined for
a whole day and in such hot weather, in so small a place.
On this journey the powers of eternity manifested themselves anew through the person of the Superintendent.
When entering the city, the concourse of people was very
great; for just at the time when the whole country hoped
the Community would go to ruin, he unexpectedly appeared
in Philadelphia. Moreover his people were better drilled in
the rules of a Solitary life than ever the royal troops understood their military exercises; they all appeared in white
dresses of most scrupulous cleanness. And although it
could be seen from their lean and pale faces that they lived
in a region where they had to suffer much for the sake of
the kingdom of God, they understood to hide their afflictions
so well under the mask of a serene countenance, that no
one could read on their foreheads what transpired in their
hearts. When they entered the house so great a number of
people followed that if a stop had not been put to it the
house could not have held them all. And when they commenced to sing in the house, you could see through the

windows that people were sitting on all the roofs. I almost forgot to mention, that as the visitors crossed a street in Philadelphia an Irish woman followed the people and said: "These persons should be left in peace, because she knew them well; they were holy persons;" for she had for a time led a strict life as a Sister in the Settlement, but was now fallen off. When the Brethren heard of it they sent after her, whether she would not like to be saved again out of the snares of Satan; but she sent word to them that she knew very well that the way of the Brethren was the right one, but she would not dare again to appear before their eyes.

After the visit at the above mentioned house and to the other friends in Philadelphia had, through God's assistance, found a blessed end, preparations for the homeward journey were made, although various other church-work was yet done. On the journey he visited his old friend Conrad Matthei, not far from Germantown. He alone was left of a venerable society, which the celebrated John Kelpius had founded, which, after his death, however, was again scattered, as has been mentioned. At this visit, when they embraced each other, a difference which had existed between their spirits, was removed. They had formerly been good friends; but after the Superintendent had permitted himself to be instrumental in this new awakening in Conestoga, a separation of their spirits took place, which was healed again by this visit, as just mentioned. Therefore he wrote a favorable letter to him as soon as he returned home and likewise exhorted John Wüster, in Philadelphia, who was also his benefactor, not to withdraw his hands from him. This journey was one of the most important the Superintendent ever undertook, on account of God's mighty presence. It was executed only through the power of the spirit, for the meagre manner of living had crushed nature in such a way that without spiritual assistance the journey could hardly have been performed. Therefore, whenever he saw their spirits yield to the weakness of nature, he used to scold them until they were revived again.

During the whole of the visit the Superintendent was entirely beyond the realm of sense and took little care of his outward life, or of the weakness of his companions, especially those of the females, who were already quite faint on account of previous severe exercises. When in hopes that they would soon reach the Settlement they were obliged to turn off from the road and go to West Nantmill, to the English congregation there, where a love-feast was held with the above-mentioned Israel Seymour. The visitors arrived at night, but the love-feast lasted till midnight, because the Superintendent talked much with them through an interpreter of the falling and rising again of man. The spirit pervaded his human nature to such an extent that he knew very little of fatigue. Early the next morning, the visitors started for the Settlement. This whole journey was made without the help of any creature.

On May 18th, 1748, a large number again visited the above mentioned W. Y. in Philadelphia, on account of a love-feast, which was held on the following 22d of May, the management of which the Superintendent put into the hands of a Brother, Jabez by name. By means of such movements this good man got so much to do that he at last imposed his whole household upon the community; for whenever he was in want of anything for his household he, without hesitation, applied for it, and he was mostly satisfied. Therefore everything had to be provided for him, flour, butter, flax, linen, bed sheets, table covers, etc. At last he made the attempt to put even his debts, amounting to £200, on the Brethren in Bethany. He wrote to the Superintendent that it was impossible for him, loaded as he was with his debts, to assist at the spiritual building up of the church, and asked to be entirely freed from them. After the Superintendent had read this letter to the Brethren, a very important work was the consequence, for they declared this demand of the man to be the greatest injustice. But the Superintendent pressed them very hard to grant it, so that they at last perceived that this man was sent to them for their humiliation. They finally held a council about the debt, and it was resolved to request a merchant in Philadelphia to advance the sum to them. Because the Brethren had thus humbled themselves under God's decree, the game was wonderfully turned; for on August 9th, 1748, three Brethren, namely, Lamech, Jethro and Gideon, were sent to him in the name of the Community with the order to take his household again upon his own shoulders. Of these Brother Jethro spoke to him thus: "We came to you in the name of the Community at Ephrata, to make known to you that we are done with your household; for we have no more money in hand wherewith to manage it any longer. Therefore we advise you to attend to your household affairs yourself, and be responsible for them and leave us. For we are not able to do this for you, because we live not for such purposes; for being an outcast people, the thing you ask us to do for you, ought to be done for us." To make it quite sure, and prevent him from abusing the goodness of the Superintendent in the future, he handed him a short letter from the same, which was couched in sharp language.

This aroused the original evil disposition of the man; and because an evil will was stirred in him he began to turn all the good he had enjoyed from the Community into evil. For instance, since the Community had an account of £123 against him he brought in a bill of the same amount for losses he had sustained during the time of his connection with the Community, which losses he chiefly attributed to his inability to attend the weekly markets in Philadelphia, on account of the Sabbath. Many to whom he formerly had given great offence, because of the support received from Ephrata, were reconciled again and were seen with him. But because none in the temporal world can live up to the principle of wrath all the time, he also turned back on himself after he had foamed forth all his badness against the Community. Accordingly he wrote to the Superintendent, and accused himself of having offended the children of God, but at the same time petitioned to have his debt of £123 cancelled, in order that after his death his children might not be held responsible. This was granted him. These are about the most important facts connected with this man. He at last tore loose again from the fraternal bond of the Brethren, and because by his actions he extinguished the few sparks of his conscience; it can be said with certainty that he was a perfect

Atheist,[2] namely, such an one as trod under foot the household of Jesus Christ.[3]

The covenant, nevertheless, which was made by him in the water will rise up against him on the last day, and witness

[2] The whole history of this man shows under what a high guidance the Superintendent must have stood at the time. He may have known all his frauds, for so much intelligence he still possessed; but it was not permitted him to see into the future. Everything that happened to him he accepted as coming from God, without his own choosing, and if his reasoning thus made a fool of him, his successors were put to the same test. In proof of it let us cite a few incidents. Once a beggar and his wife were brought before him, who desired to be baptized and received into the Settlement; herein he did not act according to human understanding, for counsel was soon taken upon it as a very important matter. All the Solitary agreed not to receive them, and represented to the Superintendent that they were already so burdened with so many people who could not support themselves, that no honest person would in the future like to have anything to do with them. But the Superintendent asked them whence they had the right to close the door against the poor? Had he done like them, and not given his possessions to the Community, Ephrata would never have been built, and none of them would be present here. Thus he compelled them through the strength of God to assent and to admit these people, and then authorized a Brother to perform the rite. But what a wonder! As soon as these people had done their work, and the Solitary thus been humbled, the angel of judgment pursued them and they decamped without waiting for baptism. O, how blessed is the man who puts his trust in God and lets his goodness rule over him! He, indeed, experiences how faithfully God takes care of his own.

Another incident, similar to this, happened some time later. Two other married people came, not much better than the former, and brought the same request. But in this case the Superintendent met with such strenuous opposition that he became helpless. At last he left it to the choice of these people to live in the Settlement without being baptized, or to receive baptism and go their way again. When they chose the former, he became convinced that baptism was not their true motive, and he let them go their way.

[3] About the year 1782 he made a new attempt at intercourse with his former Brethren, for it cannot well be believed that he was fixed in his opinions; but perhaps, if he had obtained their consent it would have been some relief to him in his doubtful condition. He sent a letter of fifty sheets to the Settlement, in which he scoffingly spoke of their household and ridiculed all the methods which they used to conquer the natural life. And that was no wonder, for since he had again put the old man on the throne, these things were of no use to him. On the contrary he said, Nature was able to bring happiness; although a fall had occurred, this did not matter much, and a proper civil government could mend this. He offered to live

against him, and it will fall heavily upon him to have licked the thorns. Those people whom he had brought to the Community also left again, and thus nothing of his work remains.

---

in the Settlement awhile. When this letter was published, the opinion was expressed that, according to the Apostle's teachings, such people should not be admitted into the houses. When this was made known to him, he thought that they were afraid of being seduced, and gave up his visit. His death occurred in 1785.

·

CHAPTER XXVII.

THE MILLS OF THE SOLITARY ARE DESTROYED BY FIRE; A BOOK OF MARTYRS IS PRINTED FOR THE MENNONITES; THE DOMESTIC HOUSEHOLD UNDERTAKES A REFORM WITH THE HELP OF THE SOLITARY; AND A NURSERY IS ESTABLISHED TO LEAD BOYS TO A SPIRITUAL LIFE.

Before I take in hand this singular event, I must make mention of the household of the Brethren in Zion, as it existed at the time before the mill was bought. I mentioned above that at the foundation of this Order, the Brethren, without exception, had dedicated themselves to the service of God and the Community, and without expectation of any compensation, which at first was a means of supporting them in their poverty, since at that time they had their support mostly from the offerings of the Community. But when these offerings began to be neglected, the Brethren fell into unbelief and bought the mill under the pretence that they had no need to live by the grace of other people. It is rightly maintained that this mill laid the foundation of their worldly household, as described above. The same, moreover, could never be brought under the dominion of the spirit which ruled in Ephrata; accordingly many Brethren turned towards the mill whenever they wished to escape the discipline of the Holy Spirit, which still was at the helm in the Settlement; since, besides hard work, they had the advantage also of being able to live their natural life, by which, however, they at last trifled away their holy calling and ran into the arms of the world.

Shortly before the mill burnt down the Mennonites in Pennsylvania agreed that their great Book of Martyrs, which was printed in the Dutch language, should be translated and printed in German. No one in the whole country was considered better able to do this than the Brotherhood in Ephrata, especially since they possessed a new printing press and a paper-mill, and moreover were able to put a sufficient number of hands to work. The contract was very advantageous for the above-mentioned Mennonites, for it was agreed on both sides that the Brethren should translate and print the book, but the Mennonites should afterwards have liberty to buy or not to buy. But as soon as this compact became known it was everywhere feared that the good Brethren might gather mammon for themselves; they even received letters of warning from friends in Germany on that account. But the good God had other designs which even the Brethren were not aware of until they were so far involved in the work that they were unable to withdraw. The Superintendent, who was the instigator of this work, never allowed a suspension of work or carnal rest in the Settlement, and therefore seized every opportunity to keep all those who were under his control in perpetual motion, so that no one might ever feel at home again in this life, and so forget the consolation from above, which purpose this Book of Martyrs excellently served, as will be told in its place.

On September 5th, 1747, which was a Sabbath, the following important circumstance happened. When, according to custom, the Brethren after supper on that day had allotted the work for the week in presence of the Superintendent, and had ordered that these Brethren should work at the printing press, others in the book-bindery, several in the paper-mill and flour-mill, and others again at shoemaking, etc, the Superintendent spoke these weighty words in conclusion: "I now withdraw again from all that has been done, and leave it to God, in order to see what kind of a trial will come to me through this whole affair. For as yet I have no proof at hand by which I could know that God approves of it," etc. But when every person in the Settlement was wrapped in the first sleep, and the millers were going to the work assigned them, on their way they saw the mill all in flames. They, therefore, gave the necessary alarm in the whole Settlement. Everybody, Brethren as well as Sisters, ran to the fire in one of the coldest nights of the whole winter, and each one strove to be the first to quench the flames. But careful examination showed that all labor would be in vain, therefore they did not make the attempt. Finally it was tried, not without danger, to life, to extinguish a wall of burning logs; and thus an advantage was gained, and the fire kept within its bounds, so that the saw-mill (which had already commenced to burn) and the paper-mill, which stood without the above-mentioned wall of wood, were saved from being burnt.[1] Many suspected envious persons of having caused it, but careful examination showed that the fire originated at the fulling-press. Within four hours in this fatal night, the whole flour-mill with three stones and a great quantity of wheat were consumed; a skillfully built oil-mill, with stones the like of which none before existed in America, besides a large store of oil, and above 500 bushels of flaxseed. A complete fulling-mill with all that belongs to it.

Thus did the fire, with God's permission, make an end of all the mammon which the Eckerlins by their flaying, scraping and miserly conduct had gathered in the former household. The old-time confidence in God was sought to be gained again, for the most of the Solitary remembered quite well how they formerly had often worked in the bakery for a long time, the supply being wonderfully increased without human help. Here the Superintendent again began to appeal to God, who had imposed such burdens on him; for all the supply of bread in the Settlement was only enough to last for eight days. This moved the Fathers of the Community to hold a conference among themselves, in which one addressed the Community in the following way: "You, Brethren, what is to be advised in the matter? You all know that the mill of the Brethren and all its contents have been turned into ashes, and in addition that the bake-house in Ephrata, from

---

[1] Although this mill was the cause of the Solitary Brethren engaging in all kinds of worldly pursuits, in oppositon to their heavenly calling, it nevertheless must be acknowledged that it was of great benefit to the household, for the poor Solitary have obtained their bread by it now for nearly fifty years. Therefore it is to be supposed that it had little favor to expect from the world-spirit and from the people who belong to it. This is proved not only by the conflagration of that time, but by the fact that after this mill had been rebuilt, in the year 1784, envious people dared to burn it down again, and to start the fire in a place which was overfilled with combustible material, occasioning a terrible conflagration, which, however, was early discovered and extinguished.

which eighty Solitary Brethren and Sisters obtained their sustenance, is entirely empty. It would be very well if we would agree among ourselves to retrieve this loss." This speech opened their hearts so that every house-father willingly sacrificed all he had that was not needed for his own household for the service of the Solitary. And because all this proved insufficient they bought of their neighbors so much besides as they considered necessary until the mill should again be rebuilt. May God recompense them on the day of judgment.

But this was not the end of their goodness. For after a consultation had been held about the matter, the whole Community offered to assist in every way to rebuild the mill for the Solitary Brethren. This was a wished-for opportunity for the Superintendent, since it had been his desire long ago to see the house-fathers have an interest in the mill, because it had thus far had the name of being the property of the Solitary Brethren, on which account he was afraid the Sisters might some day fall short. The rebuilding of the mill was, therefore, commenced with great energy by the Community and the Solitary Brethren during the coldest season of the year, so that already six weeks after the fire one set of stones was again in operation. I must not forget to mention at this place how remarkably God moved the hearts of the neighbors, so that everyone, according to his ability, contributed wood or helped with his team. And because these people were mostly people of the great religious denominations, their impartiality was all the more wonderful. The Brethren showed themselves grateful for it in later times and assisted them in every way at the building of their church.

After the mill was finished, with the help of the Community, the Superintendent became debtor before God to the domestic households, because they had shown so much faithfulness to the work of God at the time when the Solitary were so severely chastened; wherefore he sacrificed himself and all his property to the service of the Community. For, as already mentioned, there existed a disagreement between the Solitary and the domestic household, which it was not easy to remove, in which the household, because it stood nearest the world-realm, mostly had the worst; but as God had given the balance into the hands of the Superintendent, the latter preserved the equilibrium, and did not permit the Solitary to hold the married in dishonor on account of their condition. So he also brought it about that half of the new mill was awarded to the Community as a reward for their faithful services, to which the Solitary Brethren agreed. Thereupon the Community transferred their half to the Sisterhood as their particular property, and the Solitary Brethren gave a bill of emption to the afore mentioned Sisterhood for greater security. Through this the influence of the Solitary Brethren was not only sensibly weakened in the Community, but the household of the Sisters almost obtained the preponderance and commenced to get too strong for the Solitary Brethren; in consequence of which many vexations arose, of which I shall speak at another place.

After the building of the mill was completed, the printing of the Book of Martyrs was taken in hand, to which important work fifteen Brethren were detailed, nine of whom had their work assigned in the printing department, namely, one corrector, who was at the same time the translator, four compositors and four pressmen; the rest had their work in the paper-mill. Three years were spent on this book, though not continuously, for there was often a want of paper. And because at that time, there was little other business in the Settlement, the household of the Brethren got deeply into debt, which, however, was soon liquidated by the heavy sales of the book. The book was printed in large folio form, contained sixteen reams of paper, and the edition consisted of 1300 copies. At a council with the Mennonites, the price of one copy was fixed at twenty shillings, (about £1), which ought to be proof, that other causes than eagerness for gain led to the printing of the same.[2]

---

[2] This book eventually met with strange experiences during the Revolutionary war in America. When there was a great lack of all war-material and also of paper, the fact was betrayed that there was a large quantity of printed paper in Ephrata, which then was pretty soon confiscated. Many

That this Book of Martyrs was the cause of many trials among the Solitary, and contributed not a little to their spiritual martyrdom, is still in fresh remembrance. The Superintendent, who had started the work, had other reasons than gain for it. The welfare of those entrusted to him lay near his heart, and he therefore allowed no opportunity to pass which might contribute anything to it. Those three years, during which said book was in press, proved an excellent preparation for spiritual martyrdom, although during that time six failed and joined the world again. When this is taken into consideration, as also the low price, and how far those who worked at it were removed from self-interest, the biographies of the holy martyrs, which the book contains, cannot fail to be a source of edification to all who read them. Moderation and vigilance were observed during this task as strictly as ever in the convent; but everything was in such confusion, that in spite of all care, each had to submit to discipline at least once a day. God be praised that brotherly love did not suffer from it! The Superintendent visited this school of correction once every day, in order to preserve the balance among the Brethren.

About this time the domestic household had to experience perceptible changes, and certainly for the worse. Their children had in their young days lived according to the manner of the Community; their dress was simple; they also entered into the covenant of baptism; but the parents, instead of keeping them under the law during their youth, gave the freedom of the Gospel into their hands too early, so that vanity awoke within them, and being elated by their goodness, they took to scoffing, and soon to such an extent

---

protests were raised against this in the Settlement, and it was alleged, among the rest, that this might lead to evil consequences on account of the English army. They resolved not to give up anything voluntarily, but that it would have to be taken by force. Consequently there arrived two wagons and six soldiers, who took possession of all the copies of the Book of Martyrs, after making prompt payment for them. This gave great offence in the country, and many thought that the war would not end favorably for the country, because the memorials of the holy martyrs had been thus maltreated. At last, however, they were honored again, for some sensible persons bought in all that were left of them.

that none of the Solitary were willing to work with them. Having at last brought their parents to take their part, they abandoned the simple dress and clothed themselves after the fashion of the world. The Superintendent, who always was a true patron of the domestic household, took this much to heart. He spoke much with the parents, that under pretence of the Gospel they had surrendered their right over their children. But it was too late. An attempt was, however, made to stem the evil. Accordingly the 15th of May, 1749, was fixed as a day of fasting, repentance and prayer. On that day all abuses in the Community and among the Solitary were abolished as much as possible, and the parents, too, were prompted to burn the worldly dresses of their children. And because at that time the subject of matrimony was still weighing heavily on them, so that young people were obliged to follow disorderly ways in order to accommodate themselves to it, the youth were given their freedom, but so that it was done in the Lord, without consent of the parents.

About this time a young Brother, P. W.[3] by name, who wished to change his state, confided in the Superintendent and asked for one of his spiritual virgins. This, of course, was an encroachment upon the church government. But he consented, for he had as little right over the spiritual virgins as the great Apostle Paul himself. He, himself, attended the wedding and ordered one of the Solitary to perform the ceremony; but it resembled more a devotional meeting than a wedding. The Superintendent and his brother took leave of the bridegroom with a kiss, who opened his heart too far to them, and thus weakened the conjugal love between himself and his bride so much that they could not embrace each other for eight days. For the strife between the celestial Virgin and Eve's daughters for the possession of Adam's empty side is so severe that where the first takes hold all the others must give way. The bridegroom came to the Superintendent, and, with the bride's consent, asked for a separation, for they were still free. Accordingly the Brother who had united them was called for and asked whether he were

---

[3] [Peter Weitner.]

willing to separate them again? The answer was: "Rather than unite them." Thereupon he wrote two letters of divorce, which they signed, and thus renounced forever all right over each other. But it was not long before the bride repented. She took her bridegroom before court, where the letters of divorce were produced. The justices were astonished at this transaction, and one of them said: "By God, this man can do more than God and the king." Then they resolved to fetch the writer by a writ; it was, however, decided that they had no right over him, because he had only been the writer. They obliged the bridegroom to receive his bride, to which decree he submitted.

A door was also opened at that time to work upon the young people, a great number of whom were staying with the Brethren. Some had come from Germany, others attended the school. These were seized by the spirit of awakening, so that they commenced to hold prayer-meeting every morning and evening, and avoided the company of those who led a disorderly life. But the matter did not end there, for on December 2d, 1749, they immersed one another in the water, and on the same day held among themselves a love-feast and breaking of bread. The Fathers of the Community, when they saw heaven again open for their youth, took advantage of the opportunity; and when an overseer was appointed for them, they committed their boys to his care, so that in a short time their church increased to twenty-two members. Now the building of a house for them was commenced, which was to be called Succoth, for which purpose much lumber had already been prepared. For the Superintendent was anxious that this awakening should not fall into the care of strangers, wherefore also they were not permitted to unite in prayer with the Brethren, but a separate prayer-meeting was held for them alone. The house, however, was never completed.

It appears, however, that they were not satisfied with their first baptism, for they spoke with the Superintendent about it, who dared not deny them baptism on account of their youth, especially since there is proof that boys of such an age have been martyrs. Therefore he baptized six of them on December 18th, 1749. Some of the Community mutinied against it, and accused the Superintendent of wishing to introduce the baptism of children again. They also agreed among themselves not to break bread with them; but through this they fell away from charity, and left the Community. On the 22d of the same month six more were baptized, with the performance of which the Superintendent charged one of the Brethren. On the following January 30th, 1750, a breaking of bread was held for them, by which act they were completely incorporated into the Community, two of them, Daniel Wüster and Philip Beussel washing the feet of all the Brethren. After this institution had existed eighteen months, it again fell to pieces, whereby many were defrauded of their hopes; but the Superintendent was not affected by it, because he had not sought anything therefrom.

About the time that the printing of the Book of Martyrs referred to was commenced, the government of the Brethren underwent another change, and the Prior, Jethro by name, was dismissed from his office. When a new election was about to be held the Superintendent addressed the Brethren with great earnestness and admonished them to remember the future Prior in their prayers, because this office was fraught with great danger. As this was known to the Brethren none was willing to undertake it. But at last the choice fell upon one of the oldest Brethren, Eleazar. The above-mentioned Brother Jethro had indeed shown more liveliness in his administration than circumstances allowed him, and therefore was much exercised over this change, especially since he was enrolled with the printers and thus became a common Brother. He grew tired of life and longed for his dissolution. This had such an effect that he sickened, and after an illness of seven weeks and five days he laid aside his earthly tabernacle, October 12th, 1749, and on the following day was gathered to his Brethren. His leave-taking of the Brother who attended him was very edifying: "Good night," he said, "now I set out for eternity. May God reward you for the faithfulness you have shown to me; there we shall see each other again." He is still kept in blessed remembrance among the Solitary. And with this we will conclude this chapter.

CHAPTER XXVIII.

CONCERNING AN AWAKENING IN GIMSHEIM, IN THE PALATINATE, WHICH BROUGHT MANY PEOPLE TO THE SETTLEMENT. VERY SPECIAL CIRCUMSTANCES CONNECTED WITH A DROUGHT IN PENNSYLVANIA.

We now have to speak of the awakening in Gimsheim, which brought many people to the Settlement. Gimsheim is a considerable place in the Palatinate, situated between Worms and Oppenheim, on the Rhine. The Superintendent had an own Brother there, who had been converted by him. The Superintendent exchanged letters with him from Pennsylvania (see his 4th printed Theosophic Epistle, page 84), and there is cause to think that the first fire of this awakening originated in these letters. The chief men of the awakening were Lohman and Kimmel. As these, on one occasion, before their awakening, spent the night in the tavern with cards and drinking, they were so violently seized by the hand of God that they melted into tears and resolved to begin a better life. The thing was soon known by report, and they were joined by those who had a like intention. At last it came so far that they began to hold meetings in the fields or at other places, when the power of God revealed itself so wondrously that powers of prophecy were often felt among them. But since they avoided the church, the Roman Catholic and Reformed ministers sounded an alarm, and every Sunday thundered from their pulpits against these new Pietists, till at last they brought about that a commission was appointed by the chief bailiff in Altzey to look into the conduct of these people, and especially whether they were accustomed to sing and pray at their meetings, for this was forbidden under penalty. All but eighteen drew back at this examination, and the Reformed minister informed against these at the ecclesiastical council of the Palatinate in Heidelberg. The leaders of the awakening were then cited, tried, and found guilty; but before they reached home, the chief bailiff imposed a fine on them, and an execution of it was sent to Gimsheim. They paid the fine, but the affair was reported to the sovereign of the country, which had the result that the chief bailiff was ordered to remit the fine against the accused. By the death of the sovereign, however, which soon after took place, this was prevented. Therefore they were obliged to look to other places for liberty of conscience. They consequently went to Herrnhaag and Gelnhausen. But because they did not find what they wanted at those places, they determined to go to America.

In the year 1749 the first of them arrived in Pennsylvania, and soon turned their steps towards the Settlement; among these were some of the Superintendent's relations. The rest of his relatives arrived some years later, all of whom were poor people. This was a hard trial for the Superintendent, for how was it possible for him to acknowledge again the natural relationships from which he had severed himself at his first awakening. But the Community bore such love to its Superintendent, that it paid their passage. Thus every corner in the Settlement was for the time occupied by the persecuted, of whom the Brethren's and Sisters'. Houses gathered in many, all of whom eventually, however, joined the domestic household, except a few, who remained with the Sisters. The first arrivals, namely, four persons of the domestic household, were baptzied during October and November, 1749. In the year 1751 the leaders of said awakening, namely, Lohman and Kimmel, left Gimsheim, in company with some others, and arrived all well in Pennsylvania; but they experienced more difficulty in getting to the Settlement than those who had preceded them, for they were merchants, and therefore were much beset by the Pietists, who tried to entangle them in business affairs. But after they had successfully overcome this temptation, there was not one who did not go to the Settlement. This addition of new converts caused much work in the Settlement, for they hungered so after the bread of God, which comes from heaven, that their zeal roused the matrix of eternity so that powers of prophecy again were poured out. Hence several of them, in their spiritual intoxication, attempted to hand their possessions over to the Community, which, however, were not accepted. Meanwhile they professed that they had attained the aim of their awakening, and that they had no need to look for anything else.

In December of the year 1751, six more of them were baptized, namely, Henry Lohman, Jeremiah Niess and Valentine Henry, with their wives. On the 25th of that month a love-feast was held, to which said Lohman contributed the costs; but with Kimmel more difficulties arose, for it was conjectured that he would leave the Settlement again before being baptized. But at last, in the spring following, he and his helpmate also submitted to the rules of the new covenant, and his children afterwards followed his example. After having spent about six months in the Settlement, he moved to York county, in the neighborhood of the Bermudian, but after living there for several years, his helpmate was torn from him by death, which subjected him to severe temptations, since a second marriage was neither agreeable to his mind nor permitted according to apostolic church-government. When this became known in the Settlement the Solitary Brethren opened the door of their house to him; to whom he moved and where God compensated him for the loss of his wife, so that he lived with them for thirty years as a widower, and at last departed into eternity, in 1784, at a great age. These are the chief circumstances connected with the Gimsheim awakening, and how at last it was united with the awakening in the Settlement. May God grant that all of them reached the aim and end of their calling, or may yet reach it. But, to take up our narrative in proper order, all the married people of Gimsheim afterwards joined the said Kimmel and settled about the Bermudian. But because they were followed by some of the Community, of whom it was known that they avoided bearing witness to God, and could not endure its keenness, said region began to be suspected in the Settlement, so that nobody ventured to go there on a spiritual visit any more.

At that time Henry Lohman still lived in the Settlement. The Superintendent's mind was much occupied with this

Brother, because he was a man richly endowed by God, who, therefore, could be useful in building up the kingdom of Christ in this wilderness; besides he had had much experience during their awakening. On the other hand the Superintendent saw clearly that he could not make proper use of his talents in the Settlement, because the passion of Christ's body pervaded everything there and he might come in danger of losing his acquired good. Therefore he represented to him how great a want there was of faithful laborers in the vineyard of God, and how important it was to give himself up entirely to the service of God and his neighbors. Then he proposed to him that he also should move to the waters of Bermudian. "For," he said, "here I cannot any longer break bread with you, but when I seek you at the Bermudian I shall find you again and can then without difficulty break bread with you." The good Brother looked suspiciously at this talk, and could not but suppose that a pitfall was being dug for him; but when he afterwards saw by a a certain incident that it was the will of God, he submitted to the Superintendent's counsel and moved thither, where God gave so much work into his hands that he took upon himself the care of the Community. The privileges of a Community, however, were not accorded to them until Brother George Adam Martin joined the Settlement, through Lohman's interposition, of which we will treat hereafter. He was a man of great natural gifts, and for many years helped to keep the church in proper repair by his means, and he never refused his help to anyone who requested it, although he frequently received poor reward for it. We will not be responsible for his deficiencies; we put them upon the Mediator; and he himself would not wish it, if he were present. He survived the Superintendent by ten years, and was gathered to his people at the Bermudian; and may God give him there a blessed and happy resurrection!

The following was handed to the writer of this by the Superintendent himself as a fruit of his church-work, that it might be inserted here. The words run thus: The year 1751 and 1752 were so productive in wheat and other fruit that people in their thoughtlessness tried, out of mere wantonness, to waste this supply; for they fattened their pigs, which in their luxury they afterwards ate, with this precious wheat, on which many poor might have lived. Moreover distilling vessels were everywhere purchased and strong drinks distilled out of this blessed gift, which created great disorder. Thus affairs then stood in the worldly realm. But in the Settlement, especially in the Brotherhood, the Superintendent was greatly hindered in his spiritual work, wherefore he often complained that God was banished; he acknowledged also that he experienced essentially the same process through which Jonas passed in the belly of the whale. These were again difficult times for him; although the existing luxury in the worldly kingdom did not grieve him as much as to witness that sins against the Holy Ghost were committed in the midst of the sanctuary.[1]

Nevertheless he took it much to heart that the inhabitants of the country abused the gifts of God in such a manner, therefore he once wrestled with God in his prayers in this way: "Thou good God, Thou seest how shamefully the inhabitants of the country abuse Thy gifts of love. Canst Thou, O God, stand still at their doings? Thou hast means and ways sufficient to check this evil, for Thou art not honored by it but dishonored! It is indeed not for me to dictate to Thee the means and ways, because Thou art master of Thy gifts and wishes. But may it please Thee to see to it, that in future the inhabitants of the land may not be able so often to enjoy Thy gifts of love, because Thou, O God, art more dishonored than honored thereby." This happened in the year 1752. For three summers thereafter, such a drought followed, that not only plants withered but the poor beasts, too, almost died of hunger. Now it always had happened that

---

[1] After the rule of the Eckerlins in the Settlement had been overthrown, the Brethren ought to have cultivated willing obedience, because compulsion was at an end, (although the Eckerlins never abused any of the Brethren, however strict their regime had been; though they had abused their spiritual guide). After their fall, however, the whole household went too far in the opposite direction; for wherever there were any rules, they were considered remnants of the Eckerlin management. Therefore the Superintendent once said to the Brethren: God can judge the Eckerlins, for they came so near him; but your quarrels he cannot judge, because they are too far removed from him.

such public distress awakened people, who placed themselves in the breach, in order to stem the evil (see II SAM. XXI); and noboby took this severe judgment more to heart than the Superintendent. It pained him most that no one sought for the causes of this severe judgment, nor repented of the sins previously committed. He several times endeavored to better matters by prayer, in which he so far succeeded that it rained, though there was no blessing in it, because the judgment which was lying on the land was not revoked by it. Whenever he laid the distress of the country before God in his prayers, it was always brought back to his mind how he had put it before God at the time when he strove with him about the blessings he had vouchsafed the country. This embarrassed him all the more. Therefore he warned against finding fault with God on account of benefits he had bestowed upon mankind.

About the same time God brought it about that the Brethren in Bethany were again reconciled with the Superintendent, and thus a door was opened which brought a blessing upon all church movements. They had for a long time neglected their Night Watches during this dry season, but now the Superintendent said to them: "As soon as you will begin your Night Watches again it will rain," which, indeed, it did; for during the first night heavy showers fell; but it was too late, the vegetation was already dried up. When, as mentioned, a door had again been opened for good among the Brethren, the Prior applied to the Superintendent and told him that he and several of the Brethren intended to pay him a visit, in order to see whether anything could be done for the good of the country. This address gave into the hands of the Superintendent the key with which to open heaven again. And after the judgment which rested on the land, and to which the Brethren had contributed a great deal by their refractoriness, had been removed, the Superintendent also was permitted by God to take back what three years before he had laid before him in regard to the country.

A blessed year followed. The elements again proved favorable to the country; wet and dry alternated; everthing proffered its riches for the sustenance of man, for which the name of God must be praised. Amen.

CHAPTER XXIX.

CONTINUATION OF THE HISTORY OF THE ECKERLINS TO ITS END.

After the former Prior, together with his own brother and two other Brethren, namely Timotheus and Ephraim, had left their place in the Settlement of the Solitary, and had moved towards the wilderness, they built their lonely hut on the banks of the New River, on very fruitful soil, and called the place Mahanaim. When they commenced to inhabit their huts it was revealed to Brother Timotheus at night, in a dream, that the Indians were about to lay their hermitage in ruins; and because they actually arrived in a few days and laid waste their corn he revealed his dream to the Eckerlins, who answered him that if he had no faith in this way of living they would not object to his leaving them again. He, therefore, transferred his hut to them, said good night to the Solitary life, and returned to his people in Germantown, from whom he had come. The other Brother, called Ephraim, soon followed him, and ended his life at the house of a merchant of Philadelphia. These were two important proofs that a life chosen by our own will, if it appear to be ever so holy, finds no acceptance with God. Thus the three brothers alone were left, each of whom chose a special mode of making a livelihood. Jephune, the oldest, applied himself to medicine, and spent his time among the people on the border. The other, the former Prior, occupied himself with writing, of which we will speak hereafter. But the youngest, Jonathan, became a hunter, an employment which is unfit for a Solitary, and which was looked upon with much suspicion in the Settlement. Altogether they soon became aware of their mistake; but the Prior, under whose influence the two other brothers stood, was a venturesome fellow, and still hoped to bring the Community in the Settlement to bow down before him, as the sons of Jacob did before Joseph. We are assured that the said Jonathan shed so many tears that it was feared he might lose his sight, for the Superintendent loved him so dearly on account of his innocent youth that, as already mentioned, he once omitted all divine service in the Settlement until he had freed him from the snares of the tempter. His brother also testified of him that it would have been impossible for them to remain on the New River another day, such was his hunger for their mother-church. They had little or nothing to do with anything relating to divine worship, because they early fell into the fetters of free-thinking; besides they thought meanly of the church ordinances in the Settlement, such as the Sabbath, baptism, breaking of bread, etc., for they pretended to honor God in a more important way.

After the Brethren in the Settlement became aware that the rod of the taskmaster was broken, and that they were no longer kept captive under the rule of the Eckerlins, they dropped their violent opposition to them; so also the Eckerlins, who had obtained all their power in the Settlement from the opposition of the Brethren—when they perceived that this had subsided, thought it a favorable opportunity to visit the Settlement; and on February 23d, 1750, the two brothers, Onesimus and Jonathan, arrived in the neighborhood of the Settlement. As soon as this became known to the Brethren they assembled in their meeting-hall, with their Superintendent, and sent two delegates to them to welcome them, and offer them shelter in their convent, which these two Brethren thankfully accepted. Then both parties embraced each other in the Brethrens' meeting-hall, which was so edifying to behold that it did not pass off without tears, because the Philadelphian brotherly spirit was then revived among Brethren who for many a year had eaten the bread of misery together.

The Eckérlins were astonished at such kind behavior on the part of the Brethren, and offered not only to live with the Brethren again, as regarded their own persons, but also to deposit all their acquired property in the treasury of the Brethren. The Superintendent answered that they must bear patiently with us, as we had become a bad people after their departure; which gave them the more courage.

Thereafter they attended the evening meeting of the Brethren, and as many house-fathers were present at the time, these, too, received them with special love and admonished them to return again to the Brethren. After this they resolved to visit their friends here and there in the country; but because the opinion was everywhere prevalent that they were inimical to the Solitary in the Settlement, they requested the Superintendent to give them a travelling companion. He appointed one who had formerly been the best friend of the Prior, but who had separated from him on account of his rebellion. At every place to which they came the people were astonished at the sudden change, and many worked up the old lies again, namely, that the Superintendent was a sorcerer and had drawn these two brothers into the Settlement by witchcraft. And since the said Prior, during his administration, had greatly wronged the Baptists by his judgments, he now tried to make amends. This he did to Peter Becker and Gantz, near Germantown, the latter of whom was a special enemy of the Superintendent, and commonly called him an arch-heretic. But even if the good Onesimus had in some measure been guilty, this recantation would not have been necessary; but herein lies the reason why God cannot get any more witnesses to condemn the sins of men; for if the sin and wickedness of men come upon them they recant, and so God loses his honor by them, as happened to Traut, Tennhard and several others in our fatherland.

When they returned to the Settlement, after this visit, they prepared for their departure again. At the leave-taking the former Prior put £40 into the treasury of the Brethren, and it was supposed that he did it for conscience sake, either because they had robbed the treasury at their departure, or because he had formerly taken that sum out of it in order to bribe the Mother of the Sisters, as mentioned above; and therefore the money was not returned to him. After the Eckerlins had taken such an edifying farewell, they went their way back to their lonely homes. Thereupon two Brethren of the Settlement, Nathanael and Manasse, were sent after them, who were instructed to assist them in properly arranging their affairs.

But because their journey back was delayed on account of business, the time hung too heavily for the good Prior, so he started alone and came to the Settlement April 25th, 1750, which he did with good enough intentions but without sufficient consideration; for had he arrived in company with his brothers, he would again have been appointed to an important office in the Settlement, and if afterwards several Brethren had sided with them, the balance would have been restored. But he arrived alone and did not know whether or not he had a friend in the Settlement who would venture his life for him. Though as regards the Superintendent's faithfulness, that was not to be doubted, for he offered to give himself into the Prior's hands, and to go with him wherever he wished, on condition that the Prior would be answerable for him, which the Prior did not venture to do. But when it now came so far that the Prior was to be a common Brother again, the Superintendent was obliged to let the affair take its own course, and was not permitted to interfere between the schools of the Brethren. The only thing he could do was to pray and supplicate at the throne of grace for a blessed outcome. It seems, however, that a high hand impelled the Prior so that the Superintendent's innocence might come to light, because the country at large had the wrong impression that the Superintendent had persecuted the Prior. In this mirror all those awakened persons who have left their posts may see themselves reflected; for as long as the road leads to the cross God's presence is assured; but if you flee from the cross God stays behind. Thus it may happen that if God's plan is not fulfilled through the awakening the whole game is wonderfully turned around; for then first the mystery of wickedness comes out of its concealment and does not stop until it has brought to light its first and last-born son; as happened to this good Brother.

For when he had returned to Bethany, and attended their Night Watches for the first time, his old habit of long preaching, by which in former times he had rendered the life of the poor Brethren so very wearisome, again awoke within him; which showed that his retirement had benefitted him little, and had not helped to bring him to himself, and how could that have been possible? Did he not run away from his school? And because he did not endure the trial, the desire to be a minister was not killed in him. The Brethren patiently listened to him for a while, but told him at last that this might do for novices, but they who had already walked this road for many a year were not in need of it any more; at least that it was now plainly proved, that the Brethren in Bethany were able to live without the addition of any Eckerlins. Therefore he not only absented himself from the devotions of the Brethren, but the tempter succeeded so far with him, that he left their convent, and at his request a house was consigned to him in the Settlement, with the assurance that he might live there according to his conscience, without being obliged to bear the common burdens; and that he should receive his sustenance from the Community as long as he lived.

The Superintendent, it is true, saw in the spirit that the Prior would yet have a great fall; but since he had torn himself away from the Brotherhood, he was not able to help him. Nevertheless he once visited him in company with another Brother at his own house. They brought the holy bread along, and solemnly promised him not to have fellowship with any Prior or other Brother to his disadvantage. In this house he fell so deeply into the power of the spirits of temptation that he could no longer help himself. He made visits, and at one time was away from his house for three weeks; but on his return he found everything as he had left it. Moreover, men whose fathers he would not have thought worthy to be given a place among his shepherd dogs came to him to advise him. At last he commenced to alter his clothes, from which everybody saw his intentions; for, whenever a Solitary intends to leave the Order, he first alters his dress, and that is a sign that he has renounced simplicity, wherefore also he will be more readily received again by the world. After he had spent five months and six days more here he moved away on October 2d, 1750, and went to a neighbor, Jacob Sontag; at which removal he spoke these significant words: that he would rather be burned at the stake seven times than return to live again at the Settlement. But it troubled him not a little that his brothers, of whom he knew that they were on the road, might arrive at the Settlement during his absence, according to their agreement, and be received by the Brethren to his disadvantage. Therefore he spent the whole day on the public road. Meanwhile his oldest brother, Jephune, arrived in the Settlement at midnight and found the baker of the Community just at his work, whom he asked how his Brother was doing. He answered: "Your brother ran off for the second time." At this he began to weep and went back again to his team. At last they met each other on the road, when he asked them where they were going? They answered: "To Ephrata, according to our agreement." To this he replied: "If you go to Ephrata you shall have no part in me forever." Here the reader again has proof of the power a carnal relationship has to turn men away from God; for had they withstood him and adhered to the agreement they had made in the Settlement, they might have turned his mind towards better things and prevented his misfortune. But it seems the sins they had incurred were too great, therefore they were struck with blindness and could not see what tended to their peace.

After he had brought his brothers over to his side they brought their Indian wares to market and traded them for other goods and prepared for their return to the wilderness; but because winter was at the door the Brethren offered them shelter until the weather should be milder, which they modestly declined and started on their journey. However, when they came to the Alleghany Mountains they met with such masses of snow that it was with great danger that they crossed these fearful mountains and came to inhabited regions. Then they directed their journey towards the Ohio River, into the neighborhood of the place where the French at the time were building a fort, named Duquesne. Here they placed themselves under the protection of the Delaware Indians who showed them great friendship. At that time one of the Brethren in the Settlement wrote to the Prior that now one of three things would fall to his lot: he would either be obliged to return again to his people, or be an instrument for the conversion of these Indians, or would have to live in harlotry with demons. This last pained him much, for a Solitary who neither approaches a carnal woman nor the church-wife falls at last into the hands of demons, which are barren spirits from out eternity; wherefore also the natural married state, on account of its fruitfulness is opposed by them, and it is in this sense that Paul calls the forbidding of marriage a doctrine of the demons.

About this time a bloody war commenced between England and France, in which all the Indians took the part of the French. The Delawares, therefore, told the Eckerlins that they could not any longer guarantee them safety, as the French savages would overrun those regions. They, therefore, led them to a region which the Indians believed would seldom be visited by their people, and said at the same time, that they would warn them whenever danger approached. This place was high up in the mountains, on a stream called Cheat River, which empties into the Monongahela River. There they built a well-arranged hermitage for themselves, kept servants, horses, etc., as if they had to supply a large household. But there the mystery of wickedness awoke in the Prior in its innermost essence; and because a perverse spirit ruled him, all the good which he had reaped in the Settlement was turned into mockery. Therefore, instead of examining his record during the few remaining days of his life, in view of the great day of eternity, he wrote the most scornful letters to the Community. To read his first letter to the Community took five hours, and as it was full of reviling and ridicule it was resolved not to accept any such letter in future. It did not last long, however, before his oldest brother, Jephune, made his appearance at a meeting, with a writing covering fifty sheets and asked permission to read it. The Fathers of the Community gave him permission, provided it contained peaceful matter. But he had hardly commenced to read before the former things of Ishmael's church again occurred; wherefore he was forbidden to continue. Consequently he took those excrements to the friends in Germantown, so that by all means the Eckerlin's apostasy from God might be sure to become manifest everywhere.

At that time two Brothers, Henry Sangmeister and Anthony

Höllenthal, left the Settlement and settled as hermits on the river Schannedor,[2] in Virginia; but as they preferred an unfettered life to the discipline of God, which still reigned in the Settlement, they joined the Eckerlins; for like joins like, whereby they became participants in the judgment which rested on these, although they had not yet committed as many offences in the Settlement. This Sangmeister once brought a large manuscript of the Prior to the printer in the Settlement, which contained an account of the falling away in Ephrata, and desired to have it printed. The printer sent him the reply that the first writings which he had produced in the Settlement he had brought from the starry sky, but this last out of that dark region where brother-hate reigned, and that he did not want to have anything to do with such things. The messenger was ill pleased with this; he would have it printed at some other place, for the country should now realize that the Prior was a prophet. But it was not done; nor was his prophecy fulfilled, that the Indians would come to take vengeance on the Settlement, because the Brethren had resisted them, and had sought to trample under foot an innocent man and witness of God. That this same judgment should soon overtake themselves, was at this time hidden from them. In their seclusion they lived in greatest security in the midst of the war; they raised horses, cleared land and made good use of the chase and other advantages of the country. At one time the Iroquois went to war against the northern Indians; it was winter, and they were so unlucky that they had to flee in nakedness. So they took all their clothes and carpets from the Eckerlins, and then left. This should have been a warning to them. The Delaware Indians also sent word that they would no longer be secure at that place. But they took it to be a fable. They sometimes went to Virginia, and usually after their return home, the Indians invaded Virginia, which created the suspicion that the Eckerlins were spies, on which account the Prior was at one time kept captive in a fort. But when the Virginians did not want to let them live there any longer, Samuel Eckerlin tried to

---

[2] [Shenandoah?]

get permission to do so from the governor of Virginia; but it was refused, and a company of soldiers sent with him, in order to take his brothers safely to inhabited regions. They were not very far from their hermitage when seven hostile Mohawk Indians, under the command of a Frenchman, attacked it. The servant gave the alarm, but the Prior did not allow himself to be disturbed in his writing until they bound his hands on his back; they packed all their property on horses, of which these hermits possessed a great number, set the house on fire and decamped with their prisoners. Meanwhile Samuel Eckerlin arrived with the soldiers, while the fire was still glowing under the ashes. This distressing sight brought tears to his eyes; he stepped aside and allowed them to flow; an Indian who was concealed there, lying in wait according to their custom, to see whether anyone was looking after them, was moved by his tears to spare his life.

Now let us lay before the reader the further fortunes and misfortunes of the above-mentioned Prior and of his brother Jotham to their end, following the account obtained from their fellow prisoners. Because an English army, under General Forbes, was at the time on its march to besiege Fort Duquesne, the Indians made a wide detour to said fort to avoid the English. It took them eight days to make this journey, on which they were sorely maltreated by the Indians, who cut off the beard of one of them so that a part of the cheek adhered to it. At the said fort they sold the two brothers to the French; but their servant, Schillig by name, they kept for themselves. During a severe season the French took their prisoners across the lakes to Montreal, where they were for some time lodged in the Jesuit College. From there they were sent to Quebec, where they had to endure a hard winter on poor fare; yet the Canadians had so much respect for a hermit's life, that they permitted them at times to beg in the town, and thus they became an object of pity to many, for which may God reward them. They wished to leave this unfriendly region in the coming spring, but there were no "flags of truce" there, such as used to go from there to Halifax with prisoners, so they resolved to let themselves be transported to France, along with other prisoners. They indeed arrived there, but both afflicted with a distemper, which also transported them to eternity. The Prior, when he felt his end approaching, had himself received as a member of an Order of Monks of the Roman church, which is the more credible as he had always entertained a particular esteem for friars. They gave him the tonsure, and afterwards called him Bon Chretien. Soon after both brothers departed this life.

Such was the end of the first Prior of the Brethren. He lived but forty-six years, and was of a short, solid and strongly built figure. Of his awakening we have inserted his own account. We have seen his hut in the wilderness, where he lived for a considerable length of time, secluded from men, but at last had to give it up again, otherwise, he said, he would have lost his reason. After this he came under the guardianship of a Brother, Amos by name, who lived very austerely, and there, according to his testimony, he enjoyed the most blessed days of the whole period of his awakening. But because the Superintendent had selected him for a higher schooling, he was not permitted to remain in this lower grade any longer. As long as the Superintendent influenced him by his spirit, he was an humble and merciful person, and so long his own brothers were his greatest opponents. He was often seen to roll himself on the ground for grief when he saw that Brethren missed their calling, or fell back into the arms of the world. But at last he began to waver in his confidence in the Superintendent, and sided with his brothers; in consequence of which he and the Superintendent had important experiences between them, which induced him to open the door to the tempter. He determined to gain an independent position, and to obtain the privilege of his office directly from God. Those who were used for his overthrow were his most faithful Brethren. But there was no help for it, for the Prior had the seed of the spirit of Korah's rout within him, and if much care had not been taken the awakened in the Settlement would at last have been turned into nothing but Antichrists, just as the first Christians would have been seduced by the example of Ananias, and would have trampled under foot God's testimony, if vengeance had not been taken on him.

The remarkable thing in the affair is, that when the Prior had thus laid before God his purpose to break loose from the Superintendent, as mentioned above, his plan was accepted by God, and that he could not undo it until his death, although he made several attempts. God is to each man just as He is sought to be. He is pious to the pious, and wicked to the wicked; and herein lies the greatest danger in an awakening, wherefore also the good Master taught us to pray: Lead us not into temptation. And with this let us conclude the tragedy of the Eckerlins, and also this chapter.

CHAPTER XXX.

How the Country was Visited by War, and How the Solitary in the Settlement Fared by It. About the Quiet in the Land. Also the Prior's Office is Given to Another Brother.

When this bloody war commenced, and the flames of it had already seized the neighboring provinces, Pennsylvania enjoyed quiet and peace; and everybody had so much confidence in the good understanding between the so-called Quakers and the Indians that it was thought this province would not be involved in the war. But, before it was thought of, the Indians overran the back counties, and this at a time when disagreement existed in the councils of the country with regard to resistance, some advocating a standing army, others militia service. According to the situation of the land and the manner of the Indians, who always traverse a country in a straight line, the Paxton road would have led them from Shamokin to Ephrata; but arriving at the north side of the Blue Mountains they turned to the left along these mountains, and therefore the inhabitants of Gnadenhütten had to fall the first victims of their revenge. That region became for a long time the theatre of war, and much human blood was shed before the inhabitants received help, and the New Jersey militia raided across the Delaware and gained some advantage over the enemy.

At that time a good understanding existed between those at the head of the government and the Solitary, although the common people were not well pleased with them, because they did not take up arms. Whenever the Governor proclaimed a fast for the country, his secretary showed so much respect for the Solitary that he sent them a copy, and then they united with the country in divine service, and observed their fasting most scrupulously. At such times you might have heard the Superintendent fervently pray to God for the success of the King's arms. But the time had not yet come to grant these prayers, for there were sins lying upon the country which it had to expiate; therefore they had to turn their backs to the enemy, and God ordered it so that the English General Braddock was defeated. (See JUDGES Chap. XX, where the children of Israel could not humble the tribe of Benjamin, before they themselves had been humbled.) The Christian disposition of the Superintendent and of the Solitary during this distress of the country, of which it may be they also were partly a cause, gained them the confidence of many people of high and low degree; and they were anxious not to disappoint their confidence. Many a time Ephrata was full of red-coats, because everybody was intent upon learning something of their strange way of living. The officers could not see enough of the Superintendent, for the wine-press, which tormented the inner man, showed forth in his bearing and caused everyone who saw him to become favorably disposed towards him. When the officers would hand him a present they took it to be a high honor if it was accepted by him. Governor Denny, of Pennsylvania, through an interpreter, had a special conference with him in the Sisters' prayer-room, concerning the condition of the country, in which the Governor promised him and the Order all protection, and he agreed in return to remember the country before God. In the same way, whenever the enemy made a new inroad, the poor people would send messengers into the country for help, when their distress would be brought before the meeting and a liberal collection made for them in the Community.

Meanwhile the enemy daily approached nearer to the Settlement of the Solitary, and was now only thirteen miles distant. Fugitives fled to Ephrata and sought protection from those who themselves needed it. Messengers daily brought new reports of murders, which they usually augmented by further additions. Then the hearts of all the Solitary became timid; even the Superintendent turned pale, which none had ever seen before. This determined the Fathers of the Community to offer their wagons in order to bring the Sisterhood, which was most exposed to danger, further down into the country. Thereupon a council was held, in which the Sisters declared that they would be a burden wherever they went; they were determined to stay, and in case of necessity assemble in the prayer-hall and there await the result from God. It appears that this unexpected resolution touched the heart of God, for the following night the Superintendent had a revelation from God, in accordance with which he summoned the Brethren and informed them that he had received the assurance from God that none of the Solitary should die at the hands of the Indians; but that we were still in danger from our own countrymen. For many had bound themselves by oath not to march against the enemy until every non-combatant in the country had been massacred. At the same time a report was spread over the country, and nobody knows who did it, that Ephrata was to be burnt down at a certain time, so that some of the neighbors made preparation to go to the assistance of the poor Solitary. But God brought their designs to naught, for which his name be praised.

This address of the Superintendent had the effect that everybody again pursued his business as if peace reigned in the land, at which many were amazed. The Superintendent after this made several visits into the region where the danger was and spoke encouragingly to the people, as God moved him; and it always happened that the enemy came either shortly before his arrival or soon after it. Once he journeyed with a large company on account of church matters to Antitum, in Cumberland county, to which place he had been summoned. He heard on his way that the enemy had killed the schoolmaster and seven children; he, nevertheless, continued his way and attended to his work there, although not safe from the enemy for one hour. These are the circumstances attending the war.

Before the war broke out a company of awakened people of both sexes arrived in Philadelphia about midnight from Altoona under the leadership of a scholar, named Ludovic. The venturesomeness of these people was amazing. They had neither baggage nor any money for the journey; they wandered about in the city in the dark, until the watchmen seized them, and supposing them to be Moravian Brethren, took them to a Brethren's House. After more careful examination, however, it was discovered that their religious views were nearest to those held in the Settlement; therefore some sent the report thither that some of their Brethren had arrived from Germany, and that they should take care of them. Upon this, visitors were sent to them, when a distinct mutual agreement of views was revealed, although only as regards their doctrines; they had good intentions but no experience. Their leader and some of the others concluded to pay a visit to the Settlement. With this the friends in Germantown were not at all satisfied, and accused the Brethren of always attempting to fish the best men away from them, for they intended erecting a new church of the Spirit. The Brethren promised to return their visitors to them again. But they especially warned the good Ludovic against the Pious in Pennsylvania, saying that it was their way to extol a person to the heavens, but that it only lasted until they had spied out his deficiencies, then he might depart in dishonor; all of which happened to the good Ludovic in full measure.

These visitors were worthily received in the Settlement. The Superintendent especially communicated with the said Ludovic in all sincerity, for he had a pure virgin spirit, and all his people lived a life of continence. He believed in community of goods and adult baptism, according to the apostolic ordinance, although he himself had not attained to this, for in order to do this he would have had to lower himself a little before that which was inferior to him, and for this his wings were not yet grown. Nevertheless he gave his assent to everything, and confessed this to be the Community which he had sought. He several times broke bread with them, though his Sisters never did even this. When he arrived again in Germantown he earnestly engaged in the work of building up the church, for which a door was opened to him ever and anon. In particular they arranged for divine service in a house which a merchant had assigned to them, by which they first made themselves suspected to their patrons in Germantown, for these had already many years ago separated themselves from the services of the great churches. Therefore they were not a little vexed when they saw him in meeting dressed in a black coat and priestly vestments; and just as much as they had favored him before, so much they now tried to get rid of him, all of which the Brethren had prophesied of him. Honest old Saur, knowing well that Ludovic stood in high credit with the Brethren, informed them of the whole affair, adding that he had no desire to carry any more manure to this tree, as it was already too fat. When the friends in Germantown perceived that he was pregnant with a new sect, and had not abandoned the hierarchical spirit, they began to despair of his church building, while he on the other hand thought very meanly of the American revival spirit, and wrote to the Superintendent that he was now entirely at an end with the awakened in Pennsylvania, and if he had not found a true heart in Ephrata the next thing for him would be to return to Germany. The Superintendent, in answer to this, explained to him by letter the difference between American and German awakenings, among the rest in the following words: "It is an undisputed fact that in Germany the church-government of the new covenant neither can nor dare step forth, for either the little boys are drowned in the water or the little girls are smothered at birth, so that neither a priestly nor a virgin race can grow up there." And at another place he says: "Be it known, that even the magisterial office in Pennsylvania is not yet conducted in the strength of the dragon and of the great beast, but, with its judgments, stands under the authority of the saints, on which account not a few of those whom I know would soon be taught differently by the beast, should they administer their office in Germany as they do here. He, therefore, must praise Pennsylvania very highly in view of the eternal Providence of God, which so ordered it, that the spiritual lineage of the covenant, a priestly and virgin race, is again sought out, and thus a sanctuary is built, where the long dead priesthood is as a dry branch planted to grow in everlasting verdure," etc.

Soon after he and his company settled in the barony of Lancaster, on the Pequea creek; although they knew nothing either of agriculture or breeding cattle, they rented a small farm, and besides had the good luck to find a merciful neighborhood which abundantly provided for them. Here he laid aside his old name and was called Melchizedek by his people, which he most likely borrowed from the Solitary. Here he also engaged in an important correspondence, in which he, as a scholar, had the advantage over a man who possessed nothing except what he had learned in the school of the Holy Spirit. But the Superintendent caused another Brother to answer his letters. The same asked him who gave him the right to make reason the judge in divine matters? (For the said Ludovic was a good disciple of Wolff.) Whether Abraham took counsel with his reason when he sacrificed his son to God? He also told him that he would have to surrender something to God before he could enter into any degree of fellowship with him. This last vexed him most. He demanded what it was that he would have to surrender. But this nobody could tell him; he ought to have found it out from within himself. After this wordy dispute had lasted for some time the Superintendent pronounced the following verdict on it, namely: That he had vanquished the Brother with his philosophy, but the Brother had vanquished him with his experience.

Meanwhile he labored to execute his plan of a new church building, but because the human will dominated in the matter, all hearts were closed against it so that no one wanted to have anything to do with it. The Superintendent wrote several letters to him concerning it, full of unction, in which he represented to him that the household at Ephrata had been born by a holy chance, without the will of man, and that on this account the tempter had been unable to gain anything from it. Finally he frankly declared that of the following one would happen to them: either God would help them, and then sorrow would dwell with them; or it would turn out to be an ungodly success, or their ship would be shattered, and then they would have to save themselves by swimming, which last indeed happened to them. But he would not be convinced of this. He represented to the Community, that, because the establishment of such an institution at Ephrata had met with success by the blessing of God, they were bound also to assist others. This claim availed so much that it was promised to build them a large and spacious house; but as those who had promised to procure the land for the new household did not keep their promise, nothing came of the matter. Amid these strange circumstances the good Ludovic was transplanted into eternity, and their ship was shattered, according to the Superintendent's prediction. Thereupon some of his followers married, and the others returned to their native country.

Before we conclude this chapter let us mention that at about the same time a change in the church government was again made in the Settlement; for the then Prior lost his office, whereupon some of the Brethren undertook the management of the household; but since the office demanded a special person, the same was a second time put on the shoulders of Brother Jabez, during whose administration the Superintendent ended his life.

CHAPTER XXXI.

The Community at Ephrata is Extended by an Awakening, for Which Two Brethren of the Baptist Congregation, George Adam Martin and John Horn, Prepared the Way.

This awakening took place during the above-mentioned war, and may have commenced about the year 1757. The members of this awakening, as well as their teacher, George Adam Martin, before this belonged to the Baptists, but left that congregation, induced by circumstances which had their first start with the said George Adam Martin. The causes of this separation are too outrageous to call for a special investigation here, and besides it is not permitted to trouble the reader with the like of it at this place. But because the said George Adam Martin handed in a writing, in which he minutely described how he was awakened, and how he had lived for a time with the Baptists, but at last united himself with the Community at Ephrata, we will give an extract from it, and then leave it to the consideration of the reader. This document is the answer to the question of a friend, why he had separated from the Baptists and gone over to the Seventh Day Saints. He speaks thus of his conversion: In the year 1733 I was strongly moved to repentance and a change of life, and all without any man's intervention, which confused me so that I did not know what to do. For my heart was troubled. Wherever I went or was my conscience was so disturbed that I avoided all company and felt grieved at any vanity I met with. I was constantly frightened and alarmed, for my conscience smote me everywhere; besides I was young, bashful and timid. I therefore went about like a lost sheep, and thought all people better than myself, which opinion indeed I still have. I never looked for much from men, and if I occasionally listened to some one preaching, I was not frightened by it, because I felt myself more damned than any preacher could damn me; nevertheless some little hope remained, and I thought perchance I might yet be saved. Being in such a condition I was baptized on my faith in the year 1735. This I did to honor God in Christ Jesus and intended to follow him; but had no further thought about the piety of a Community, because my inner troubled state did not permit me to think about other things. All my thinking and striving were only as to how I might enter the kingdom of God.

After my baptism, when alone in the woods, I knelt down behind a tree and prayed. After I had finished it came into my mind to open the New Testament, and whatever I found under my right thumb that should be my precept during life. Then I turned up: "Study to show thyself approved unto God, a workman that needeth not to be ashamed, rightly dividing the word of truth" (II TIMOTHY, II, 15). This troubled my mind excessively; sometimes I took it to be a temptation; then, again, as if I had tempted God; and again that the Spirit had mocked me. Taking all together I did not know what to make of it. To become a workman in the church of God, that I dared not harbor in my mind. Soon after I was led into such temptation for about sixteen weeks that I incessantly heard nothing but: "You are damned! you are damned!" This frightened me so that I enjoyed neither sleep, nor eating or drinking. My father asked me what was the matter with me, but I dared not tell him, for I thought that never before had a person lived on earth in such a damnable state. At last I was delivered out of this bondage, received pardon, and became a recipient of the gracious visitation of my God in Christ Jesus, and of the power of regeneration, of which before I had known nothing. Thus by grace and compassion alone I became one of the redeemed of the Lord. After this I became cheerful and joyous in my Saviour, Jesus Christ, diligently read the Bible, exercised myself in prayer, took pleasure in divine things, and meddled with nothing but what concerned my salvation; besides I held the Brethren in high esteem and had a sacred regard for everything good.

It happened in the year 1737 that my Superintendent was

called upon to go to the great Swamp, in order to baptize several persons. When he announced this at the meeting and asked who was willing to go with him, I was willing to go. After our arrival, when the meeting was over, the persons to be baptized were introduced, and a passage from Luke XIV was read to them, about the building of towers and waging war, which also was customary among them even in Germany; for when I was baptized this surprised me, and I did not know what to think of it. It was done as often as persons were to be baptized; so that you did not know whether you were to build or not, to go to war or not, or whether God had 10,000 and the devil 20,000 men. As soon as you came to the water the hymn was usually sung: "Count the cost says Jesus Christ, when the foundation Thou wouldst lay," etc, which A. M.[1] had composed already in Germany. When these confused transactions were now also enacted here, as was customary, it suddenly seized me so that my limbs trembled, and it flashed like a flame through my whole being, and before I knew it I heard myself speaking in an overloud voice. I was frightened at myself, for I thought of nothing less than of speaking. I said that it was not the Lord Jesus' intention to bring such things before candidates for baptism, for their purpose was to enter into their covenant with God by baptism, and to build upon the rock Jesus Christ; those who wished to build a tower besides the temple of God might have such things brought before them. This speech frightened everybody, and all were silent and dumb. At last our Superintendent, M. U.,[2] of blessed memory, said, "What shall we do then, for something must be said to the people." Without taking thought I answered: "The 18th Chapter of Matthew, about exhortation and punishment, might be read;" which proposal was adopted from that hour, and is still customary with them to this day.

This was the first stumbling block I found in their doctrine. But because they adopted my suggestion throughout the whole country, and no person moved against me, but all were surprised and thought that this movement on the part of a young man which they saw and heard was the work of

---

[1] [Alexander Mack.]   [2] [Martin Urner.]

the Spirit of God, I greatly honored them, since they in so childlike a way gave all the honor to God. Moreover they now noticed me more, especially did my Superintendent love me until he died, and he was much grieved when he had to lose me. But I did not respect the household of the Congregation, and nothing of the kind touched me; but I was earnest in my calling to gain favor before God by my life and behavior. I took no offence at any person, nor did I seek their esteem; I only endeavored to follow the dictates of my conscience. But it happened by and by that they, contrary to my wish, chose me as their Superintendent, after I had already obediently moved across the waters of the Susquehanna. Before this occurred it happened that Count Zinzendorf and many of his Brethren came into the country and occasioned a great stir, especially by his conferences. And because all denominations were invited to them, I too was deputed by my Superintendent to attend them. When I arrived at the conference, which was held at Oley, I found there some of our Baptists, Seventh Day men, Mennonites and Separatists. The Count himself was president, and for three days I heard queer and wonderful things there. After my return home I went to my Superintendent and said that I looked upon the Count's conferences as snares, for the purpose of bringing simple-minded and inexperienced converts back to infant baptism and church-going, and of erecting the old Babel again. We consulted with each other what to do, and agreed to get ahead of the danger, as some Baptists had already been smitten with this vain doctrine, and to hold a yearly conference, or as we called it, a Great Assembly, and fixed at once the time and place. This is the beginning and foundation of the Great Assemblies of the Baptists.

After this general meeting had been established, the opportunity was offered to speak of various matters whenever we met, and since most of the Baptists who had laid the foundation of their Congregation in Schwarzenau, were uneducated arch-idiots and ignoramuses, their followers, of course, brought their absurd notions also to this meeting, always appealing to their predecessors, saying the old Brethren in Germany did so, and we must not depart from their ways.

When I heard this I contradicted them, which occasionally gave rise to disputes, in which I always had P. B. and M. U.[3] and most of the common people on my side. But among other things something once occurred which appeared to me to be heretical, for when A. D.,[4] who still was one of the first, once said that our old Brother A. M. had believed the same, I was at once aflame and boldly contradicted it. But another Brother, M. F.,[5] took the affair out of my hands and said: "If it had not been for this I should not have joined the Brethren." To this I answered: "Then you have a poor reason for your change of religion." Meanwhile ears were pricked up and the matter was talked about, and I said I did not know how Christ Jesus could call himself a son of man if he had not taken upon himself something from the Virgin consecrated for this purpose, for it was evident that she never had known a man. Then M. F. answered that he had not received more from the Virgin than a wanderer who passes through a town receives from the town; or than a ball which passes through a gun, or the water which runs through a pipe. I was frightened at such an expression. M. U. sat alongside of me and said: "May God protect us against this!". But he whispered into my ear: "Speak out against this, it is heretical; do not spare it." I then said that if it were as they said it would have been all the same whether the Virgin was holy or not; a wanton might then as well have given birth to him since he received nothing from her, which is blasphemous to think and far more to say. This frightened them so that they left off defending this thing; the dispute, nevertheless, lasted two days before this Mohammedan Goliath was slain. It may be thought that I have deviated too far from my reasons why I left the Baptists; but no, these are the very reasons, for I took offence at the foundation and origin, because the originators deviated from their aim and basis, which in my opinion is the love of God towards all men, and formed a sect, like the Inspired, out of the great awakening which had taken hold of them in Germany, and aroused strife and hatred by their disputes. This George Gräben told them to their faces, and

---

[3] [Peter Becker and Martin Urner.] [4] [Abraham Diboy (Dubois?)]
[5] [Michael Frantz.]

especially to A. M., at a public meeting in Holland, being
inspired to it, saying: "You and all of you are dead, and
have died to the life of God;" all which was listened to by
W. K.,[6] who had just been liberated out of the prison in
Gülch, where he had been incarcerated for the sake of the
truth; he told me all this. At the very commencement they
adopted needless restrictions, in that they did not allow anyone who was not baptized to partake with them of the
Holy Sacrament. Had they not been so sectarian in
this matter, and been more given to impartial love,
they would have found entrance to more souls in their
great awakening and largely promoted the glory of God.
But, instead, sectarianism, quarrelsomeness and discord
spread through their whole awakening in Germany as
far as to Switzerland. Therefore, also, the incomparable
teacher, J. N.,[7] separated from them, and stood alone,
until he went to America and arrived in Philadelphia, to
which place A. M. went to meet him, and entreated him for
God's sake to forget and forgive what had happened in Europe; to which the same agreed. A. M. by his diligence
also prevented the above mentioned J. N. from coming to
Ephrata at the time of the awakening, otherwise he would
have been a victim of it too, for his testimony concerning the
renunciation of the world was as similar to the testimony in
Ephrata as one drop of water is to another. He afterwards
moved to Amwell, in New Jersey, and superintended the
Community there. I visited him there several times, and was
much edified by his conversation, and pleased and surprised
at his great and sound mind and the gifts which God had
bestowed on him. I might here mention many things
which he made known to me. He told me that A. M.
had been an honest and faithful man, but that he lacked
enlightenment. Perhaps this was because they had fallen
out with each other about the incarnation of Jesus Christ.
He said to my face, "You will not agree with these people,"
meaning the Baptists; "either they will reject you, or you
them, for a truly converted man cannot live with them; and
I," he added, "should I live another year, shall again with-

[[6]Will. Kebinger.]   [[7][John Naas.]

draw ftom them." But he died within that very year, and is buried in Amwell, among twenty children, all of whom lie buried around him.

With Christian Libe, who also was a preacher among them, strange things likewise happened. He was taken prisoner in Basle, where he was engaged in divine affairs, and was sold into the galleys, but ransomed after two years. At last he settled in Creyfeld, where he and the above-mentioned J. N. superintended the Community, until they at last had a fall-out, because J. N. called him a pill-monger publicly before the whole Congregation, and then left. But Christian Libe tried to continue the Congregation, although everything wasted under their hands; the Brethren who had been prisoners withdrew, the whole Congregation was given up, and everything went to ruin. He himself became a merchant, and even at last a wine merchant, and married out of the Congregation, against their own rules, and not a branch is left of their Baptist business in all Europe. Such matters, and many others not mentioned, prove to me that their fundamental principles cannot endure before God and the world; for they neither know, nor are they able to conduct the office of the new covenant, because they have no true knowledge of salvation, nor of the righteousness which avails before God, and is reckoned to us as faith; but they want to force and perfect everything through righteousness, by punishing, condemning and avoiding, which is not according to the new covenant, but the letter of the law, consisting of commandments and laws.

If God had not spared a branch of the root of Hochmann from Hochenau, the whole brood would have died at birth, like the Baptists of Munster. This innocent branch was P. B., who was a spiritual son of Hochmann, but was baptized, and came to live at Creyfeld, where he energetically exercised the gifts he had received from God, in singing and fervent praying, to the benefit of the Congregation; although he was otherwise no orator, but led a quiet life. Soon after he had to experience what he had not expected, for his spiritual Father had taught him peace and love; but here he heard much quarreling and strife, which soon deeply grieved him. It happened that a young Brother, Häcker by name, who had studied, and who was full of love and an intimate friend of the said P. B., wanted to marry the daughter of a merchant, who also had been baptized into the Congregation, but still served the Mennonites as preacher, because they did not wish to lose him, and gave him a yearly salary of 800 Gulden. This man was glad for such a son-in-law, and married them with great pleasure, not thinking that it would produce such a great excitement in the Congregation. But when the affair became known the tumult in the Congregetion became so great that Christian Libe, the second teacher, and with him four single Brethren, rose up against it and excommunicated said Häcker, though J. N. and the Congregation wished only to suspend him from bread-breaking. This godless excommunication ruined the whole Congregation in the town of Creyfeld. I heard the blessed teacher, J. N. say that more than 100 persons in Creyfeld had been convinced in favor of the new baptism, but on account of this ban everything was ruined and killed. And since no Moses was there, who might have sent Aaron with the censer, the fire of the ban burned on and consumed the whole Congregation, which still pains my heart whenever I think of it. But it touched poor Häcker most, who took all the blame on himself. The spirits took possession of him so that he fell sick and died of consumption; as they were converted people they were able to accomplish something. His good friend P. B., however, was with him in his utmost need, up to his death.

After this P. B. concluded to move to Pennsylvania, and when this became known several others moved with him; but the spirit of discord and ban also moved with them, and so wounded and corrupted them on the other side of the ocean, that they could hardly be cured in America. But God, nevertheless, took care of this branch, that it should bear fruit from the root, and brought it about that the German ban-branches were broken off, in order that this branch might have room to grow, and at last it blossomed and bore fruit in America, as in a garden of God. But the dear soul, P. B., could not attain his object, for the wild Baptist ban-branches always tried to paint a European shadow before his eyes; so that he died having fellowship with hardly anyone, for none of them understood his nature. Now I return to our yearly meeting, at which the European ban-branch continually became a topic of conversation, so that you always had to contend with these quarrels, until A. D. and M. F. at last died. Then other and thinner branches came forth, with which it was still more difficult to deal, until at last they put me out. Then I thought the affair would end, but it only commenced in earnest; for as quiet as ever I kept they let me have no peace. I was heartily tired of their affairs. Some, however, still adhered to me and could not leave me. They also were suspected and were avoided on my account, for whoever would not ban me himself had to be banned.

Now I became puzzled, for the wild European ban-branches threw such a shade, mist, darkness and gloom over the eyes of my mind that I could not see the light of the sun in the Gospel. I still lay buried under the hellish ban-doctrine, and my conflict was very great, for I was even afraid to doubt the ban-doctrine. In Germany I should willingly have entered the highest classes of the high schools, but here I had to attend high school against my will, had to learn the language of Canaan, and to begin with A. This, indeed, appeared very strange to me, because nearly everybody who knew me considered me a great doctor of Holy Writ. There I lay under a heavy rod, severely beaten both by God and men, for the treacherous dealt treacherously with me and I was so lean. (ISAIAH XXIV, 16.) For the justice of God pursued me and all the good in me was turned into evil, because I had taken it as my own. Here my earnestness was turned into hypocrisy, my singing and praying into boastfulness, my preaching into vanity, my journeying and visiting into an outrunning of God before He had sent me. My friendliness was dissimulation, my weeping and my tears a sectarian longing, my conversation with men on religious subjects a fraud, my piety a mere show, my reading and my studies a prying art, my desire to convert men a rebellion against God. For the cursers cursed me (namely, the old Baptists), and those who are ready to awaken the Leviathan (JOB III, 8); for whoso banneth he curseth. Here I had to learn the language of Canaan, willing or not willing, like Balaam, who, whether he wished or not, was compelled to bless and could not help it, however much he wished to curse. (NUM. XXIII, 20.) Here, then, God severed all fellowship of my conscience with the European ban-teachers and showed me how their foundation was laid in cursing and blessing. For, if a person does not wish to be blessed by them, they curse him like those who curse and who awaken the Leviathan, and they rejoice in the ruin of such people and say that that is the judgment of God (see A. M.'s little book, pages 107, 108, 109; also the answer to Gruber's twenty-second question), at which talk any one instructed by God should verily grieve in his heart. May God preserve mine and everybody's heart from such a doctrine, because it is so far removed from the doctrine of Christ, which teaches: "Love your enemies; bless them that curse you!" May God, the Almighty, have mercy.

Therefore I believe that the European Baptists have no business in America, but that they escaped hither as fugitives from the Spirit of God, which would not allow them to build their nest in Germany, because they were corrupt in their principles; for without knowing it they had been cheated by the spirit of Balaam, who rode and struck the she-ass before he was sent. (NUM. XXII.) I further believe that it would have been better for the American awakenings if they had never come to America; but flight is permitted in the Old and New Testaments. However, had they fought out their fight in Europe, since they were there awakened, it would have been more to their honor. For although I disagree with their fundamental principles in time and eternity (except baptism, the Lord's supper and the rite of feet-washing), I nevertheless respect them before God, but especially A. M., a man who suffered much for God, in spite of the great and grave errors which he had, like many of the saints; for a man who with his congregation leaves his inherited religion, leaves Babel and Egypt, experiences what one who is no leader cannot experience, as did Moses, John Huss, Martin Luther, Ulric Zwingli, Menno Simon, Count Zinzendorf, Conrad Beissel, etc.

There never was a false prophet, who had not also some truth.

There never was a godless person, who had not before been converted.

There never has been an accuser of his brother, or a despiser of his mother's son, who has not had the covenant of God on his lips and proclaimed the laws of God.

There never was a calumniator, who had not before known the truth.

There never was one who cursed, who had not before known how to bless.

There never went a person astray, who had not before been on the right way.

There never was a liar, who did not before fall from the truth.

There never was a bitter envier, who was not before in the bonds of love.

There never was an enemy, who was not a friend before.

There never was one who recognized the truth, before he recognized the lies in himself.

Now I will briefly answer a second question: How and why I might have joined the Seventh Day Baptists? Although you might as well have asked: How and why I might have joined the children of God? For my Congregation is the largest of all, since I am at one with all who belong to the kingdom of God. (MATTH. XII, 50). But I must begin my narrative at the beginning. On my account nearly sixty souls were banished (a likeness to JOHN, IX, 22), because they would not believe in lies, nor follow the envy of their preachers; therefore we formed a Congregation. However I continued to preach as before, and there was great commotion throughout almost the whole land, so that I was in demand at Conestoga, Philadelphia, Germantown, Conewago, Monocacy, as far as Virginia. And although I kept up fellowship with all unsectarian souls, I, nevertheless, was most intimate with my own trusty Brethren and Sisters. About this time Brother Frederick Fuhrman held a love-feast, to which all this little flock gathered and some were baptized; this was the first love-feast. But the Congregation increased in membership by baptism, so that during a journey of four weeks twenty-six were baptized and twelve love-feasts held. But as the affair progressed it happened that I was expected at Conestoga. I, therefore, got ready, and three Brethren with me. I long before had intended to see the Brethren at Ephrata. When we arrived at Lititz I sent two of my Brethren by another way to those who expected me, to announce to them that I was there, and if they wished to have a meeting held the said Brethren should come to Ephrata before the meeting and notify us. I and my Brother, John Horn, however, with staff in hand, went direct towards Ephrata. Following the road we first arrived at the Sisters' household, though we did not know who lived there. We went to a worthy matron and asked where Friedsam lived. She showed us the way. We went straight to it and knocked, when old Nägele came out and asked where these men came from. I answered that we came from far, for I did not wish them at once to know who we were, for they knew my name but not my person. Then he said: "Come in then," and opened the door. The old Father reverently rose and received us with a kiss, and the others did the same, for he had visitors at the time. Then he made us sit behind the table, he sitting before it, and said: "Where do these dear men come from?" I answered: "We come from far" (for I restrained myself). He asked: "But from where?" I said: "From Canecotschicken."[8] He said: "Then you know George Adam?" I answered: "Yes, we know him well." He spoke: "Ah, how is he?" I said: "As you see," for I could no longer hold back. "Ah," he said to this, "are you George Adam? here lies the letter which you wrote; we were just speaking about you when you knocked." We continued the conversation, and nothing was said on either side to which we both did not agree.

While conversing thus animatedly, a Sister entered, brought a tub of water and an apron, put them down and silently left; who she was, and who had ordered her to do so, I do not know even to this very hour. The old Father rose and

---
[8][Conococheague?]

said: "Come Brethren, sit down here, I will wash your feet." So he washed our feet, and Brother Nägele dried them for us. Then I said: "You have washed our feet, now let us also wash yours," to which they consented; so I washed their feet, and Brother Horn dried them. When this was done, he said, "Let us go into the Sisters' house." I said I should like also to visit my old pastor M. and Brother Obed. He said that could also be done, but desired that we first should go to the Sisters' house. We went there, and they prepared a splendid meal for us, during which we all the time continued our conversation; but nothing was said on which we did not agree. After this we ascended the hill where Brother Obed lived. On the way up he said to me, "God has done this, that you had to come to us, for with us everything lies prostrate, and we have for years been unable to hold any meetings; I hope you have come to raise up again the fallen down hut." I was surprised at this candor, and thought perhaps there was some trick behind it. But I afterwards learned that it was sincerity, and through all my life until his death, I never heard of unfaithfulness in him.

When we arrived there, and had welcomed each other, he said, "How do you do, Brother Obed? How about heaven?" Such speech continued and all was harmony, which pleased my Brother Horn so much that he afterwards remarked: "You will not bring me away from these people again, do what you please;" which I heard with pleasure. At the close of the visit the old Father asked whether we would not like to visit the Sisters? I said we had no time now, we expected two other Brethren who had left us at Lititz, who were to inform us where and when the meeting was to be held. "Why, do you know what," he said, "I will make them assemble in their prayer-hall, so that you can see them all; it is also desired that you should make an address to them;" and this it was resolved to do. After this we visited our old pastor Miller, who reverently received us, and met us with all the modesty becoming an honorable man. In the course of conversation I asked him whether he did not still owe something to the R.[9] He said, "I no longer have a

---

[9][Reformed.]

drop of blood in me that is R——d." I said, "That is not what I ask." "Oh!" he said, "I understand; not only to the R——d but to all men, whatever I have and can;" which pleased me.

Meanwhile it was some time before our two Brethren arrived, and reported how it was to be. At the same time news arrived that the old Father and the Sisters had assembled in their prayer-hall, and were waiting for us. Since our number of visitors was now again complete, we were all conducted thither by the old Brother Eleazar, and were shown to our seats. An inward emotion here seized me; my spirit felt the presence of a divine majesty; the veil was removed, in which all the nations are enveloped. I saw the pathway of the saints into the holy of holies; the spirits kissed each other in stillness, and a divine, holy, mutual, and profound unity was entered into without a word, voice, utterance, or speech, for there reigned silence for a long time as if no person were there. Smell, taste, feeling, even seeing and hearing, all were one, just as I have seen two small flocks of sheep unite in which there were no rams.

At last my spirit was called back again. My eyes were full of tears when the Sisters began to sing a hymn, as well as I remember: "The streets of Zion are desolate;" which brought tears to many eyes. After this was finished, I spoke: "You sang a hymn for us, let us now also sing one for you." Then we sang the "Song of the Lilies,"[10] but as it had

---

[10] We will here communicate this song to the reader on account of its strange expressions.

    1. The heavenly drama, the perfume of lilies,
       Awakened anew the spirit's desire ;
       The roses of Sharon, though low on the ground,
       Bring heaven to spirits for the covenant bound.
       The apple tree's shade bends forward in pleasure
       And seeks in the field of the lilies its treasure.

    2. The color of lilies, their figure so fine,
       Aroused all the love in this bosom of mine.
       The roses of Sharon that bloom in the field
       Are kindred to me, 'neath God's holy shield.
       So away with your crowns and treasures so rare,
       With lilies so beauteous you cannot compare.

escaped my memory, I asked Brother Horn for the words, and he told them to me; then we sang it to the end, which simplicity astonished the Sisters. After quiet was restored, I made a short address, although I felt no particular inclination to speak. I had various impressions from the spirit of prophecy, but since our time was limited we had to accommodate ourselves to it. Thus everything passed most pleasantly. A fellowship was formed, and the unity of spirits concluded without a word, without conditions, without questioning as to how or when, without care, without labor, without fear, without distrust, without consideration; in love, with love, through love, out of love, and for eternal love; and neither world nor time, neither flesh nor blood, neither friend nor foe, neither the present nor the future, neither fear nor death, neither devil nor hell can break it, for Two became One, and were One before they knew it. And thus it is with all who are truly born again; for they are children, sons and daughters of God Almighty. So far the record.

---

3. Oh heaven, how rich and how happy am I,
For the beauty of lilies you showed to mine eye.
She groweth as straight as the smoke on the plain,
And love-like she clings to me, now and again.
I stay with her always, because she so charms,
As long as I breathe she'll rest in my arms.

4. Thine odor divine, thy heavenly form
My poor sinful heart did wondrously warm.
My heart how it longeth to join in the hymn
That swells from the throngs of Mahanaim.
Oh might I, low bowing, without any fear,
Pluck off all the roses so plentiful here.

5. My life I would give it forever to thee,
With heart and with soul; yea so it should be!
For thou art the lily, else nothing can clothe
My poor naked form in peace to repose.
If Prince I were called, I'd wish nothing more,
Nor care for aught else that I wanted before.

6. Enraptured I am by this beauty of thine,
I sway like one drunken and vanquished by wine.
The apple tree casteth its shadow so still
Where the lilies abound by God's holy will.
The carpets of Solomon ever so fine
Are nothing compared to these beauties of mine.

Such are the particulars of this important union, related by the Brother himself. It must be known, however, that in spite of his banishment he still had a strong following among the Baptists, who were honest people, and began to think that he had been unjustly treated; and who, therefore, were disposed to stake their lives on his innocence. The most prominent of these were John Steiner, John Horn, Peter and Abraham Knipper, Frederick Fuhrman, George Scheitler, Peter Zug, Finck, etc. But the reception of these two Brethren brought about great changes; for, in the first place, these two visiting Brethren were seized with holy wonder when they saw that the union was made in the spirit without any words, as they had thought that articles of agreement would be laid before them. Afterwards the old hatred between the two Communities was again revived on this account, for the reception of Brother G. A., nullified the ban which the former Brethren had laid on him; all of which happened in the prayer-hall of the Sisters, as above men-

7. Melchizedek's altar, here also it stands,
   As master it guardeth this purest of bands ;
   As oft as he thinks of them in his abode
   The manna of Paradise falls to their lot.
   The strength of the lilies, like secret-kept fire,
   Springs forth with new force in the virginal choir.

8. Come dearest ! oh come ! and make me thine own,
   To rest on thy heart and have there my home.
   Oh give me the juice of the lilies so mild,
   The balsam of love and heaven's strong child.
   Baal-Hamon, my vineyard, brings splendid new wine,
   It robbed thee of life, oh beloved of mine.

9. Let, therefore, the virgin by all be extolled
   As long as of crown and of scepter we're told.
   Although she despised the hot and the small,
   Through shame she high honor hath brought to them all.
   The little ones feed in the dale with the rose,
   For brides and espousal the Lamb did them choose.

10. The flowers of Sharon are counted no dross,
    Because they're bethrothed to the Lamb on the cross ;
    And follow his footsteps through danger and chance,
    Drawn closer to him through the love of his name.
    Yet they are the virgins Christ chose for his brides,
    He made them his own and set others aside.

tioned; for there the holy Mother came down from above with the oil of anointing, and healed his wounds; wherefore he was often heard to say: "Rejoice with me, for I have found the piece which I had lost." It appears that the Superintendent had received, as a trust from God, a blessing for the B—— Community, of which they would have become partakers had they humbled themselves; for he was the greatest stumbling-stone which their Community ever encountered. But because they failed to endure the test, the choice fell upon another. For we must concede to this Brother the honor that he was the first among them, who arrived at a holy harmony and yet remained a Baptist. For all of this people who had joined the Community before him, sent their letters of withdrawal to their people, but Brother G. A., above spoken of, was faithful to their statutes, and neither a second baptism, nor the Sabbath, nor any of the various other ordinances of the Community, were urged upon him. Therefore it was ordained by God that Brother G. A. was to earn the blessing, which their whole Community might have had; and the Superintendent once addressed the following impressive words to him: "You shall be blessed, and also remain blessed." When, shortly before his death, he once more visited the Superintendent, the latter said to him: "My salvation rests in your hands." All this created an extraordinary esteem for the Superintendent in this good Brother, and all the letters he wrote to him were full of special expressions of love, while the superscription sometimes contained the title: Pontifex Maximus.

Some of the Baptists who saw a little further, expected that the Superintendent's bearing towards this man would subdue him sooner than all their bans; but in the Community in and around Ephrata he occasioned great excitement, especially in the households. For up to this time the priestly office had been in the hands of one of the Solitary, but now the domestic household also wished to have part in it, which brought with it such temptations, that one housefather, J. S.,[11] declared on his death-bed that this Brother would be the cause of the Community's destruction. But

---

[11][John Senseman.]

because the Superintendent was the first to condescend to him, there was no help, everybody had to follow suit; and if any one had not done so, judgment would have come upon him, so that he would not have dared to lift up his hands towards God. All this was not unknown to the said Brother, therefore he once declared that all the good in Ephrata rested in his hands. After the visit was now concluded with blessing, the Superintendent dismissed them with letters of recommendation to the Brethren at the Bermudian. Soon after, moreover, he sent two of the oldest Brethren, Jehoiada and Lamech, to the Brethren at the Bermudian, and expressed himself in the following manner, namely, that they should receive Brother G. A. as if it were himself. This was saying as much as that they should take him as their priest, which greatly troubled them, so that they protested that their priests lived in Ephrata. A venerable house-sister was even seized with a fatal sickness on that account, of which she died; it happened to her like to the wife of the son of the priest Eli, who, when in labor, was more concerned for the glory of God, than for her own child, and said: "The glory of Israel is taken captive," (I Sam. IV, 19.) But after they had learned to submit to God's wonderful guidance they became one Community, for before this they lay under suspicion, because most of those who had moved away from the Community at Ephrata had done so for improper reasons. If you wish to build churches you must lay the foundation on the lowliness of Christ, else you build in the air.

Through this movement a door was opened for a new church-period, during which much important spiritual work was transacted. The Superintendent called the awakening at Antitum from this period on, the Eagle church, after the fourth beast in the Apocalypse; although these good people considered themselves too lowly and unworthy of such a high title; but there was another secret connected with it. The Superintendent, who, during his whole awakened condition, stood in the service of the four beasts, about this time came under the dominion of the Eagle, wherefore the renewal of the Eagle's youth showed itself so much in him that he was entirely pervaded by it during his old age. During his first journey from the Settlement to Antitum he carried all his ecclesiastical vestments with him, because not only the oldest Brethren from Bethany, and the house-fathers, but also the oldest Sisters of Sharon, with their Mother, were his companions. They who beheld the glory of these two flocks of lambs when they united into one at Antitum (and many who saw it must still be alive), will well remember that then their mountains leaped for joy like sheep, and their hills like lambs, at the generation of the celestial Mother, which shall at last take possession of the Kingdom, when the adulterous seed is destroyed from the earth. The Superintendent made this whole journey on foot, except when they forced him to make use of a horse, and then he said: "In this way I cannot be edifying to anyone." In this lively spirit he was seen to travel over mountains and valleys, and no hut was too poor for him to enter with his company. And now the fire of the awakening spread over the whole region of Antitum. Many secretly stole away from their houses and ran after this wonder, for the former Brethren of Brother G. A., in order to put a stop to this awakening, sent two of their Brethren, John Mack and Staub, to all their houses to warn them against being seduced.

During the whole journey the Superintendent gave strange evidences of his humility and obedience. He never sat down in a house until the father of the house showed him a seat, which some observed and remarked: "He is more strictly led than we." But the circumstances forced him to this, for he was hired in a vineyard which already had its husband-men with whom he might easily have interfered; on which point also a law was made in the *Jure Canonico: Quod unius ecclesiae unus debeat esse Sacerdos:* that each church should have but one priest. When it was resolved to hold a bread-breaking, and a priest was required for it, his humility taught him to make room for Brother G. A., who, in consequence presided, though their love-feasts were at the time still held in Corinthian fashion, and not in the manner in which they were held at Ephrata. Soon after another breaking of bread was held, the administration of which they conferred on the Superintendent, which he promised to undertake on condition that they would permit him to break in the manner in which he had been taught. To this they would not agree. They said: "It is strange that you make such a difference in such small matters;" to which he answered: "It is also strange that you, to whom I yield in all points, cannot yield to me in this one point, which my conscience demands." Then they gave him the permission, and from that time they celebrated all their love-feasts in the same way that is customary with the Brethren at Ephrata. The reason why the Superintendent took offence at their way of breaking bread was because they were of opinion that all must be equals; and, therefore, they did not wish to allow any prerogative or privilege to any one person among them. On this account some of them were not pleased when the Superintendent, at a large meeting, held in the house of a Brother named Joseph Greybühl, while the whole congregation were on their knees, consecrated this Brother by laying on of hands, and thus confirmed him in his office. After the Brethren of Antitum had dismissed the Superintendent and the other visitors in peace, they went on their homeward journey. The spirit of awakening about this same time caused so much work between Ephrata, Bermudian and Antitum that visitors were continually on the march to and fro, which nourished the mutual love. For the Superintendent had scarcely settled down in his seclusion again when a new visit to Antitum was prepared for, which started six weeks after the first. The Superintendent charged another Brother with it, and ordered some Brethren and Sisters of the Settlement and some of the oldest house-fathers to accompany him. The Superintendent himself was at Antitum three times, and this in his old age, when his task was fast approaching its end. But those at Antitum reciprocated by many a fatiguing journey to Ephrata. For at that time the fire burnt in the Philadelphian church, which each and everyone at Antitum tried to keep up, even at the risk of his earthly possessions. At this time the before-mentioned Brethren, G. A. and H., paid a new visit to the Settlement, in order to see the Superintendent once more, for they expected that he would soon leave his earthly tabernacle. The Superintendent received them with open arms and held a lovefeast in their honor. After this the said Brother G. A., accompanied by some of the Fathers and some Sisters from Sharon, paid a visit to Philadelphia, but his companion meanwhile remained quietly in the Settlement; and after their visit was ended in blessing they gave the last kiss of peace to the Superintendent, for they did not see him again after this. Thus they returned in peace to their home. And with this we will conclude the chapter.

CHAPTER XXXII.

CONCERNING VARIOUS STRANGE AFFAIRS WHICH OCCURRED IN THE COUNTRY ABOUT THE SAME TIME, AND IN WHICH THE SUPERINTENDENT WAS INTERESTED.

At that time an old Separatist who had been the Superintendent's travelling companion across the ocean, Simon König by name, joined the Community, and thus another opportunity was given the Superintendent by spiritual alms to help an unfortunate, who had failed in his calling, to rise again. The way in which the said König was brought to the Community was quite extraordinary; for he had lived seventy days without any natural food, which produced such a change in his nature that he afterwards could not live in society any more. He published in print his own account of his reception, in which he calls the Ephrata Community the most noble in the world, at which his Separatist Brethren took great offence; but it happened to him like the new wine which bursts the new barrels, for the Pentacostal wine had intoxicated him. It is however to be deplored that such a paradisiacal foretaste was followed by such sad consequences; for not long after this he fell under displeasure, and left the Community again, which he had extolled to the skies; and although several attempts were made to snatch him out of the fire, everything was in vain, and he passed into eternity during his alienation.

Now we come to the history of the spirits, which took their beginning in Virginia during January, 1761, and were laid at Ephrata in the following spring; but to understand it several other circumstances have to be mentioned also. There were two young married persons in the Community of Ephrata who were anxious about their eternal welfare; but because, according to the usage of those times, the wife entered upon the practice of continence without consent of her husband, he fell into great temptation, and at last sinned with a neighboring widow whom he had served in many ways. Because on this account he lost his fellowship with the Community, he took his children and the said widow with him to Virginia, and left his first wife in the Community. After he had three children by that widow, she died, and he married a person of noble birth, who had just arrived in the country, and who called herself Henrietta Wilhelmina von Höning, but who did not bring the best character with her into the country.

It happened in January, 1761, that as this third wife of the man mentioned (his name was C. B.), was slumbering, an old woman appeared to her, who, according to the description given by her, must have been the above mentioned widow. She took hold of the arm of said third wife, and placed her on a chair, and that part of the arm which she had taken hold of was blue for several days. Then she said to her: "Don't go away, but remain here with my husband, I am an old woman and do not mind it; I shall go away again; you are the third and legitimate wife. And because you are good to my children, I shall reveal everything to you, for you will not be here much longer. Go into the kitchen about the twelfth hour; there behind the tin closet you will find money." Afterwards she and her husband searched the kitchen and found there £3 hidden, in paper money. After this the spirit played a strange comedy with this person for four weeks, so that she thought it would cost her her life, as she suddenly spit half a pint of blood. Every night the spirit revealed some of the money which the woman had during her lifetime purloined from her husband, and which was found in the places where she had hidden it. But it appears that the spirit must have been greatly under the influence of a fierce temper, for whenever it was not obeyed, it would tear the clothes from the body of the wife; and that was a common thing. If she rode behind her husband her shoes and stockings were taken off her feet while sitting on the horse. Did she go to a neighbor, it always cost her part of her dress, which was torn; but if she remained at home, there was a continual racket all around the woman. Sometimes all the books were thrown down from the shelf, and hardly was this done when the tea-service followed and was broken to pieces. At length the report of these strange matters spread over the whole country, and a messenger, B. by name, was sent from Winchester to inform himself accurately about the thing. He spent the night there; but during the night the spirit rioted in throwing, knocking and pounding so that the afore-named B. commenced to curse on his couch, which so exasperated the spirit that it dragged the couch on which three persons were lying around the room, though B. resisted with much force. Then the spirit took hold of his arm and tried to twist it, whereupon he cried out in fear: "Lord Jesus, what is this?" Now the spirit fell down upon its knees before him, pushed him back with both its hands, and disappeared.

They several times heard the spirit utter the word Conestoga, at which place they had formerly lived; and because the wife was always seized by the arm by the spirit they interpreted it to be the spirit's meaning that they should go to Conestoga. In this they were not deceived, for as soon as they had resolved on this move two spirits appeared; the last stood behind the first and was quite tall and lean, which made them think it was C. B.'s first wife. Whenever the first said to his wife, "Come!" the second would stand behind and beckon with its hand that they should come, and behaved very devoutly. After the wish of the spirit in regard to the journey was divined it plainly told them the whole affair, namely, that they were to go from Ephrata to Conestoga; about the twelfth hour of the night they should enter the great hall over the church, and to this place Conrad (this was the Superintendent whom the deceased during her lifetime had highly esteemed), Nägele, her husband, and a Sister who had long ago died (most likely Anna Eicher), should also come; it and Catharine (the first wife of said C. B.) would also appear, for they had died unreconciled with each other. Then the following two hymns were to be sung: "Oh God and Lord," and "Dearest Father, I Thy child." After this they should clasp each other's hands, but she should put her hand on them and say: "Christ is the reconciliation of us all; may he help you and forgive you your sins, and wash you with his blood." On this journey to

Ephrata it was observed that as often as she tarried longer than necessary the spirit became uneasy and threw her shoes towards the door; and in Lancaster it also tore her clothes in sight of all the people in the tavern.

When they arrived at Ephrata the Superintendent was away from home on official duties, and of those present none was inclined to meddle with these things. A Brother, therefore, was sent to him to tell him that his presence was required in the Settlement. At first he refused and said there would be a meeting next day, at which he had to be present. But the night following he received other instructions and travelled home with the Brethren. He considered that these people and their important experiences had been sent to him by God, and as such accepted them. The meeting was held February 3d; it began at the eleventh hour of the night and lasted two hours. Besides those three persons from Virginia, eighteen from Ephrata were present, and among them those whom the deceased had especially named; but the chief person with whom the spirit had had to do refused to be present until she was at last persuaded to it after much trouble. The meeting was commenced by reading the last chapter of JAMES, and after the first hymn had been sung, all knelt down; but when the spirit was mentioned in the prayer, strange emotion took possession of her, and she was seized by great fear, so that her husband and step-son had to support her. It was noticed at the time that her neckerchief became sprinkled with blood while they were on their knees; there were thirty drops, but where the blood came from did not become evident. This was the only extraordinary circumstance that happened at this meeting, for the spirit did not appear according to promise. But when the reconciliation was about to take place, the above mentioned person refused to do anything in the matter, and tried to put the management on others; but she was told that it was her duty, and that none else could do it. At last it was thought advisable that the two daughters of said C. B. (the one by his first wife, who was a member of the Sisterhood, the other by his second wife), should perform the act of reconciliation instead of their mothers. They clasped their hands, and the third wife spoke the above-mentioned words over them; then the exercises closed with prayer.

After this act the spirit did not trouble this person any more. The opinions which were now and then passed on these occurrences we will leave untouched; but as the Superintendent clearly expressed his opinion on them, we will lay it before the friendly reader for further consideration; it was as follows:

I cannot help but say a little something about what happened to me last night during my spiritual labor, especially since I expressed myself pretty plainly yesterday. In the first place, yesterday I had a very strange revelation to my spirit before the mercy seat, and in my usual manner, in the spirit of the prayer. I went to lie down to sleep at the proper time and woke up again at midnight, as, indeed, is commonly the case. I looked at once for the mercy seat and put my incense on the altar, and it filled my house. After a while I again lay down to rest on my bench, but soon I had to get up again in order to offer incense, so I took my golden censer and made the fire burn high; but myself remained bent low to the earth in prayer and intercession for the oppressed and innocent, and that God might vindicate his great mercy, goodness and compassion towards the innocent, just as he had sought to vindicate his honor on the unrighteous through his righteousness.

After this sacrifice I lay down again to rest, slept for a while, and when I awoke looked around and waited in spirit for my watch-word; when it was told me that we labored in vain about this spirit; that we would be rid of it if the stolen goods were returned to their proper place; not indeed as the spirit had ordered, for then we would become partakers of its sins. For no part of them can be laid on the altar of God; it would not bring honor even to use them as alms, for it is written: "I hate robbery for burnt offering;" and again: Who restoreth to the debtor his pledge and payeth back what he hath robbed. Without this neither sacrifice nor prayer can be pleasing. It was further told me that if it were right, nobody could for conscience sake take away any of the money from the children for whom it was intended, for this would deprive the father of his honor and parental right, and they, the children, would rob themselves of the father's blessing, for it is written: "The father's blessing builds houses for the children, but the mother's wrath plucketh them down."

Now I will speak: It came to my mind, after deep reflection, that N. N. is the first-born child, who in this affair is nearest related to the mother. If now this should be so, then she (of course, if the others agree to it), instead of the mother, should gather up all, and should lay the money away in an unclean place (he meant a secretary) until seven periods had passed, and should give up the mother and try to gain the heart of the father, where thus far she had been a stranger through the mother's fault, and therefore could not fully love the father, which brings upon us the mother's wrath which plucketh down houses. For by such work the kingdom of heaven is not gained; and so likewise, as I understand it, the spirit had not had a hair to give for the kingdom of heaven while it was in its body, and had nothing else to do but to torment innocent hearts, and so assist in the evil design, etc.

If the dear heart, N. N., cannot agree to this as above explained, to give up her mother with her evil doings and try instead to lay hold of the father's heart, which has as it is been sufficiently wronged by the mother, then it may happen that good fortune will not be with her in her future course, for the mother's curse destroys it. Should it, however, come to pass that the money could be disposed of as explained, and the spirit should continue to lay any claim to it, then we must do what we can. I also considered whether the spirit would not have lost its right if the money were only kept at those same places where the deceased had put it.   F., One who Possesses
Nothing on the this Earth.

The history and revelations of Catharine Hummer follow now in order of time, and although we may have no right to connect them with this chronicle, especially since they began outside of this Community, they, nevertheless, deserve to find a place here, partly because they are edifying and partly because the Superintendent esteemed the person worthy of his favor; the account however is taken from her own confessions and is as follows:

While sitting in the kitchen near the fire on the night of October 3d, 1762, between ten and eleven o'clock, somebody knocked at the door. I looked out, but nobody was there. It soon knocked again, and I again went out but found nobody. At last it knocked the third time, and going out and looking about I saw an angel standing at my right hand, who said: "Yes, my friend, it is midnight and late; the hour of midnight is approaching; alas, what shall I say? love has grown cool among the members. Oh, that this were not so among those who are Brethren in the faith!" Then he sang, that it echoed through the skies, and I thought it must be heard far and wide. When he had ceased, I said: "Shall I go in and tell my friends that they may rejoice with me?" He said: "No; they have lain down." I said: "They are not asleep." He said: "Yes, they sleep." Then I kept silence and thought, how well I feel, how well I feel! Thereupon the angel began to sing: "How well I feel, how well I fell, when our God doth show himself in spirit to my soul, so that within I leap and jump for joy, and bring all praise and honor to the Lord, although the tongue oft silence keeps." At the middle of the verse he told me to join in the singing; then he knelt down and I with him; he prayed fervently and beautifully for the salvation of believers. Now I wept for joy, and he dried my tears; but I dared not touch him. Then I said: "Shall I go and tell my friends?" He laid his hands upon my shoulders and answered, "My dear child, they are asleep." I said: "My dear friend, they just now lay down, they do not sleep." After this we again commenced to sing: "The children of God indeed sow in sorrow and in tears; but at last the year yieldeth what they long for; for the time of the harvest cometh, when they gather the sheaves, and all their grief and pain is turned to pure joy and laughter." Then I again said: "Shall I go in and tell my father that he may rejoice with me?" He said: "No, all your friends are asleep, and their hearts also want to sleep." Then I wept bitterly, and the angel asked: "Why do you weep?" I answered: "I have committed many sins and often grieved my Saviour." He said: "Do not weep, your Saviour forgave you your sins, for he knows that you have gladly listened to the good, and that you did not delight in the greatness of this world, that you have no pride in your heart, and that you have kept lowly company with the believers." Then the angel and I began to sing: "Who knows what shall come, what shall be our lot, when the Lord one day his own will take, his chaste bride so full of honor; he hath already known her in his mind, she follows well his guiding hand and much augments his honor." Then we knelt and prayed again, and he prayed for the sinners. Then I asked for the fourth time: "Shall I go in and call my friends?" He said: "This is asked once too often; do you not know that the Saviour awakened his disciples three times?" I said: "This is too much;" and I wept. He said: "Weep not," and I kept silent. Then we began to sing: "O blessed he will be who shall enter in with me the realms of bliss; it surely is but right that we should here below us always well prepare." Then the angel began to speak and said: "My dear child, did you ever see such ungodly display? Did you notice the daughters of Jerusalem walking about in gay calico, of which things they have much on earth. They will be sent down to the wicked if they do not turn back, for they will not enter the kingdom of God; and there is still a great deal of this godless display upon earth; they will be shown down into hell. Then the Lord will say: Depart from me, ye sinners! I know you not! And then you will burn to all eternity and will be tormented from everlasting to everlasting."

Then he ceased to speak of these things, and we again began to sing: "They all will see at once with pleasure and joy the beauties of the heavenly realm; and the beautiful throng will walk two by two on Zion's meadows." Then, for the third time, we knelt down on the ground and he prayed about the sufferings and the death of the Saviour, and then we got up. Now he said to me: "Go in and lie down;" and said: "Hallelujah! hallelujah in Christ Jesus! Amen." Then he ascended towards heaven and spoke in a loud voice, so that it reached to heaven: "Father, father, faithful father!" and called out three times in a loud voice saying: "I ascend into heaven." I looked after him until he disappeared from my sight; then I went in and lay down.

After this I lay in a trance for the greater part of seven days and nights, so that my spirit was separated from the body. In this state I was led through strange conditions and dwelling places of spirits, and I saw such wonderful things that I greatly hesitate to reveal them. After this it became quite customary for me to talk with good spirits and angels, and also to be transferred in spirit out of my visible body into heavenly principalities, just as if it had happened bodily. The Almighty God in his mercy also allowed me to translate myself in spirit into eternity as often as I wished, either by day or night, and there to see, hear and touch the divine wonders. My body was always as if asleep until my spirit returned. I wandered through indescribable habitations of the blessed, and saw innumerable hosts; and once I was told their number, but I could not remember it. Oh, what joy and happiness did I there behold! There you feel a bliss that is inexpressible and cannot be described. Now I will describe a few of the divine wonders which Jesus Christ, who had joined me and was my guide into eternity, revealed to me.

In the year 1762, on November 12th, my spirit was taken from this visible creation, and out of my body, up into invisible eternity. There I saw all the prophets and apostles, together with all the saints and patriarchs, and heard one of them say these words to the pious: Hallelujah, hallelujah, highly praised, highly honored; gather ye pious, gather all ye pious to the great supper; rejoice ye all and triumphantly declare how kindly the Lord leads you. To the godless the Lord will say: Depart ye wicked, I do not know you, go with him whom ye have followed. Then they will try to excuse themselves and implore the Lord, but he will say to them: Depart from me, ye evil-doers. And the Saviour then will say: Come, all ye pious, to the great supper. And they will hasten with gladness, and triumphantly shout and say: Highly, highly be praised the Lord's precious name! Then they will walk two and two on the meadows of Zion; then they will walk even by fours. Oh, how will the pious rejoice when the Saviour says: Come hither, ye pious! Then they will hasten by fours, and the gross, godless sinners, by hundreds, and on the middle path by sixties; and the unbelieving children, under seven years old, by twenties on the middle path. Then they are again divided on the middle path. What is here said about three paths is to be understood as follows: We human beings know what is meant by morning, noon, evening and midnight; in the same way this is also to be understood in the other realm. A great water runs from Noon between Morning and Midnight which divides the earthly from the eternal realm. When man dies and leaves this earthly realm he imagines himself alive and does not know anything of his having died, and yet finds himself a stranger on earth. Then he comes to a great road that leads from Evening towards Morning; after he has travelled some distance on this road a broad road branches off to the left, leading to damnation and hell. The road ascends a little until it reaches a certain height, when it suddenly descends, and there hundreds on hundreds are travelling. But on the road which leads towards Morning there sixties on sixties are travelling; this road leads to the water mentioned, but the other one, almost directly towards Noon, brings you to the water sooner. On this road none but adults walk towards the temple of Mount Zion. Then the angel said: "And then the Lord will say: Come ye pious and baptized, who have persevered to the end, come over here; come, you are baptized and have persevered to the end." Again the angel spoke: "Behold the five chosen ones! Oh, how glorious and how mighty! Behold the Father, and the Son, and those three with him, God Abraham, God Isaac, and God Jacob!" And one of the three went into the water and baptized (what is not fulfilled here in this time must and inevitably will be fulfilled in the time to come). And the Saviour and the Father stood on the other side of the water, and the Saviour called the innocent by name, one after the other, to go in. Those who had here repented and believed in baptism he also called in. But those who had transgressed the Word of God, after having been baptized on earth, they must tarry at the water until they have repented anew. Those whom the world had bought, and who clung to it with their hearts, they must anew repent upon earth, for they must wait by the water and listen to what the Father preaches to them. These two, the Father and the Son, stood together on the other side. Then they also came to the water and preached, the Father to the godless, the Son to the pious. Now the pious also went into the water and were baptized, and the Saviour called to them to cross also; and they were glad and joined in the triumphant shout of the angels; and the angels stood in the water up to their hearts. I will yet add something important about baptism. I know a man, it is not necessary to mention his name, who when he died and came to the water was told that before he might cross he would have to be baptized. He answered that he had been baptized in his infancy, and had always thought that immersion was not so essential. Then he heard the words: Jesus too was circumcised on the eighth day, and nevertheless was also baptized in his thirtieth year; therefore he would have to follow, and so indeed he did. I saw him moreover until he had crossed.

After they had come out of the water they went away from it, the Father first, then the Saviour and the Three, and after them the angels. The further they went the more beautiful it was, bright and shining. These five sat down, then the baptized, then the angels singing most charmingly. The Saviour preached the Gospel; he did not preach as he had to the Jews in their synagogues. And after he had preached the Gospel, he also preached faith. Then they stood up and prayed mightily and gloriously, and Jesus told the pious to go their way, and they all departed; but the five chosen ones returned again to the water, and the angels accompanied them, and did as they had done before at the water. But the multitude of the pious, whom Jesus told to go their way, numbered one hundred; they departed and were prepared. Then one of the Three went into the water, and also the angels up to their hearts. Then the Lord of innocence called out and said: "Come hither ye innocent, ye must be baptized." Then they will hurry into the water and be baptized; and when they come out, the Lord will call to them: "Come over here!" and they will go to the

T

Five. But those who are baptized here, and fall away again, but repent again and are converted during their lifetime, to them the Father will say, when after death they come to the water: "Halt, halt!" and will preach to them and tell them what they have done; but the Saviour will preach to the pious. Then the Saviour will say: "Come also into the water, you must be baptized again;" then they will go into the water and be called over to the other side, shining and glorious in their beauty. Thereupon they all will rejoice with shouts and jubilation, because the Lord has led them so kindly. But to those who but half repented the Lord will say: "Depart, depart, depart from the middle road!" And when those come who here on earth stood by themselves, the Lord will say to them: "Depart from me, I know you not!" He will say: "No standing alone availeth here!" and they will be turned off with the godless.

Then the Saviour will say: "Come ye pious, rejoice and triumphantly shout, because the Lord leads you so kindly;" and he who baptized in the water said to me: "Behold Peter, and John, and James!" They were of the same degree; Peter and John had friendly countenances. Peter said to me: "Are you glad that your spirit will soon depart?" I said: "Yes, my friend, I am very glad." I sighed: "Come, Jesus, take me up." I was so happy, my heart was never quiet. Peter said: "Yes, my dear child, you shall soon join the five chosen ones." He continued: "They may keep your body, but not your spirit; I shall soon bring you up to me, as soon as your spirit departs from you; but your friends will sleep, and not see it." I spoke: "I am glad, my heart is never quiet; soon I shall rejoice and shout in triumph, because the Lord so kindly leads me." I was very glad that I had seen the believers in eternity; but my heart was very sad as they took leave of me; and yet I was glad, and hoped to see them again in eternity. It also gave me much joy that two of them returned with me to the water. Then one of them spoke: "The Lord will say to them that are exalted: Go down, you stood high in the world, you must now be made low; you were not satisfied with shelter and food. But to the humble he will say: Ye must be raised up, you were low upon the earth. But woe to them who purchase the world; they must go with the godless. Oh, how will the humble rejoice! for those who purchased the world and are citizens thereof, they will cry woe! over themselves; hallelujah, amen." When I came to this side of the water I began to sing: I shall love my Jesus until I am carried to the grave, and until he shall awaken me, and they shall write on my coffin: Jesus is my hope and my light; I my Jesus shall never leave.

Anno 1762, on December 6th, my spirit was again carried out of this visible creation and frame of flesh, up into the invisible eternity, again to hear something new. Then one spoke the following words, and spoke very loudly to those in heaven and on earth: "Rejoice and shout triumphantly, you will soon be led to your rest; rejoice with might, ye pious, you soon will find your rest. Hallelujah, rejoice with might! High, high, as high as you can extol, rejoice ye all and triumphantly shout, for the Lord so kindly leads you! Oh, how glorious and how mighty! Rejoice ye all and shout in triumph: come all ye pious, come to the great supper! Hio! hio! hallelujah! Oh, how glorious and how mighty; rejoice ye all and shout in triumph; soon all the pious and all the lowly will find their rest! Oh, what joy! oh, what delight! rejoice ye all and shout in triumph, hallelujah, hallelujah! Come ye pious, come ye all, come to the great supper!" The angel further spoke to me: "Behold the angels without number, behold how splendid and shining; behold how they protect the pious on earth! Oh, how glorious and how mighty! Who can number the angels who sit above and protect the pious on earth? Rejoice ye all and shout in triumph, the Saviour will come soon to take home all the pious, and with him his angels in white array; then heaven shall be barred. Hallelujah, hallelujah, rejoice with might ye pious, you soon will come to your rest! High, high, extol as high as you can! High, high as he can be extolled! Rejoice ye all and shout in triumph! Oh, how glad the pious will be! Oh, how blessed are they who believe that the Saviour died for the world and who are baptized in His name," etc.

On December 13th my immortal spirit was again carried

up to eternity, and again heard the voice of a watchman resound aloud like a trumpet; the sound seemed to go through all the heavens and the earth. He again spoke: "Oh, how glorious and how mighty! Rejoice ye all and shout in triumph; behold how the Lord so kindly leads you! Rejoice with might, all ye pious, and ye pious all at once, come to the great supper!" etc., etc.

I find that these visions continued at least till April, 1765. The father of this person was a respected Baptist preacher. He, because he also had a great desire to build churches, made use of this circumstance and travelled through the country with his daughter, baptizing and preaching God's kingdom, whereby many were awakened from their spiritual sleep, some of whom he baptized in the stream Codorus, at Yorktown. It is beyond description how quickly this awakening spread through the country; people came from a distance of more than sixty miles to the house of the above-mentioned Hummer, so that the too numerous visitors emptied these good people's house and barn of their provisions. Night services were then arranged, to which people came every night; but if some tried to steal in from impure motives, the Instrument[1] was so keen to find it out that they were exposed and excluded from the service. That at the same time most charming hymns were sung by angels in the air, I give on the authority of those who allege that they heard them. Catharine Hummer, before mentioned, and her sisters, showed from the very beginning of this awakening a particular esteem for the Solitary in the Settlement; therefore it was hoped that this awakening would be of great advantage to Ephrata; for as the Superintendent with a considerable following of the Solitary was at this time officiating at the altar in this region, these daughters invited them to visit their house, and entertained them in Christian love, even without their parents' knowledge, who at the time were not particularly favorable to the visitors. May God repay them for this faithfulness on the day of judgment, because they without fear went to meet the reproach of Christ and sheltered under their roof such scourings of the world.

---

[1] [Catharine Hummer.]

Thereupon it came to pass that two of them, namely, the chief person, Catharine, and her sister, Maria, paid a visit to the Solitary at a time when there was a service at the altar, so that they were initiated into its mystery, which produced great excitement in the whole Settlement as well as in the Congregation, because the hope was entertained that such respectable lasses would help to make up the church of the 144,000 virgins of the Lamb, that so the new world might the sooner become manifest. These matters at last induced the Superintendent to write an edifying letter to the Instrument, in which he, with his usual modesty, spoke in a very Christian way of this movement, and laid before this person certain signs by which to recognize whether the Spirit of Jesus Christ were its impelling force. He wrote as follows: "If our beloved and respected friend, or rather Sister, C. H., wishes to be fully assured of the spirit of her divine youth, or of what she has further to expect of the whole affair which happened to her, then let her preserve right relations with her virginity. If so be that the Princess on the throne is using her sceptre in this affair, then let her be of good cheer, the matter is all right, and no doubt concerning it need arise in all eternity; for the Virgin never deceives, because she is the mother of the eternal Wisdom, through which all things were created. If, however, the Virgin should have to lose her princely hat through the affair then it may be a result of the official or judging spirit of the fallen angel, administering his office for good and ill over the apostate life. But he does not get into the city of God or the New Jerusalem with his office, but has to live and lodge outside the boundaries of Israel; and at last will even be utterly expelled, when the mother-church or the church of the Holy Spirit shall wield the sceptre and the kingdom. Then, of course, all the offices created by the fallen prince of angels shall be abolished."

But it appears that after the above-mentioned person had changed her state and married, the spirit retired into its chambers again and the whole work stopped and fell into decay, which is usually the case with all angelic visions and revelations. May God grant that it may turn into a plentiful harvest in eternity.

CHAPTER XXXIII.

Concerning the Last Circumstances Connected with the Life of the Superintendent, and How at Last He Laid Aside His Earthly Tabernacle.

A father of old, when he was about to go home, and it went hard with him, raised his hands to God and said: "Lord, thou knowest I never let my prisoner escape." This can justly be conceded to the Superintendent also, namely, that he kept a sacred watch over his life from the first awakening unto his end. And as he was obliged to desist from his austere way of living, when compelled by God to mingle with the flood of humanity, so it was also observed that towards the end of his life, he again withdrew himself from close fellowship with any one, and led so secluded a life that even those nearest to him could not reach up to him in spirit. All his aim was not to stand in God's way in reaching the consciences of those who were intrusted to his care. For even as the good Master himself had to stand off, in order that the Spirit might be imparted to his disciples, so the Superintendent had to withdraw his fellowship even during his life-time, in order that his successors, weaned from him, might learn to walk on their own feet. The most important fact to be noted of his walk through life is, that all the strange situations into which he was brought during a pilgrimage of many years, could not turn him aside from the purpose once taken, to live a life disdainful of the world and serving God; of which he thus writes in a certain letter: "I know by this that I did not forsake my calling, because all carnal and worldly-minded people are still my enemies, just the same as at the time when I first entered upon this road." And to one of the Brethren who visited him shortly before his end, he said: "I am now again the same that I was when first exposed to the world-spirit, namely, an orphan." It surely is saying a good deal when a spiritual warrior can boast that during so long a time neither the flatteries nor the malice of men could lead him astray from his holy calling. But because he has been accused of having been addicted too much to strong drink for several years before his end, something would be wanting if this charge were not duly met. It appears that Providence ordered that he had to help his Master carry his shame even in this; for that God had lost sight of him so far as to permit him to again fall under the power of the things from which he had freed himself by his first repentance, is not easily to be believed, although one might, if it were necessary, make excuses on account of his old age and great bodily infirmities. This report he made excellent use of, and bore himself in appearance in such a manner that men were confirmed in their conjectures; for shame was his outer coat which he wore on his long life-journey so that his inner, pure white garment might be kept unspotted. But what great temptations this occasioned in the Settlement cannot be described; for if God intends to humble a people, he allows contempt to be heaped on its priests, and makes fools of its princes. And now all the Solitary revealed their real feelings towards him. His spiritual daughters who formerly would have gone through fire and water for him, now withdrew themselves from him; some of them who meddled too much with his frailties, had great cause to thank God that Noah's curse against Ham did not fall upon them. All of this, however, came from God, for had he died in the midst of the churchly honors which he had formerly enjoyed, his loss would have touched the Sisterhood most of all, for next to God, they esteemed their spiritual Father above everything. He once appeared to two of the Brethren in the form of one who is drunk, when they put him under severe discipline; but he went straight home from them, and composed a hymn about this occurrence, which soon after was printed and distributed in the Settlement. This hymn shows that at the time he had full possession of his senses. Two of the verses are as follows:

>Once when I thought that I was from the illness freed,
>In which for days and years I'd suffered grief, indeed;
>Some travellers came to me, all weary from the road,
>And gave me bitter gall, with blows a heavy load.

> Oh, God! I bring to Thee my woe and bitter pain,
> Since Thou my Saviour art, to whom I ne'er in vain
> Did come, from early youth, for help to bear my cross,
> For heavenly bliss instead of pleasure's earthly dross.

Nevertheless some, especially of the domestic household, would have nothing to do with the matter, but kept their senses in Christ Jesus, and said: "The Superintendent stands directly under God's orders and is responsible only to him." Herein he can be compared with David, whom the Sanhedrim also wished to strangle; but David well knew with whom he had to deal, and said: "Against Thee, Thee only have I sinned;" and whoever of the Community reads this will remember that all who laid hold of this presumed weakness of the Superintendent fell under judgment. He once came to a Brother in the likeness of one who is drunk, and took him along to another Brother, where they prepared a love-feast. After this was done, the Brother, as was customary, accompanied him to his house, where he had a very edifying conversation with him; so that the Brother perceived that his drunkenness had been a holy pretence.

It was observed of him that towards the end of his life he endeavored to remove all stones of stumbling out of the way of the Solitary. His quarrel with the Prior, which had lasted for years, he put entirely aside, and said: "I am done now, and dare not go one step further." He also took a Sister into his house, and went to the former Mother, Maria, who also had stumbled over the rock of offence, and called her his Sister, and offered her reconciliation in Christ; but she in no wise accepted it.[1]

---

[1] Because the whole life of this Sister, even her stumbling and falling, contains much of edification, this work would be incomplete if it were not given to the kind reader. It has already been said that when the Spirit, who at that time wooed people who were to act in this strange drama, seized her, she and her elder sister fled, in tender youth, out of their father's house and placed themselves under the Superintendent's guidance, and that a small house was built for them at Mill Creek, where at that time stood the first Settlement of the Solitary after their exodus out of Egypt. When the Superintendent afterwards settled in the wilderness where Ephrata is now situated, they were the first of their sex who followed him thither, where on the banks of the Cocalico, a small house was built for them, so that this stream formed the boundary line between the Brethren and Sisters. There the Superintendent had much fellowship with them and dined with

He attended to his official business up to within eight days before his death, when he officiated for the last time at a love-feast, being already so weak that he said on the way to it: "I am sick, I could just lie down and die." Three days before his decease one of the oldest house-mothers, Barbara Höfly by name, who thought very much of him, and was also breathing her last, sent to him and asked for a visit, even though he were not able to speak with her, if only she might be permitted to see him. Although he was at the time already wrestling with death he took a Brother along

them several times during the week, for the miracle-play of eternity was before his eyes and was to be applied to them. Her elder sister, Anna, was of an austere and imperious disposition, by means of which she exercised a severe guardianship over her; many, therefore, thought that this Anna would become Mother in the Sisters' convent; but here it came to pass just as with the election of David, for because the elder had the purpose to deprive the Superintendent of the locks of his hair, she fell out of favor into contempt and died in this state; while the choice fell on her younger sister, Maria.

When the Sisters' convent was erected and filled with spiritual virgins the Superintendent installed her, with special church solemnities, in return for the faithfulness she had shown towards him; and all the honor due to such an exalted office was portioned out to her. About the same time the Superintendent wrote several letters to her, which are full of unction. The following memorable words occur in one: "Because your person, during the time of severe and hard sifting and trials, risked not a little danger of loss; and because you perseveringly helped us to endure in times of sorrow as well as joy, up to the present day, therefore I am obliged by all means to give you notice that like as the net of love then captured a prize and made you partaker of such high and important processes of suffering, therewith granting unto you to be faithful until now, so the intention is now to make another catch, by which you may at once be crowned with the captured prize and will consequently be doubly repaid for your shame and pain. And this it is to which my love and highly esteemed governess invites you as guest, namely: to the enjoyment of that heavenly harvest of joys, which only yonder will be manifested to its full extent. (See his printed epistles, page 201.) The spirit of prophecy was very strong at that time, and it appears that the heavenly Mother greatly rejoiced over this little band of people, and therefore sought again to perform the miracle she had done at the time of Jesus Christ's humiliation. For when all the Sisters changed their names Mother Maria was excepted as being the representative of the Virgin Mary. And as then the Virgin Mary had two sons, two spiritual sons were also given to our Mother. But since her first-born, after the type of his Master, had to be crucified, it was time now to give another son to the Mother. Therefore the Spirit proceeded and said to another Brother: "Behold thy Mother!" It must be con

and fulfilled her wish; she was buried yet before him. Another Sister, who had only lately joined and came from a foreign country, was also breathing her last at this time. She prayed to God that he might let her die with this holy man, and she also died yet before him. These are the travelling companions who accompanied him to eternity. At last the 6th day of July of the year 1768 came, when he laid aside his mortal raiment. On the morning of that day he had yet been in the Sisters' house, and nobody, therefore, thought that his departure was so near; nor could the powers

---

fessed, however, that these two spiritual sons were a source of many sorrows to her in the future.

She conducted her office with great authority, and during her term she saw four Priors deposed among the Brethren, who therefore felt ashamed that so weak a vessel should have more godliness than they. Some said to the Superintendent that they were sure the Mother would yet be deposed, even should it only happen in eternity. The reason why she could maintain herself in office so long was because she knew how to profit by the mistakes of each Prior; for she watched everything the Prior did, and as soon as she noticed a mistake, she went to the Superintendent and said: "Oh Father, the Brethren have a child in the cradle again, and it will most likely be sacrificed to the world-spirit." When thereupon the Superintendent in his zeal uttered something rash, this was at once known to the Prior. Thus she had incautiously given too great confidence to the first Prior, so that he raised himself up against his spiritual Father, and so she kept up continual disagreement between the Superintendent and his Prior, to her own advantage. But at last the game took another turn. The Superintendent got a Prior who walked in harmony of spirit with him, and after some unsuccessful attempts to turn one against the other, she became suspicious of her spiritual Father and closed her heart against him, and also induced some of those under her to do the same; so that for several years her house was not open to the Superintendent as formerly. All this came from God; for the time of her fall was near at hand, and she herself had to pave the way for it. The fire lay smouldering under the ashes for a long time and only broke forth on the visit to Antitum, during which she behaved so reservedly that the Superintendent at last said to her: "The worm of hell is sticking in you." Then she plotted to separate the Sisterhood entirely from the Brotherhood, and publicly declared that their Prior must be overthrown; which was the chief cause of the succeeding unedifying land dispute in the Settlement. The Superintendent who had learned to sail with all kinds of wind, took hold of this opportunity and declared himself publicly against the Brethren and their Prior. Whoever is anxious to know the reason for this action of his, is referred to the story of Job; let him ask God how He could justify His entering into a compact with Satan against His faithful servant. But according to the wonderful government of our God, the right to the land in the Settlement was given into the hand

of darkness prevail upon him to lie down on a sick bed. Meanwhile a constant watch was kept, for strange happenings were expected, and that the powers of death would have a fierce struggle with him, especially since he was an old soldier, who was accustomed neither to call on men for mercy nor to yield to the powers of darkness. But at last the news came of his approaching end, whereupon all the Solitary assembled at his house. The Brethren stood nearest to him; behind them the Sisters, and those who were of short stature got upon benches to witness his sacrifice. In his

---

of an outspoken enemy of the same, who was faithfully supported in all these transactions by the Mother. Possibly she may have done all this more out of a holy zeal against the other sex than out of malice; for Abdias writes even of her Principal, the Virgin Mary, that she cursed all males. In this wise the Mother may in a measure be excused. This man and some other antagonists took possession of his land in the Settlement, performed various acts of violence, and in general wielded such hellish power that the Superintendent, usually not in the habit of running away, forsook his house and tarried for eight days in the Sisters' prayer-hall; during which time he published the following notice among the Solitary:

> The victory comes from on high,
> A strong and mighty leader nigh
> Commands the battle forces.
> He breaks the teeth of the evil host
> That mocks his gospel truth the most,
> That none by them be tempted,
> To enter sinful freedom's way
> Where all do act just as they may:
> Old Adam's things they take,
> And with the stuff themselves adorn
> In fashion new, quite lately born,
> That scarce they can be known.
> A mocking laugh is the comment,
> And this they but deserve;
> E'en when their building shall fall down
> With all its false and glittering crown,
> For nothing else it is,
> Or was, but idle lust's display
> Which with his sins in full array
> Did Lucifer then show.

But the opponents disregarded this accusation, as much as they could, and hung this notice up in their dwellings. At last the Brethren complained to the Superintendent of the Sisterhood, because the evil had originated in their house; the Superintendent heard their complaint, and promised an investigation. The Mother was called to appear for judgment before the older Sisters, who were innocent of this affair, in presence of the Superin-

last trouble he clearly showed that he was anointed with the priestly spirit of Jesus Christ, for of all the adverse circumstances which had occurred during his administration in the Settlement, he declared himself to be the sole cause, and thus freed and acquitted all from every charge, and especially those who accused themselves of having misunderstood him. Then he desired the Brethren to bless him, and to receive him into their fellowship, which was done, for the Prior gave him his blessing with laying on of hands, and thereafter all the Brethren gave him the kiss of peace to take

tendent. They spoke affectionately with their Mother, saying that the two societies could never be separated, because they had been formed by the Spirit, as a miracle of the times, into an inseparable unity ; and that if she were willing to again break bread with the Brethren, everything should be peaceably adjusted. But she refused, and was, therefore, dismissed from her office. After this she dwelt in a corner of the Sisters' convent, because she was long in doubt whether she should not live in a holy separateness. After a considerable time, however, she again joined the Sisterhood, and died as one of its worthiest members. That the Superintendent offered her peace which she would not accept, has already been mentioned ; and so the matter stood until the Superintendent departed this life. Then a Sister admonished her quickly to make up with him, as he would soon leave this world, but she said: "I have nothing to make up," which certainly was a great loss to her; for he had hardly died when she was seized with great remorse. But she could not undo it; the man was gone with whom she ought to have made her peace. Still, she went to the coffin and touched him, when one of the Sisters called out: "It is too late now!"

After she had been divested of her official dignity, she commenced anew a rigorous life of penitence in her seclusion, and shed so many tears that her eyes were always swollen. It may well be believed that she pleased her bridegroom better, when bathed in this flood of tears, than at the time when she was the honored matron of an order of virgins; and if, during her long pilgrimage, she got some spots on her bridal dress, she surely washed them all out by her tears of contrition. He who scattered Israel, will gather it again. May God not repent him of his gifts and calling.

In person she was small, but she had keen senses. She was a great admirer of the humble life of Jesus Christ, and when still clothed in her dignity she often wore a garment with one patch upon the other. At the same time she kept herself very distant from the other sex and was never called to account on that point, although she once delivered her faithful leader out of the hands of the recruiting officer. Besides she had fine gifts in writing letters and hymns. In her letters she usually signed herself: "Maria, God's servant;" and her hymns are full of unction and spiritual thought. Her translation to eternity was sudden, for being missed for some time her door was broken open, and it was found that she had departed, which happened December 24th, 1784. Her age was 74 years, 3 months.

along on his journey. Then they persuaded him to lie down on the bench, and he was heard several times to repeat the following words: "Oh woe, oh woe! oh wonder, oh wonder!" But he did not explain himself about it, because his voice failed him; and soon after he fell asleep without a motion. Now the cry was, "My father, my father! The chariot of Israel and the horsemen thereof!" Yet nobody was seen to shed tears, but all thanked God most fervently that after so long a martyrdom he had delivered his servant from the body of this death.

These are the most important events in the life and blessed death of a man who was a great wonder in this century. The first impregnation for a spiritual life he received at Heidelberg in the Palatinate, when the great weight of the Spirit was laid upon him, which was one cause of his many succeeding passions. Many awoke to a spiritual life through his labors, and many strove earnestly to follow his footsteps; but they could not keep step with him, for he had so completely given himself to God, both body and soul, that he passed his life in wonderful strictness, even up to his death. The reason why most of the awakenings of our times come to such sad ends is, because people rely upon themselves, and do not renounce self more than their own interest demands, so that it may truly be said: All plans of self-interest bring death. It nevertheless remains a great wonder that, after God called him from his blessed life of seclusion to bathe in the flood of humanity, in order to fish for people, he had so much faith that he could risk his salvation on God; and it is a still greater wonder, that surrounded by so many dangers in this human flood, he did not forfeit his calling. And on account of this his faithfulness did God crown him with praise and honors, and ordain him to replace on the candlestick, at the sixth period, both the priesthood of Melchizedek and the heavenly virginity. Because this could not be done in Europe, on account of the Beast's great power, God ordered it that he came over the ocean into this country, where his doctrine of the heavenly virginity and the priesthood, after some opposition, gained a firm footing, and where an altar was built to the Lord in such wise that all awakenings not in harmony with his testimony have no other effect than to bring forth children into servitude.

Before him the wisdom of God attempted to reveal the mystery of eternal virginity in the old countries, through many precious instruments, of whom those dear men of God, Godfried Arnold and George Gichtel and many others, may especially be mentioned. The latter's success was great, and I may well say that he had borne the light before the Superintendent; but he remained a virgin, nor did he attain to the secret nuptial couch of the Virgin Sophia, where children are born; still less did he reach the covenant household of Jesus Christ, but ended his life in a holy separateness. It is known that he and his first co-warriors were so severely sifted through the envy of the tempter, that he, in order to prevent similar siftings, did not want to allow two to live in one town. When we consider that the Superintendent for about fifty years stood in a visible organization in which under God's decree one rebellion after the other broke forth against the testimony of God which was entrusted to him, it must be confessed that he fought on many more battlefields against the Prince of Wrath than did the venerable Brother Gichtel of blessed memory, and that he extended the borders of the generation of the divine Mother far more than he. It must also be conceded that the venerable John Kelpius, who had settled near Germantown with a company of spiritual wooers of the hand of the Virgin, as already mentioned, did much in spirit to assist the Superintendent in his church building. The same spirit inspired the sainted Kelpius that afterwards descended on the Superintendent; but when the good Kelpius departed this life, his work fell into the hands of the tempter to be sifted, and the spiritual ship broke up, so that Selig, Conrad Mathäi and some others, had to save themselves by swimming. The Superintendent's work, on the contrary, with better success passed to posterity; for eighteen years have passed since he was transferred to eternity, during which time the Order and the Community have been built up in the unity of the spirit, although with much opposition.

And if, as he maintains God promised him, a seed of his

labors is to remain until the second advent of Jesus Christ, this does not mean that the Settlement of the Solitary shall stand so long; although they are just as well entitled to this as any congregation of Christ on earth. But we believe that it is to be understood more in a spiritual sense than literally: that wherever there is anyone in this country who has a matrix ready to conceive, there the Spirit, who in the beginning overshadowed the Superintendent, will also overshadow and impregnate him. All of which, however, must be taken figuratively and not literally. And because this country at last, after much opposition, received this ambassador, who had been driven out of his fatherland, and granted him and his whole family complete liberty of conscience, therefore it will always be blessed and be a nursery of God, which shall bear him much fruit, for the promise given to Abraham must be fulfilled: "In thy seed shall all generations of the earth be blessed." He was small in person, well formed and proportioned, had a high nose, high forehead and sharp eyes, so that everybody recognized in him an earnest and profound nature. He had excellent natural gifts, so that he might have become one of the most learned men if pains had been taken with his education. All secrets were opened to him, just as he wanted; and wherever he saw a piece of skillful work he was not satisfied until he had examined and understood it; he used to say it would be a shame for the human mind if it would be defeated in anything. He likewise was endowed with such a keen perception that he was enabled to discover with ease whatever might be hidden to others. But after he had dedicated himself wholly to the service of God these gifts were sanctified, and were used by him for the upbuilding of the temple of God in the Spirit. What he accomplished in the art of music, which he learned without any human instruction, has already been mentioned; he composed not less than one thousand tunes for four voices, of which none interfered with the other.

His printed hymns number 441. The reader will see his enlightened nature from them; many of them are prophetic, representing the near approach of the Sabbatic church, and the gathering together of the people of God.

Of his printed discourses there are 66; besides which you will find many of his spiritual lectures printed. He also wrote many spiritual letters, of which 73 are printed; the rest are still in manuscript, but will also be communicated to the reader, though *sub conditione Jacobœa*. In conclusion we will here give the inscription on his tombstone, from which the reader may learn both his natural and spiritual age:

"Here Rests an Offspring of the Love of God,

FRIEDSAM,

a Solitary, but later become a Leader, Guardian and Teacher of the Solitary and of the Congregation of Christ in and about Ephrata. Born at Eberbach in the Palatinate, called Conrad Beisel: Fell asleep July 6th, Anno 1768; aged according to his spiritual age 52 years, but according to his natural, 77 years and 4 months."

THE END.

www.ingramcontent.com/pod-product-compliance
Lightning Source LLC
Chambersburg PA
CBHW022111230426
43672CB00008B/1350